Education and the Making of a Democratic People

Education and the Making of a Democratic People

Edited by
John I. Goodlad,
Roger Soder,
and Bonnie McDaniel

Paradigm Publishers
Boulder • London

Copyright © 2008 Institute for Educational Inquiry

Published in the United States by Paradigm Publishers, 3360 Mitchell Lane, Suite E, Boulder, Colorado 80301 USA.

Paradigm Publishers is the trade name of Birkenkamp & Company, LLC, Dean Birkenkamp, President and Publisher.

Library of Congress Cataloging-in-Publication Data

Education and the making of a democratic people / edited by John I. Goodlad, Roger Soder, and Bonnie McDaniel.
    p. cm.
  Includes bibliographical references and index.
  ISBN 978-1-59451-528-6 (hardcover : alk. paper)
    1. Citizenship—Study and teaching—United States.   2. Education—Aims and objectives—United States. 3. Democracy—United States. I. Goodlad, John I. II. Soder, Roger, 1943– III. McDaniel, Bonnie Lyon.
  LC1091.E3843 2008
  370.11'5—dc22

                                                                        2007049334

Printed and bound in the United States of America on acid-free paper that meets the standards of the American National Standard for Permanence of Paper for Printed Library Materials.

Designed and Typeset by Straight Creek Bookmakers.

12 11 10 09 08   1 2 3 4 5

Contents

Acknowledgments

This book emerged from an invitational conference at the Institute for Educational Inquiry in Seattle that brought together educators interested in and working on the close relationship of education and democracy. Most of those in attendance subsequently wrote chapters. We thank the six individuals who did not contribute chapters to this book but made significant contributions to the purposes, substance, and structure of the manuscript: Donald Ernst of the Stuart Foundation, Bruce Field of the University of South Carolina, Gary Howlett of the Edmonds (Washington) School District, Bruce Novak of Northern Illinois University, Marjorie Serge of Marysville (Washington) Alternative High School, and Allen Trent of the University of Wyoming.

Without the weeks spent by Paula McMannon of the Institute staff in communicating with the authors and editors and attending to every conceivable detail (like cleaning up what each of us thought to be the final draft), publication would have been delayed several months or would not have occurred at all. We are deeply appreciative.

—*The Editors*

Introduction

Kenneth Alhadeff and John I. Goodlad

This book focuses on a condition of our country that urgently needs attention. The democracy that holds us together as a moral community, that embraces our guiding principles—liberty, justice, and a good life for all—is showing serious signs of stress, of not living up to what we celebrate. For many of its people, the American Dream has faded away.

This is not a condition for which we need a national commission's report to set us right. Nor is this a call for another summit meeting of our states' governors. It is instead an argument for continuous care and renewal of this democracy so that it will take good care of us.

The central problems are educational ones, as is the agenda of renewal—an agenda for all of us but particularly our children, who will constitute, we hope, a democratic public. The authors of this book believe the mission and much of the substance of this agenda to be nonnegotiable—that is, they are not to be cast aside for some other political and social mode of life that makes no commitment to liberty, justice, and a good life for all. It is, however, an agenda that depends for its well-being on inquiry-based discourse, innovation, and diverse opinions that

1

inevitably provoke disagreement. It is an agenda that calls for a broad, general education of everyone.[1]

A democratic public is an educated public. Consequently, our system of public education constitutes the front line for the development of democratic character in our people and democratic functioning of our government and institutions. Democracy embraces how we are with one another, and how we are with one another entwines with how we conduct all of our affairs. The necessary learning begins with the very young and should become habitual in our preschools, nursery schools, and kindergartens and increasingly rigorous in later years.

★   ★   ★

The oxygen we breathe each moment keeps us alive. The culture in which we breathe determines the nature and quality of our lives. Here in the United States of America we are blessed to live in a culture grounded in moral principles that the several great religions of the world largely agree are necessary to human well-being. As historian Warren Wagar states this agreement, we "can find a common core of truth in all of the positive religions."[2] Ideally, these principles, taken together, define the moral community we refer to as a political and social democracy.[3]

In practice, however, the American democracy, like all democracies, is a work in progress and, one might hope, always will be. Philosopher Paul Woodruff writes that democracy is a beautiful idea but one that cannot be put fully into practice.[4] Nonetheless, it appears to be the best vision we have managed to come up with for guiding individual and collective behavior.

Then why should we hope that perfection will elude us? Because, once we come to believe that all is well, that we have reached the zenith and improvement is neither needed nor possible, we will be content with only sustaining, not renewing, where we are on the scale of possibility. Once renewal ceases, decay commences.

We take great pride in what often has been described as the great American experiment—our democracy. We celebrate it in myriad ways: in school and college graduation ceremonies, in recognition of the nation's achievement of independence, by the singing of the national anthem before the first pitch at baseball games, by a great display of flags on memorable occasions, at the swearing-in of freshly minted citizens, in the morning exercises of kindergarteners who often sing "my country *tisabee*"—not perfect but fervent nonetheless. But are pride and eloquence sufficient?

We expect the democracy we celebrate to take care of us, just as we expect the air we breathe to keep us alive. But if not taken care of or if treated carelessly, this invisible air can and frequently does disable us. Similarly, this democracy of ours, when ignored or not carefully cultivated, can quickly run amok, leaving in its wake the weakening or destruction of what we celebrate. In a monograph read by millions of people worldwide shortly after what we now need only refer to as 9/11, wise observer of our culture Wendell Berry warned us of how easy it is to give up our hard-earned freedoms in the face of fear.[5] And that fear may arise out of sources as ubiquitous and intangible as the air we breathe.

★ ★ ★

Is the American democracy in trouble? There have been since the beginning of this century a great many economic, political, social, educational, and ethnographic analyses claiming that it is. But it would be difficult to claim the winning side were the debate over whether or not our democracy is in *deep* trouble.

There are serious, thoughtful analysts and pundits who view the nation to be in accelerating decline toward a much lesser status in the economic world, a markedly lower standard of living, and a disappearance of the American Dream for an expanding percentage of the people. Many of these are mute on the question of whether this downward slope can be turned around. And few of those who envision a turnaround see it coming soon or without enormous sacrifice and effort. The year 2050 is often the chosen one for the depiction of dire consequences as well as, for the more optimistic of this doomsday-lies-ahead group, the year of significant turnaround.

The history of this country, from the time of the first European settlers, has been one of crises experienced, crises overcome, and optimism characteristically prevailing. And, not infrequently, it was optimism that led to a new course at the brink of a precipice. Pessimism has played at most a cameo role in the history of this country. Let us hope that it continues to be only a minor player in the future.

Although pessimism is a dangerous enemy of renewal, it falls far short of being the major obstacle to significant change. Far more significant is incorrect or superficial diagnosis of the problem. A closely related one is simplification of the solution. The well-being of our democracy is at its core an educational matter. Unfortunately, the most recent decades of attempted educational reform reveal a succession of incorrect diagnoses and inadequate or missing strategies of improvement. Consequently, it is folly for us to assume that simply assigning responsibility to our primary, secondary, and tertiary educational institutions for renewing our democracy will ensure it a robust future. Education and democracy are entwined. The two must be renewed together.

Schooling is increasingly becoming a minor player in our learning. The highly informational role it once featured is being taken over by the media. This could be all to the good *if*—and it is a big "if"—our schools were successfully addressing the thinking, reasoning, and evaluating processes we all need in order to live rich lives in today's and tomorrow's complex world. Currently, the relationship between what goes on educationally in the classroom and what children and youths encounter beyond their hours at school is modest, to say the least.

Calling for the schools to raise test scores will not produce the desired outcomes, nor will parental pressure on their children and their schools to gain entrance for their offspring to a clutch of our most prestigious colleges and universities. And such expectations certainly will not advance the public purpose of educating "the whole person" for living a responsible, productive, satisfying life—for understanding and participating in the kind of social and political democracy we celebrate. Such a mission for our schools is, however, essential.

Advancing this public mission is what the chapters of this book address. All the authors are in various ways engaged in advancing it. Because of the work they do, they were brought together by the Institute for Educational Inquiry (IEI) to share and then write about their goals and experiences. The IEI has drawn together lessons from three decades of inquiry in designing an agenda for renewing simultaneously schooling and democracy. This agenda guides twenty-four school–university partnerships in nearly as many states and Canadian provinces—the National Network for Educational Renewal (NNER)—in the simultaneous renewal of those institutions and the teacher education programs they jointly conduct. The IEI has produced over a dozen books on the democratic mission, the conditions necessary to its advancement, and strategies to be employed in implementing this agenda of developing democratic character in the young.

The threats to our democracy and to a public democratic mission for our schools in recent years appear to have aroused significant interest in the importance of thwarting their expansion. The relatively new Forum for Education and Democracy is attempting to provide at local and national levels forums for public discussion, inquiry, and action in strengthening the role of schooling in sustaining and renewing our democracy. The First Amendment Schools focus particularly on the nature of our freedoms and the importance of understanding and sustaining them. Grassroots enterprises such as the League of Democratic Schools and the well-established Coalition of Essential Schools at the national level and the League of Professional Schools in Georgia are helping, for example, to maintain education of the whole child in the face of federal mandates that have cut short curricular attention to the arts, health and physical education, history, geography and the social sciences, and more.

The above does not by any means exhaust the list of initiatives that include in their mission attention to the critical relationship between education and democracy. But their efforts probably have contributed to the generally positive tone that pervades the chapters of this book. The early ones sound warnings regarding the possible shift in tomorrow's status of the major nations in the global economy, against giving up cultural features of our country that have served us well, about the growing gap between the rich and the poor, against underestimating the necessity of carefully guarding the hard-earned freedoms we celebrate, and more. But even these chapters are upbeat about the prospects of strengthening the moral grounding of the democracy that Abraham Lincoln said must be of, by, and for the people. The chapters that follow on the necessity of cultivating a well-informed public, morally conducted institutions, democratic schools and classrooms, and close links between the public and school boards and between journalists and educators also point the way toward increasing refinement and strengthening of the American democracy. This is a book of hope and what must be done to fulfill it.

In chapter 1 John Goodlad sets the stage for the rest of this book by reminding us that democracy requires an educated public. The time has come, he argues, for Americans to stand up and insist that educating the young for participation in our democracy is a nonnegotiable agenda for our schools.

Alan Wood expands on that idea in chapter 2, placing America's educational challenge in global perspective. Education is central to our very humanity, he insists, and it must balance cooperation with competition, assume moral responsibility for the well-being of the whole, and take place in a democratic community committed to freedom and opportunity for all.

In chapter 3 Jane Roland Martin observes that education and schooling are not the same. She argues that school-based educators must reach out to form cooperative relationships with educational and social agents outside the schools if they are to serve the interest of democratic renewal.

Chapter 4 addresses the close relationship among the political, economic, and educational functions of nations and the need for these three functions to come together in common cause. Paul Theobald calls for improved public understanding of and involvement in advancing the democratic purpose of schooling.

Conversation is the lifeblood of democracy, an idea that forms the basis of Bonnie McDaniel's essay (chapter 5). A conversation among parents, educators, and community members about the challenges of democracy and how they are worked out in the context of their local school reveals that when we talk together, we form a moral identity capable of giving direction to our public life and engendering a sense of responsibility for our democracy.

In chapter 6 Gary Daynes investigates how we have arrived at a condition in which most institutions fail to educate the young to behave responsibly in our social and political democracy. He provides concrete and theoretical examples of moral education that is fostered by some institutions in America today—examples that support the themes of hope that pervade this book.

As Jim Strickland and Dianne Suiter have seen firsthand, democratic school cultures can help our children and youths find meaning, voice, and direction in a rapidly changing world. In chapter 7 Strickland and Suiter posit that the young learn about democracy by participating in a democratically organized community.

Chapter 8 takes the form of an interview with school superintendents James Lowham and William Mester conducted by Barbara Lippke and Eugene Edgar. As the conversation reveals, superintendents of school districts hold considerable power in influencing the mission and conduct of our schools. Lowham and Mester explore the challenges of democratic renewal from the perspective of the district leader.

Chapter 9 reflects on the unique role that school board members can play in advancing the public purpose of our schools and renewing our democracy. As authors Michael Resnick and Anne Bryant note, school board members are in a strategic position to broker the interests of the several subcultures of the schooling enterprise.

The common equating of education and schooling ignores the reality and potential of such institutions as the news media, which are increasingly influencing what the people believe and do. Richard Clark and Clifford Rowe argue in chapter 10 that the media need to become major players in advancing the well-being of our democracy.

Chapter 11 is not the chapter initially intended. With the writing of the book well along, the three editors came up with the idea of including a chapter by someone who might have a perspective quite different from that of the several other authors. The name of a former head of a corporate philanthropic foundation came to mind—a foundation that had given support to the Institute for Educational Inquiry, the sponsor of this book. The invitation sent to him was accompanied by a copy of the first draft of chapter 1.

His response provided a different perspective indeed—very sharp criticism. Our invitee disagreed strongly with the level of engagement expected of people in local communities. He viewed the author, John Goodlad, as contradicting himself in advocating better care of our democracy but a lesser role for policymakers in the nation's schools. And this was only the beginning of a lengthy critique of disagreement.

After recovering somewhat from the unexpected, Goodlad suggested to his colleagues that they take advantage of a unique opportunity to provide a lively ending to the book that might stimulate the conversation recommended in its pages: bring our critic to Seattle for what most assuredly would be lively, educational debate. Our long-term friend and supporter could not come; he and his wife were packing for a long stay abroad. We settled for a telephone conference, which proved to be only a chummy chat. Friendship won out over critique.

What to do now? Editors McDaniel and Goodlad conspired in reminding Roger Soder that he had agreed to write the concluding chapter. The reader will see that Soder did not give up on the possible usefulness of a sharp critique. Goodlad then critiques the critique and moves on to a concluding message of hope.

★　★　★

The chapters that follow present a challenge to us all—children, youths, adults, and especially those who have chosen and been chosen to lead us. Troublesome issues and problems abound. We do not now share a common public democratic mission for our schools. There is not in our communities an ongoing public dialogue about school renewal, let alone an informed one. Policymakers at federal, state, and even local levels appear to be either unaware or uninterested in the polls that reveal that adults, especially parents, desire a balance of personal, social, vocational, and academic development in the teaching of the young.

The current narrow focus on achievement tests as the prime or only indicators of school quality and students' learning reveals policymakers' monumental ignorance regarding several decades of research on cognition that shows scarcely any relationship between test scores and the human virtues we most value. It is essential that the several subcultures of schooling—that of policy and reform, of local communities, and of scholarship and practice—simply must be brought together in and for discourse and action.

The authors of this book view public involvement in advancing a democratic agenda for our schools as a promising entry point for greater community conversation and action regarding the well-being of our democracy as a whole. The terrain to be addressed is lumpy, fascinating, and of great importance to us all. Perhaps the thorniest domain of potential agreement and disagreement is that of implementing a democratic culture of, by, and for the people. What are the strengths and weaknesses of representative government? How do we bring an end to the sobering situation of registered voters not being able on Election Day to connect their personal values and beliefs to those of the candidates? That is, what can be done about voters who do not yet know for whom they will vote as they prepare to drop their ballots in the mail or ballot box? Awareness of this phenomenon, not limited to an insignificant segment of the population, is sufficient to pronounce nonnegotiable the participation of young and old in an agenda for education in a democracy.

Notes

1. For more on the mission and substance of such an agenda, see John I. Goodlad, Corinne Mantle-Bromley, and Stephen John Goodlad, *Education for Everyone: Agenda for Education in a Democracy* (San Francisco: Jossey-Bass, 2004).

2. W. Warren Wagar, *The City of Man: Prophecies of a World Civilization in Twentieth-Century Thought* (Boston: Houghton Mifflin, 1963), 163. See also W. Warren Wagar, "Religion, Ideology, and the Idea of Mankind in Contemporary History," in W. Warren Wagar, ed., *History and the Idea of Mankind* (Albuquerque: University of New Mexico, 1971), 196–221.

3. Kenneth A. Sirotnik, "Society, Schooling, Teaching, and Preparing to Teach," in John I. Goodlad, Roger Soder, and Kenneth A. Sirotnik, eds., *The Moral Dimensions of Teaching* (San Francisco: Jossey-Bass, 1990).

4. Paul Woodruff, *First Democracy* (New York: Oxford University Press, 2005).

5. Wendell Berry, *In the Presence of Fear: Three Essays for a Changed World* (Great Barrington, Mass.: Orion Society, 2001).

Chapter 1

A Nonnegotiable Agenda

John I. Goodlad

> Democracy, I believe, is a dream. The ancients did not fully realize it, and
> neither have we. The job of thinkers is to keep the dream alive, come what
> may. And the job of doers is to keep trying to approximate democracy as
> well as circumstances will allow.
>
> —*Paul Woodruff*

On Friday, December 1, 2006, the editorial column of a Seattle newspaper
began with the following sentence: "Whatever became of the idea that
representative democracy is the essential starting point for public education?"[1] One might also ask the question, "Whatever happened to the idea
that public education is the essential starting point for addressing the well-
being of democracy?"

A robust, renewing democracy requires the presence of a *well-educated*
public. This is not necessarily a *much-schooled* public. But the only institution in the United States capable of providing this education for everyone

is what was once referred to as the common school. The American people are being taught by political and business leaders that the purpose of our schools is to prepare workers who will ensure the nation's leadership in the global economy. A closely related but more important purpose is the public democratic one of sustaining a wise populace. The renewal of our democracy and the role of our schools and communities in sustaining renewal are what this book is about.

★ ★ ★

The American democracy is a work-in-progress. It always will be. And so have been and so are whatever other political and social human constructs have laid claim to democracy. All have envisioned ideals of dreamlike qualities, none has achieved them, and yet all probably have claimed existing qualities more tangible than dreams. Indeed, the symbols brought into play in celebrating this work-in-progress often convey images of dreams attained. Herein lie the seeds of the work-in-progress's self-destruction.

Philosopher Paul Woodruff alerts us to the impossibility of making democracy perfect.[2] It will always be a work-in-progress. Without understanding this hard truth, the people of an assumed democracy are likely to expect more from it than they give to it. The hard lesson for all civilizations to learn is that things left unattended soon decay.

A major problem in seeking to take care of democracy is that so much of it is an abstraction. There are no invading troops climbing over our walls. Many people who were watching on television the surreal destruction of the World Trade Towers on September 11, 2001, at first thought they were seeing a clip from a movie. Wendell Berry's little monograph *In the Presence of Fear,* read by millions around the world in the aftermath of this shocking tragedy, for many of us converted democracy as an abstraction into shocking reality.[3] He opened up to us the prospects and the dangers of yielding our freedoms in the face of fear.

The nation paid dearly for the events of 9/11 in lives lost and lives rent apart. What happened that morning proved to be a wake-up call. There has been during the intervening years more talk of our freedoms, of the First Amendment, of the constitutional limits to the authority of government officials, of the moral grounding of democracy, and of the shortcomings in democracy's functioning than there had been for several preceding decades. What is becoming increasingly apparent, even if often obscure, is that renewing a democracy requires a well-educated, responsible public. Such is essential to government of, by, and for the people and to a nation where freedom and justice for everyone are to prevail. Each of us must become democracy's caretaker.

"America is a collection of multiple communities defined by different interests, races, ethnicities, economic stratification, religions, and so forth."[4] From time to time, we celebrate the moral ecology that holds us together as a nation. But we are far too casual about ensuring that the populace understands both the political fabric and the fundamental values that make up this ecology.

There is only one institution with the capacity to provide the education necessary to the existence and renewal of a democratic public—the common school. Currently, that institution is guided by a narrow academic curriculum that only by incidental teacher attention embraces this public purpose. There are no data to suggest common attention to the personal and social attributes most people expect schools to develop in the young: dependability, honesty, compassion, fairness, good work habits, ability to work independently and with others, creativity, civic-mindedness, and other traits of the well-educated individual. The current call across the nation is for raising test scores, not wise graduates of our educational system. We will pay a high price for this neglect.

We do not want any more wake-up calls such as that of September 11, 2001. What we need is continuous renewal of the social and political infrastructure we celebrate from time to time. But celebrations alone will not sustain renewal. We must have a populace that understands what a *political* democracy is and is not and that practices social democracy. We must have a populace committed to an agenda of participating in the political process, righting the injustices that inevitably exist, eliminating poverty and homelessness, ensuring equal opportunity, and providing for all the education required to forge a democratic public. Such an agenda must be ubiquitous, a nonnegotiable part of the fabric of daily life in a functioning democracy.

The chapters of this book endeavor to flesh out the agenda by addressing what democracy and education are, the role of educational institutions in their renewal, the moral mission of schooling in advancing this agenda, and more. Running through the whole is an urgent message: that of renewing America through renewing the mission of our educational institutions.

Educating the young is a critically important but insufficient component of this agenda. We must not wait a generation for the creation of a democratic public. We will not even get started on what must be done in schools unless there is widespread support from the people who sustain the infrastructure of their communities—people who have been too little involved in conversations and decisions about how their tax monies are expended. They must become good listeners, learners, crap-detectors,[5] and decision makers. They must join with educators (who, up to now, have not commonly assumed educational leadership roles in their communities) in advancing the public democratic purpose of schooling. Absent this joining, our schools will continue with the regularities and systemics of yesterday. Let the conversation begin, and invite policymakers to join in. They will come, they will listen, and perhaps they will learn that the continued failure of politically driven school reform is the result of the repeated use of a flawed model of change.

What Education Is and What Schools Are For

Many thousands of educators attend conferences each year to learn from one another, listen to speeches, check out new publications, visit with friends, and so forth. These meetings address specialized work or fields: the elementary or secondary school principalship, research, music education, early childhood education, the teaching of reading, physical education, multicultural education, special education, educational leadership, adult education, and on and on. I recall only once encountering a conference on *education,* such as what education is. I have noted a good many on school improvement or reform. These appear to me to assume that everyone knows what education is and so there is no need to define it. But the topics usually turn out to be closing the academic achievement gap, or including more or fewer elective subjects in the curriculum, or preventing high school dropouts, or ensuring better teaching, or creating better linkages between secondary schools and colleges, or whatever. The topics frequently are the same ones that have appeared on conference programs for decades. One would think that, as a result, school-based education today is much better than it was yesterday.

One wonders, however, what participants in these conferences view education to be. Learning the letters of the alphabet? To add two-digit numbers? The uses of a period, colon, semicolon? Learning the names of the major bones of the human body? To sew on a button? These appear to me to be training exercises—and rather low-level ones at that. Yet many hundreds of these were a very large part of my "educational" menu at school, whether as pupil or as teacher.

Some of these lessons appear to me to be useful in the marketplace and, perhaps, appropriate for schools to teach. But they had little or nothing to do with our becoming uniquely human beings, and certainly not all we could be. A chimpanzee could learn much of what I learned in the early years of school, and certainly a computer could perform these and more complex exercises better than I. These lessons did not help me think about who I was and wanted to be. Education should make me a person for the better rather than the worse.

I am reminded of the time my wife, Lynn, had a rather distressing experience. Arriving home from her first lesson in painting from the Russian artist Sergei Bongart, she broke into tears. She was angry as well as unhappy and said she would never go back to his class for another lesson. A requirement for admission had been that she bring some of her paintings. He had examined them and exclaimed (with a strong accent), "This isn't painting; this is coolooring."

I encouraged her to go back, and she did (although she probably would have without my urging). On that second day, she began the arduous, satisfying journey of becoming an artist. But she also strengthened her resolve to continue to be the person she knew she was and wanted to continue to be. When asked for more "cooloor," she gave him more color. But at home, she usually painted in softer tones and, when painting children, sought to bring out what she thought to be characteristics of their feelings and personalities. Nearly every canvas provided a gratifying learning experience that enriched her daily life. She put to good use much that she was learning from Bongart. From her I learned to tell my students not to let a teacher or anyone else get in the way of their education. "Education" and "schooling" are not synonymous.

Scholars who have sought seriously to define education come together on its being a growing process, one of shaping individual character for good or ill. Philosopher John Dewey wrote, "Education is all one with growing; it has no end beyond itself. The criterion of the value of school education is the extent to which it creates a desire for continued growth and supplies means for making the desire effective in fact."[6]

British philosopher R. S. Peters agreed in saying that the appropriate word is "training," not "educating," when we are seeking to attain a specific extrinsic learning objective.[7] Historian Lawrence Cremin's succinct definition of education takes us nicely into what schools are for: education is "the deliberate, systematic, and sustained effort to transmit or evoke knowledge, attitudes, values, skills, and sensibilities."[8] These categories of learning shape both the cultural and the human character and must discipline the curriculum and teaching of the school. Clearly, reading, writing, and arithmetic will not suffice. Since good and bad struggle for control of the individual psyche, the education provided by the school must not remain morally neutral. Democracy does not flourish in an ecosystem of moral neutrality.

Nonetheless, many people believe that a school should be such an ecosystem. They fear the teaching of values other than their own. There is a paradox here in that nearly everyone polled on expectations for schools wants social, personal, vocational, and academic development of the young.[9] Such development requires educating, not just training, and education is by definition and functioning a moral endeavor. Schooling is in part a political endeavor—a struggle for what values will prevail. The late Neil Postman concluded in 1995 that the "god of economic utility" was winning the struggle for the soul of the U.S. public school:

> It is a passionless god, cold and severe. But it makes a promise, and not a trivial one. Addressing the young, it offers a covenant of sorts with them: If you will pay attention in school, and do your homework, and score well on tests, and behave yourself, you will be rewarded with a well-paying job when you are done. Its driving idea is that the purpose of schooling is to prepare children for competent entry into the economic life of a community.[10]

Harry R. Lewis, former dean of Harvard College (the very core of the soul of Harvard University) shook the academic world in 2006 with the charge that his and other universities regarded as excellent have lost sight of what education should be and have turned to the cultivation of consumer satisfaction.[11] It is long past time for the American people to regain the conversation of what our schools are for and establish education at the core of the soul of our educational institutions.

The Public Purpose of Schooling

There are two distinctly different levels of parental interest in the purposes of schooling. One is private and usually looms large. Parents want to know how their offspring are doing and that each is safe and gets his or her share of teacher attention. The other is public, has to do with the scope of the school's responsibility, and commonly is voiced if the parent is polled or attends a rare meeting on the subject.

An unfortunate result of the obscurity of public interest is that it rarely enters into either the making of school policies or the conduct of school practices. Put bluntly, parents are out of the loop in regard to determining the ends and means of schooling. The same can be said for the rest of the people who provide the financial support for sustaining schools.

For several decades school reform reports have taught the people that we have a failing system of schooling. Each year, the Gallup Poll reports that the public gives a low rating to the overall enterprise of schooling but a surprisingly high rating to the local school. It appears that a significant percentage of the populace has come to believe that there are many weak schools "out there," but the school their children or their neighbors' children attend is just fine. It is little wonder that bond levies to support entire school districts so often fail, with the result that these local schools are underfunded.

What school personnel hear from parents is a mixed chorus of personal expectations that the primary *function* of schooling is child care. The structure of the curriculum and the quality of instruction rank low in parental concern.[12] But this should not be interpreted to mean that parents are uninterested in the purpose of schools. The reality is that forums for discourse about what education is and schools are for are rarely built into the infrastructure of our nation's communities. The creation of them is overdue.

As stated above, public expectations for schools' educating of the young are very comprehensive, and there is high agreement. What we want is education writ large—development of the whole child. The phrase "the whole child" became repugnant to critics of "progressive" education a half century ago and only now is coming back into fashion.[13] And what do we mean by this phrase? The beliefs, attitudes, skills, passions, knowledge, and sensibilities that make the whole of an individual's unique being.

And what should be the educative context within which the desired human characteristics are honed? The Founding Fathers spelled out the specifics: a context of freedom, equity, justice, and more that make up the moral ecology that holds this nation together. Combine these educationally with the moral traits we want everyone's children to develop in their homes, and we are well on our way to defining the essential curriculum for our schools and their public purpose—the making of a democratic people.

This public democratic agenda must be immune to political intervention and manipulation. In other words, it is not negotiable. The more than two dozen Amendments to the Constitution of the United States of America spell out, among other things, an array of freedoms and rights of the people. What is not included is the right to an education that seeks to ensure for each of us the full development of our capacities, the very best we are able to be. Studies and polls have consistently revealed the American people to want schools that address the personal, social, vocational, and academic development of the young. Should we have an Amendment that seeks to ensure this public expectation as a nonnegotiable right?

Today, our elementary schools are being held accountable for student test scores in reading and mathematics, thanks to the No Child Left Behind (NCLB) Act passed by Congress soon after George W. Bush took office. Because of the act, the already narrow academic curriculum narrowed even more. As Richard Rothstein and Rebecca Jacobsen point out in their excellent piece on the goals of schooling, NCLB put "curricular coverage ... at odds with the consensus about the goals of public education to which Americans historically have subscribed.... It is also starkly at odds with the apparent intention of school board members and state legislators, who are responsible for implementing the policy, and with the intentions of the public whom their leaders represent."[14]

While one might quibble over "the intentions of state legislators," the fact is that much of school policy and practice has been at odds for a century with the breadth of "whole child" expectations in the rhetoric of school purpose. In their appropriately titled book *Tinkering Toward Utopia: A Century of School Reform,* David Tyack and Larry Cuban document little change in the regularities and symbols of schooling.[15] The layered structure of authority and responsibility inhibits change and innovation. Promising ideas come and go and often return for brief attention but rarely even dent the deep structure.[16] Change is cosmetic rather than significantly real.

A Formidable Challenge

During the concluding three decades of the twentieth century, colleagues and I conducted comprehensive studies of educational change and innovation, elementary and secondary schools, and the education of educators that led us to six major conclusions, which are highly relevant to the central theme of this book. First, nothing is more important to the well-being of the United States than the continuous renewal of our democracy. Second, the natural and currently only agency potentially capable of educating the people for this renewal is our system of public schooling. Third, although the rhetoric of the public democratic mission of our schools can readily be traced back to the nation's founding, it has been at odds with schooling's policies and practices. Fourth, school personnel do not view the development of democratic character in the young as a major purpose of the schools for which they are stewards. Fifth, the infrastructure necessary to responsive school renewal and innovation is not characteristic of the system. Sixth, preparing teachers and administrators for advancing a democratic mission for schooling and continuously renewing the schools in which they will serve are not significant priorities for educator-preparing programs. The overarching message emanating from these six major conclusions is that securing the necessary support for tying our schools to an agenda for developing democratic character in the young and cultivating a democratic public is as great a political, social, economic, and educational challenge as any this country has ever experienced.

The 1983 report of the National Commission on Excellence in Education, *A Nation at Risk,* charged the schools with responsibility for the nation's place in the global economy.[17] The strategy was time-worn: ratchet up the curriculum and teaching, push the schools much harder, but leave the basic structure essentially as it is. The commission presumably assumed "that the public and the polity, for whatever reasons, were largely satisfied with the existing shape and routines of the familiar place called school."[18] There was nothing in the report to suggest that greater participation of the public in the destiny of their schools might create a readiness for very fundamental change. Nor was there any indication that the members of the commission were aware that public expectations for our schools are very comprehensive.

At the time of this writing, *Tough Choices or Tough Times,* the report of an independent commission, is stirring the pot of school reform as did *A Nation at Risk.*[19] More arrogant than that earlier report, *Tough Choices or Tough Times* would relinquish district control to private companies, allow some students to graduate from high school after the tenth grade and enroll in technical-vocational schools, and let the more academically competent take advanced courses and then after graduation enroll in college as sophomores and juniors. A half century ago, the Conant report, *The American High School Today* (1959), similarly recommended a comprehensive high school in which the more and less academically able students would be separated into differentiated curricula.

Are these the best routes for ensuring a wise democratic people? Are commissions, made up largely of political and business leaders, the bodies to whom local communities should grant their proxies in the making of policies for schooling and forging of school practices? Are these the ideal processes of a democratic society? I think not.

Ironically, much of the current rhetoric of political and corporate would-be school reformers speaks of bringing our schools into the twenty-first century. During the second half of the twentieth century, their forerunners in such rhetoric spoke of bringing schools into the radio age, the air age, the television age, the global age, the space age, the computer age, etc. But little in the conduct of schooling changed. Study after study shows that out-of-the-box thinking and boundary-breaking initiatives, such as there were, came out of the heads of educational researchers and thinkers whose ideas motivated and guided those creative school staffs able to take advantage of periods of freedom from external authority. Most were encouraged and supported by private philanthropy. In 1975 I wrote the following:

> The single school with its principal, teachers, pupils, parents, and commu-
> nity links is the key unit for educational change.... The school is a social
> system with regularized ways of behaving for those who inhabit it.... No
> matter what the approach to change, it must reckon ultimately with the
> functional reality of this social system.... The school itself is an agent for
> change, potentially or actually.... External change agents, instead of trying
> to insert something into the school's culture, first should be trying to help
> that culture develop an awareness of and a responsiveness to itself.[20]

Commission-driven school reformers either ignore or simply do not understand this reality (or both). They are guided by a linear model of change
that inevitably fails to achieve its ends in a human-intensive ecosystem. The
too-frequent galvanic reaction is to destroy the school's responsiveness to
itself and make it into a robot. I am fascinated to observe that the alternative
processes of school renewal I have studied and recommended for decades
have so much in common with the processes Jim Collins and his colleagues
found to characterize their samples of corporations that progressed from
good to great over a period of fifteen years.[21] In every instance, significant
leadership and change came from within.

More than six decades ago, when I began my teaching career in a
one-room rural school, I had this kind of freedom. But there was nobody
available to share ideas—no experienced teacher, no principal, no superintendent—only my instincts regarding what was right and what was wrong.
The annual one-day visit of a school inspector was the only check on my
competence and compass. Fortunately, he approved of my radical departure
from the eight-grade schedule I had learned to construct in normal school,
which required me to plan and conduct more than fifty lessons each day.
My entire family of thirty-four pupils came together around a comprehensive organizing center of learning that left me teaching in "graded"
lessons only what appeared not to be accommodated by this central whole
of planning, reading, writing, figuring, and discussing. We constituted
every day a compact social democracy that simply took care of what are
commonly referred to as discipline problems.[22]

Much as I enjoyed the absence of restrictions on my behavior, the risk-
laden nature of teaching the young calls for a more communal context
than was available to me. That tight little social democracy could have
benefited and been benefited by conversation with the larger ecosystem of
which its members were individually a part. The parents and other adults
of that ecosystem could have enriched and extended my sparse classroom
learning environment and simultaneously discussed their understanding
of what schools are for and what makes them good.

But there are thousands of schools, big and small, scattered across the country and concentrated in the cities. Don't they need to be tied together in a system of common requirements? My answer is NO! We speak of our system of public schooling, but we do not have one. A system implies connections among the parts, each a link in the whole. But linkages from one to another are extremely rare, even when schools are near neighbors. Take away half of them, and the "system" is little affected.

State and federal regulations, promulgated on the assumption that there is a system, are frequently ignored. They gain attention when there are penalties, especially financial, for not conforming. The current federal No Child Left Behind Act is a classic example. The penalties are substantial, and the complaints are legion. Ironically, what the disconnected array of individual schools scattered like seeds across the landscape most need to serve the people and this nation well would be what our so-called system of schooling lacks: a common public democratic purpose. What we would then expect of our schools is common commitment to this purpose and creative attention to the personal, social, vocational, and academic development of the young.

There is nothing overwhelming about this one-school-at-a-time concept multiplied by the number of schools functioning nationwide. Indeed, it represents quite the opposite: patrons of each local school joined with the responsible stewards of that school in ensuring both the public national and the individual private purposes of schooling. Going back to where I began this writing, the concept seeks to implement the idea that public schooling is the essential starting point for addressing the well-being of democracy.

The Challenge to Education Beyond Schooling

This message cannot be overstressed: *public schooling is the essential starting point for addressing the well-being of democracy.* It embraces a large majority of the young; it surpasses all other institutions in its commitment to and accountability for education; and its rhetoric of mission embraces the personal, social, vocational, and intellectual development of children and youths. What better place might we turn to for advancing the public purpose of ensuring a democratic people?

Nonetheless, even most of those who graduate from secondary schools are still early and limited in their apprenticeship into the social and political democracy of which they are a part. And there is little on the road of life lying ahead to ensure that the passage of time will move them beyond this apprenticeship. In general, the populace is, at best, well informed about a quite narrow range of the social, political, and economic issues with which the nation must continuously grapple. Most of us, in addressing the domains of human discourse and endeavor, are informed by the friends and colleagues with whom we associate daily, among whom none may be well informed in the rubrics of the ongoing conversation.

In other words, we are much guided in what we store in our mental ecosystems by conventional wisdom, not the books and papers that arise out of serious inquiry into our habitat and behavior. A disturbingly high percentage of voters are so unclear about their own beliefs that on Election Day they are unable to sort out candidates on the ballot who appear to align with them from those who do not. The most cleverly scripted and presented television message wins the day.

Were easy exchange of informed views the essence of our democracy, I would not be writing what you are reading here. But, as the late communications specialist Neil Postman reminded us, we largely solved the information-getting problem years ago and are now overwhelmed by the consequences.[23] We have instant access to whatever we want and, more gratifying to many of us, unbridled participation in what writer and award-winning cartoonist David Horsey refers to as an "unfiltered cacophony of opinions" on the Internet. He "worries about the intellect and analytical skills (plus spelling ability) of [his] fellow citizens. In so much of this populist punditry there is an overabundance of ill-informed spouting off infused with incredible rudeness, paranoia, bias, and bile. . . . With everyone holding a virtual megaphone, will we be able to hear the wiser voices amid the din of full-throated free expression?"[24] Over time, we must become adept at this process of belief selection.

In most domains of human endeavor I tend to see the glass as half-full rather than half-empty. We have the needed tools to explore together every nook and cranny of the human conversation. There always will be inexcusable misuse of the media as we seek to democratize it more productively, skillfully, and artistically. It is my glass-half-full belief that a significant percentage of the people are hungry for freewheeling interpersonal verbal exchange. We flock to town hall meetings and other gatherings in order to listen to and perhaps interact with well-informed individuals who share their knowledge and carefully phrase their arguments. We follow up with buying a book that was referred to or further explore the views of a speaker on her Web site. Implementation of the Renaissance café concept brings together small groups of people interested in hearing and talking with the evening's speaker, who presents the topic briefly and invites conversation.

The Institute for Educational Inquiry (IEI), the sponsor of this book, is committed to advancing the agenda of educating the young in the social and political infrastructure of democracy, with special attention to that of the United States. Its inquiry-based Agenda for Education in a Democracy that guides the renewal of schooling and the education of educators in school-university partnerships scattered across the country—the National Network for Educational Renewal (NNER)—has been spelled out in books, papers, and visual presentations.[25]

At the core of the IEI's strategy of implementation is a leadership program that has introduced educators to the Agenda who, in turn, have trained new leaders in the settings of the NNER. Carefully planned readings and conversations are focused on the substance and processes of introducing the young to the moral grounding of social democracy—how we interact with one another—and political democracy—how we manage our affairs. The overall intent is to change our elementary and secondary schools from a reactive to a renewing mode and prepare teachers and administrators for their role of moral stewardship.

What the leaders of the Institute for Educational Inquiry had concluded from their studies in the 1980s into the 1990s and what stimulated their creation of the IEI in 1992 is that our nation does not have the necessary infrastructure for renewing either schooling or democracy. The purposefully representative schools and teacher education programs we studied across the country were not engaged in appraising their strengths and weaknesses, identifying promising new ideas, planning changes, implementing them, and studying the consequences. They were remarkably similar in their basic structure even as they differed in the circumstances of their existence.

Our findings were very similar to those of David Tyack and Larry Cuban, studying the history of school change over the twentieth century,[26] and social psychologist Seymour Sarason, studying the nature of change.[27] Almost all of the school-based educators we studied believed that no policy or public expectations exist for them to be educating their pupils in the principles and responsibilities of democratic citizenship. Most of the university-based educators believed that a public democratic purpose of schooling is desirable and that teachers should be prepared for advancing such a purpose. However, their programs were not geared for fulfilling it, and neither the public nor state and district authorities expected that they should.

Both groups appeared to be unaware that most parents, when polled, express very comprehensive expectations for the educating that should go on in their schools; they mention qualities embedded in social democracy such as honesty, compassion, trustworthiness, independence, teamwork, kindness, and more. As educator Ernest Boyer concluded following his study of adult expectations for our schools, "We want it all."[28]

But today's federal requirements under the Elementary and Secondary Education Act and its current manifestation, NCLB, hold schools accountable for very little breadth but considerable depth in a narrow slice of academic performance. Teachers who passionately believe that caring for each child and educating them all in the social, personal, vocational, and intellectual wholeness that the great religions and our democracy advocate for humankind risk censure if they take class time away from preparing their pupils for what will be tested.

The American people are not accustomed to having nonnegotiable mandates for their schools (like NCLB) imposed by federal authorities, mandates that, if not observed, call for monetary penalties. There is a void regarding information-seeking queries and debate. The people responsible are invisible. Schoolwide, districtwide, and statewide test scores take the place of informed discourse. Neither individual schools nor school districts nor state education departments play discretionary roles in expenditures of the 7 percent of the total educational budget contributed by the federal government. The essence of political democracy is cut off at the ankles.

Enough already!

The IEI and the NNER are committed to an educational agenda that encompasses much more than simply terminating NCLB and avoiding its near replication. Simply returning schooling to where we thought it was at the beginning of this century is unacceptable. It needs comprehensive overhaul: mission, educational conditions, structures and systemics, and, above all else, the development of a renewing mode throughout. We can no longer afford the comfort of allowing change to stop short of the familiar symbols of schooling. Such symbols must be relegated to our memories of how we recall our schools to have been, memories that help to retain what is commonplace.

Even given widespread agreement with an agenda for renewing education and its role in promoting democratic values, the imminent danger is that we will follow the familiar linear model of school reform in seeking to put things right: the presidential appointment of a well-funded all-star commission or a national summit of political and business leaders that might even include a few educators. Been there, done that—over and over. The warning to be heeded at the outset is that we cannot "put things right." Things must make themselves right, with enormous support from "the people": policymakers, school boards, philanthropists, the disenchanted and disillusioned educators. Renewal is not a project; it has no time limits and no ending. It is an essential characteristic of a robust democracy.

Several years ago, colleagues and I in the IEI and the NNER decided that others essential to our work were missing: parents and all those childless adults who live alongside everyone else's children. We need the input of those who pay for public schooling. For years, we had been fostering a tripartite joining of school personnel and teacher educators in both colleges of education and the arts and sciences departments of universities. We began to talk of a fourth partner: representatives of the community context within which the schools of the NNER are located.

Surely, our Agenda for Education in a Democracy is as relevant for these adults as it is for children and youths. We should not have to wait several decades to experience the fruits of our work. The education of a democratic public touches the lives of everyone. To restate what I already have written a couple of times: the idea of renewing public schooling is the essential starting point for addressing the renewal of democracy.

Supported by a grant from the W. K. Kellogg Foundation, three of my colleagues gathered together other colleagues and entered into an initiative entitled Developing Networks of Responsibility to Educate America's Youths (DN), built upon the IEI's Agenda for Education in a Democracy. Four years later, they began a report on the lessons derived as follows:

> The DN initiative asked persons from schools, universities, and communities to work together to create a constituency of the whole and to develop the capacity to address issues arising from efforts to educate all students equitably and excellently. The initiative built on the belief that not only educators but also community members are stewards of our schools and as such hold responsibility for bringing the young into full participation in our social and political democracy. What better way to do that than by participating democratically themselves?[29]

What better way, indeed.

In her chapter in this book entitled "Education Writ Large," Jane Roland Martin effectively reminds us that each of us is educated by much more than schooling, that education and schooling are not synonymous. In her recently published book *Educational Metamorphoses,* she expands this important theme:

> Important as school has become, it is still only one of society's educational agents. Home is another. Church, neighborhood, police and fire departments, museums, historical societies, libraries, and archives; zoos, parks, playgrounds ... ; banks, businesses, and the stock market; newspapers, magazines, book clubs, book stores, publishing houses; ... TV, the Internet, and the media in all its multitudinous forms: these and the myriad other institutions of society also educate young and old.[30]

She makes a powerful case for the early educative environment of infants and the teachings, for better or for worse, of parents. A nonnegotiable agenda of schools committed to advancing democratic public purpose is insufficient promise of a democratic public. The necessary human conversation and accompanying action must embrace "multiple educational agency," to use Martin's language, and both children and adults.

Renewal and the Great Turning

The chapters of this book are guided by four organizing propositions. First, if our democracy is to take care of us, we must take care of it. Second, the care of our democracy is primarily an educational enterprise grounded in moral principles and embracing more than the core element of schooling. Third, the comprehensive general education provided by schooling for all children and youths must address their understanding and appreciation of the public democratic purpose of our schools. Fourth, for the schools to effect the sweeping changes necessary to this learning, the people of their communities must share commitment to and participation in this public mission. Schooling provides an apprenticeship that launches lifelong learning and engagement in social and political democracy. Collectively, the chapters that follow this one seek to deepen understanding of the themes I have sought to introduce.

In addressing the obvious need for fundamental change in the policies and conduct of schooling, colleagues and I reject the word and the concept "reform." Why this nasty word has become attached to virtually all references to needed school improvement and hardly at all to needed change in other domains of human endeavor is an unfortunate puzzlement. It implies ill-guided people doing undesirable things and needing to be redirected by other people.

Except when referring to this abomination, we use the more-uplifting concept and word "renewal." Renewal is a process by which motivated people seek to do better because they want to, whether or not directed or assisted by others. Problems or alternatives are discussed, decisions are made, actions are taken, consequences are evaluated, and the cycle continues. Many self-introduced school initiatives supported by private philanthropy have gone through processes like this with considerable success. The theory supporting it is ecological in character, hence geared to the ecosystems of schools. Reform, however, is inevitably a linear model of defined outputs and anticipated (often mandated) inputs that is almost always out of sync with the realities of individual schools. Failure repeats itself.

Unfortunately, schoolteachers and administrators have rarely been introduced to or experienced the renewal model. In the foregoing, I introduced the work of the National Network for Educational Renewal in seeking to advance the IEI's Agenda for Education in a Democracy: schools and both colleges of education and departments of the arts and sciences of universities are engaged in partnerships dedicated to advancing the public purpose of schooling, processes of renewal, and educating a new corps of school personnel capable of integrating purpose and process. They are breaking new ground.

But the story of seeking to break new ground in schooling has been an exceedingly disappointing one, overshadowed as it has been by reform eras addicted to an ill-guiding linear model of change. There has been reluctance on the part of reform leaders to challenge the long-standing symbols, structure, and systemics of our system of public schooling.[31]

Ultimately, processes of educational renewal confront the need to change these symbols, structures, and systemics. It is essential, therefore, that partnerships such as those of the NNER, committed to advancing the critically important public democratic purpose of schooling, engage their communities in the renewing process. Subsequent chapters reinforce this assumption.

It would be folly to await policy-driven directives for launching a school reform era of community involvement. Indeed, such a development would signal, one more time, that school reformers from the worlds of politics and business are in the driver's seat and would probably do more harm than good. Of course, there will come a time when they will find it desirable to claim ownership of the idea that the stewardship of public schooling must be returned to local communities, and the renewal of schooling is a promising avenue to the necessary renewal of our democracy. And they will learn that participation in the ongoing conversation will give them political traction. But let us remember that they will no longer be key leaders on whom the rest of us are willing to wait for support and approval.

I am not arguing that the direction of school policy and practice be turned over to the sole responsibility of local communities. Nor am I assuming that our democracy will be well taken care of both politically and socially by exclusively local discourse, planning, and action. The Founding Fathers did a superb job in designing the three branches of federal government. I like what we have. This is why I want us to ensure the intentional education necessary to the development of a democratic public. This will necessitate the coming together of the several subcultures of the schooling enterprise in a common mission of education for democracy. The good news is that the call for change is rising and the necessary renewing processes have begun.

Borrowing the title of David Korten's seminal book, I would say that the coming of The Great Turning is palpable. He sees the democracy that has been taken over by the few being recovered by and for the many:

> Beneath the political stresses in the United States that at times threaten to tear our nation apart, we can see the emergent outlines of a largely un-recognized consensus that the world most of us want to bequeath to our children is very different from the world in which we live.... It is within our common means to create a world in which families and communities are strong, parents have the time to love and care for their children, high quality health care and education are available to all, schools and homes are commercial free, the natural environment is healthy and toxin free, and nations cooperate for the common good. It is about renewing the democratic experiment, liberating the creative potential of the species, and coming home to life. It is an idea whose time has come and the foundation of a true political democracy.[32]

Bill Moyers sees the power of the word as being central to effecting the great turning:

> Here in the first decade of the twenty-first century the story that becomes America's dominant narrative will shape our collective imagination and hence our politics.... It is that the promise of America leaves no one out. Go now and tell it on the mountain. From the rooftops tell it.... From the workplace and the bookstore, tell it. On campus and at the mall, tell it. Tell it at the synagogue, sanctuary and mosque. Tell it where you can, when you can and while you can—to every candidate for office, to every talk-show host and pundit, to corporate executives and schoolchildren. Tell it—for America's sake.[33]

It is my hope and expectation, as well as that of the other authors of this book and colleagues beyond, that this telling will inspire and inform conversations about the moral grounding of our democracy, just as April showers nourish our gardens. Some of these conversations have begun, and many more are incubating. The agenda is compelling and nonnegotiable.

Notes

1. "Trust the Voters," *Seattle Post-Intelligencer,* December 1, 2006.

2. Paul Woodruff, *First Democracy* (New York: Oxford University Press, 2005), 5.

3. Wendell Berry, *In the Presence of Fear: Three Essays for a Changed World* (Great Barrington, Mass.: Orion Society, 2001).

4. Kenneth A. Sirotnik, "Society, Schooling, Teaching, and Preparing to Teach," in John I. Goodlad, Roger Soder, and Kenneth A. Sirotnik, eds., *The Moral Dimensions of Teaching* (San Francisco: Jossey-Bass, 1990), 307.

5. In their book *Teaching as a Subversive Activity* (New York: Delacorte, 1969), Neil Postman and Charles Weingartner startled readers with their introduction of crap-detecting as an essential skill for both teachers and the lay public.

6. John Dewey, *Democracy and Education* (New York: Macmillan, 1916), 53.

7. R. S. Peters, *Ethics and Education* (London: George Allen and Unwin, 1966), 27.

8. Lawrence A. Cremin, "Further Notes toward a Theory of Education," *Notes on Education* 4 (March 1974): 1.

9. John I. Goodlad, *A Place Called School* (1984; repr., New York: McGraw-Hill, 2004). See chapter 2.

10. Neil Postman, *The End of Education: Redefining the Value of School* (New York: Knopf, 1995), 27–28.

11. Harry R. Lewis, *Excellence without a Soul: How a Great University Forgot Education* (New York: PublicAffairs, 2006).

12. See Goodlad, *A Place Called School,* chapter 3.

13. Both the National School Boards Association and the large educational organization the Association for Supervision and Curriculum Development have come out strongly for school purposes and programs directed to the total development of children and youths. The latter formed a commission of prominent educators and lay citizens to promote educational attention to "the whole child."

14. Richard Rothstein and Rebecca Jacobsen, "The Goals of Education," *Phi Delta Kappan* 88 (December 2006): 264.

15. David Tyack and Larry Cuban, *Tinkering Toward Utopia: A Century of School Reform* (Cambridge, Mass.: Harvard University Press, 1995).

16. Barbara Benham Tye, *Hard Truths: Uncovering the Deep Structure of Schooling* (New York: Teachers College Press, 2000).

17. National Commission on Excellence in Education, *A Nation at Risk: The Imperative for Educational Reform: A Report to the Nation and the Secretary of Education* (Washington, D.C.: U.S. Government Printing Office, 1983).

18. Theodore R. Sizer, "Back to *A Place Called School,*" in Kenneth A. Sirotnik and Roger Soder, eds., *The Beat of a Different Drummer: Essays on Educational Renewal in Honor of John I. Goodlad* (New York: Peter Lang, 1999), 112.

19. National Center on Education and the Economy, *Tough Choices or Tough Times: The Report of the New Commission on the Skills of the American Workforce* (San Francisco: Jossey-Bass, 2006).

20. John I. Goodlad, *The Dynamics of Educational Change* (New York: McGraw-Hill, 1975), 81 and 177.

21. Jim Collins, *Good to Great: Why Some Companies Make the Leap—and Others Don't* (New York: HarperCollins, 2001).

22. For further information, see John I. Goodlad, *Romances with Schools: A Life of Education* (New York: McGraw-Hill, 2004), chapter 5.

23. Neil Postman, *Technopoly: The Surrender of Culture to Technology* (New York: Vintage Books, 1993).

24. David Horsey, "Horsey's Burning Questions: Unfiltered Cacophony of Opinions a Good Thing?" *Seattle Post-Intelligencer,* December 30, 2006.

25. For an introduction to the Agenda for Education in a Democracy, see John I. Goodlad, Corinne Mantle-Bromley, and Stephen John Goodlad, *Education for Everyone: Agenda for Education in a Democracy* (San Francisco: Jossey-Bass, 2004).

26. Tyack and Cuban, *Tinkering Toward Utopia.*

27. Seymour B. Sarason, *The Culture of the School and the Problem of Change,* 2nd ed. (Boston: Allyn & Bacon, 1982).

28. Ernest L. Boyer and the Carnegie Foundation for the Advancement of Teaching, *High School: A Report on Secondary Education in America* (New York: Harper & Row, 1983).

29. Institute for Educational Inquiry, *Engaging with the Community* (Seattle: Institute for Educational Inquiry, 2006), vi.

30. Jane Roland Martin, *Educational Metamorphoses* (Lanham, Md.: Rowman & Littlefield, 2007), 56.

31. James H. Nehring's historical research has led him to the conclusion that six destructive tendencies in our culture have conspired to inhibit change and innovation in our schools. See Nehring, "Conspiracy Theory: Lessons for Leaders from Two Centuries of School Reform," *Phi Delta Kappan* 88 (February 2007): 425–32.

32. David C. Korten, *The Great Turning: From Empire to Earth Community* (San Francisco: Berrett-Koehler, 2006), 340.

33. Bill Moyers, "For America's Sake: A New Story for America," *Nation,* January 22, 2007, 17.

Chapter 2

What Is Renewal? Why Now?

Alan T. Wood

Never have the United States and the world been more prosperous. Never have they been more vulnerable. For a century the United States has been the largest market economy and the most powerful nation on earth. Its preeminence in world affairs has come to be understood—at least by Americans—as virtually a natural right. That period at the summit of world power and influence, however, is about to end. In one generation the United States will become only the second largest economy in the world, behind China. In another generation it will become the third largest economy in the world, behind China and India. The changes are even more profound on a global level. For the last two hundred years humankind has witnessed a vast increase in its productive and destructive capacities, but for most of that time the consequences have been only local in scope. Now advances in technology have reached the point at which our human propensity to slaughter each other, foul the environment, and squander our natural resources carries with it truly global consequences. To prosper in the future (and even to survive), therefore, we citizens of America and of the world—for we are both simultaneously—need to reassess our priorities in a fundamental way. In short, we need to relocate education from the periphery of our collective consciousness to the center.

The rise of the United States to global preeminence began in the closing decades of the nineteenth century. The Industrial Revolution, which had propelled Europe to world dominance between the 1830s and 1890s, crossed the Atlantic and transformed the American economy from an agricultural powerhouse into an industrial one. That same Industrial Revolution has now crossed the Pacific to China and India. The center of the world economy and global power is shifting back to Asia, where it in fact resided for most of human history (even as recently as 1830, China produced one-third of the world's total Gross Domestic Product). The playing field, in effect, is being re-leveled for the first time in almost two hundred years. The consequences of the economic rebirth of Asia will be profound. No longer will America dominate the world like a colossus. No longer will it be able to act unilaterally on the international stage.

America also faces two additional challenges, one internal and the other external. Internally, the disparity between the wealthy and the poor in American society has increased to a degree not seen since the Gilded Age in the last two decades of the nineteenth century. For reasons that remain unclear, we seem to have lost the commitment to equality—a fundamental basis for any common standard of equity and justice—that for so long was one of the defining characteristics of American society. Over time, these inequalities will corrode the connective links that hold American society together. Externally, we have embarked on a series of military campaigns—from Vietnam to Iraq—that have dissipated our power, drained our resources, multiplied our enemies, and alienated the world. The impact of the destruction of the World Trade Center on September 11, 2001, which might have stimulated the United States to open up to the outside world, appears to have had the opposite effect, making us more defensive, more insular, and more inclined to use violence to protect ourselves than ever before. The unintended consequences are notable for their ironic quality. In the name of fighting terrorism, we seem to have abetted it; in the name of building democracy, we seem to have undermined it.

The worldwide change we confront is even more fundamental. Humankind now faces a challenge unique to its entire existence on this planet. For the first time the lethality of our weapons and the degradation of our environment endanger not just individual societies but the world as a whole. The very survival of *Homo sapiens* hangs in the balance. Meanwhile, the central ideology of our time—nationalism—and the central institution of our time—the nation-state—are inadequate to the task at hand. Both grew out of a highly competitive, bloody stage in European history that is long since past. We face the twenty-first century, in effect, with eighteenth-century tools.

Cooperation and Interdependence

If the picture I have painted above—of great challenges and self-defeating actions—is true (and I would be the first to celebrate if I am wrong), then where should we go from here, and what does it all have to do with education? Our predicament calls to mind H. G. Wells's insight that civilization is a race between education and catastrophe. Those words continue to ring as true now as they did when he wrote them. And yet the urgency of the task is widely ignored by a polarized American public whose attention is easily distracted by politicians from both the left and the right eager to exploit legitimate fears and false hopes. As the Industrial Revolution moves to a new stage in which workers who once got by with practical skills are being replaced by those who require greater knowledge and creativity, and as the demands of responsible citizenship expand to require higher levels of cooperation to deal with truly global challenges such as climate change, disease, and war, then education will become more vital than ever before.

The path out of the predicament in which we find ourselves lies in rediscovering the centrality of education not only to our national welfare but also, and far more profoundly, to our very humanity. To do that will require more than just a minor recalibration of our national priorities. It will require, to some degree, a fundamental rethinking of the intellectual assumptions of the modern world. This essay's four sections—on renewal, on the moral component of social life, on education, and on democracy—share the overall assumption that we need to replace our present worldview stressing the value of competition alone with an ecological and organic worldview stressing the value of a balance of both competition and cooperation. Like the wings of a bird, they need each other. Our modern obsession with the partial truth of competition obscures the equally valid truth of cooperation.

It must be said at the outset that an organic worldview of the kind I am proposing here, which stresses the vital importance of relationships, implies a broader view of education than is encompassed by schooling alone. Here education is used in a larger context that includes the contributions of all those institutions—including business, the family, the media, the church, the courts—that through their influence on young people shape their personalities and either inspire or confuse them. Education is the key to renewing America only if it is seen in its broadest possible application and in its manifold connections to all other major aspects of American life and to the core values of American society.

In 1776 the Declaration of Independence announced the birth of a nation that dedicated itself, in Thomas Jefferson's immortal words, to the truths "that all men are created equal, and that they are endowed by their Creator with certain inalienable rights, that among these are life, liberty, and the pursuit of happiness." Embodied in that phrase is a dual objective—to promote both equality and freedom—that was echoed by Abraham Lincoln in the Gettysburg Address, in which he reminded us that we live in a "nation conceived in liberty and dedicated to the proposition that all men are created equal." If true, then education is central to the bedrock values of this republic, as well as to the essential qualities of our very humanity.

Education gives us the eyes to see and the knowledge to understand the choices (freedom) and opportunities (equality) that might otherwise lie hidden by the veil of ignorance. If we truly believe that all children on this planet have a fundamental right to a life of human dignity, then we must recommit ourselves, every day, to building the road of education that will lead them to a new land of freedom and opportunity. What we need now is a new statement of principle—a kind of Declaration of *Inter*-dependence—that realigns our national and global priorities to respond to our present array of challenges. We need nothing less than a new constitutional convention that would bring together representatives of all the chief institutions in American life to rededicate the nation to the renewal of the human potential through education.

Why Renewal?

The thesis of this essay—that education is the key to the renewal of American and global society—rests on a fundamental set of theoretical assumptions about the nature of the world that is different from the dominant worldview of our age. It might be worthwhile, therefore, to identify exactly what those assumptions are. In doing so I am inviting the reader to see theory and practice not in terms of a dichotomy, but in terms of a mutually interactive whole. Ideas are not just abstractions with no practical relevance. They matter. Theory and practice reach their fulfillment only in relation to each other, never by themselves. To understand the roots of

American behavior, one needs to look first for the unexamined theoretical assumptions on which that behavior is based.

Those theoretical assumptions are usually encompassed by the term "mechanistic." In a broad sense, this worldview—the hallmark of the modern age—holds that nature operates more or less like a machine, the parts of which are related to each other much as the parts of a machine are related to each other. The whole is assumed to have no identity or existence other than as the sum of those aggregate parts. This view also posits that natural phenomena influence each other in a linear, cause-and-effect fashion, such that every effect can ultimately be traced to one cause, and every solution reduced to a single problem. Thus social scientists narrow down complex factors to one "independent" variable so as to identify more clearly the relationship of cause and effect. One consequence of this outlook is to foster the notion that the only valid method of discovering knowledge is by breaking phenomena down into ever-smaller, bite-sized chunks—that is, by analysis. The modern American university is a monument to this mechanistic and reductionist view of the world. It reduces knowledge to disciplines and studies them largely in isolation from other disciplines. There is no need for synthesis, that is, for putting the pieces together, because the whole is assumed to be no more than the sum of those pieces. It has no other reality. Any high-level synthesis that is done—to create interdisciplinary collaboration, for example—is accomplished in spite of and not because of the bureaucratic structure and culture of the university. Door prizes in the academy continue to go almost exclusively to those scholars who focus on breaking knowledge down into its analytical components.

This mechanistic, sometimes called "atomistic," view became dominant in modern Western civilization for a very good reason—it worked. As early as the Scientific Revolution in the seventeenth century, it was spectacularly successful in revealing and subsequently controlling many of the underlying processes of nature. Its counterpart in political thought was an individual-based notion of human society, of which Thomas Hobbes's *Leviathan* (published in 1651) became the preeminent example. In Hobbes's view, society itself was not "natural" at all but merely an artificial construct of the human will whose primary function was to fulfill the needs of the autonomous individual. It was a social contract. The individual came first and society second, consisting of nothing more than an association of individuals.

This mechanistic and atomistic model, together with its corollary assertion that the social good was no more than the total of individual goods added together, gradually evolved into what came to be known as classical liberalism and formed the basis of the Enlightenment. Adam Smith's *Wealth of Nations* (published in 1776), for example, which became the Bible of classical liberalism and modern capitalism, was based on the principle that the most efficient economy emerges out of unfettered competition in the marketplace among individuals maximizing their self-interest. The impact of these ideas on America—whose founding documents were written by admirers of the Enlightenment such as Thomas Jefferson—was profound and provided the intellectual basis for the experiment of radical individualism that still remains one of the most important identifying features of American society.

Charles Darwin gave classical liberalism further credibility when he applied its focus on competition to biology, making struggle appear to be not just a human attribute but a phenomenon essential to the basic evolutionary processes of life itself. He therefore built not only on the views of Adam Smith but also on those of Hobbes (who had described life in the state of nature as a "war of all against all"). This doctrine fit perfectly with the needs of the newly emerging middle class and with the rise of the new nation-states of Europe, the latter of which owed their very existence to violent conflict and war. Even Karl Marx, hardly a believer in the virtues of capitalism, adopted his notion of class struggle from this fundamental tenet of classical liberalism.

Although I will challenge the dominance of this mechanistic and reductionist worldview below, it is not my intention to argue that it is invalid. On the contrary—it is not only valid but necessary. We need to study the parts of a whole. We need specialists. Believe me, if I require brain surgery, I want it done by a specialist who may not know a lot about Western political thought or Chinese history but knows a great deal about how to remove brain tumors. I acknowledge the obvious value of studying the parts of a whole in great depth.

My point is that the mechanistic view of the world, while it is undeniably successful and necessary, is only partially valid. There is another view, which we might call "organic," "ecological," or "systemic," that is equally valid. This view of nature favors not just the parts but also the whole. The relationship between the mechanistic and organic worldviews is therefore not adversarial but complementary. Analysis without synthesis has no meaning. Synthesis without analysis has no substance. They need each other.

That this is so is because the natural world is both simple and complex. There are often many causes, with effects that loop back and change the causes. All the parts affect each other. Nature, in practice, does not favor competition alone but a dynamic balance of both competition and cooperation. To be sure, competition is important. Over time, and in many differing circumstances, it provides a means of promoting successful over unsuccessful organisms. But an equally valid case can be made for co-operation as well. Let us imagine that the organs of your body decide to compete with each other rather than cooperate. Your feet resent the fact that they get no respect and have no power. Fed up with unfair taxation and lack of representation in the governing organs of the body, they declare independence. Soon other parts of the body follow suit, on the principle that they are also free and autonomous units and deserve to be in charge of their own destiny and seek their own happiness. In time, the health of the whole is compromised, and eventually the body dies (including, naturally, the very parts that precipitated the revolt in the first place).

Okay, you say, that analogy may be clear, but reasoning by analogy is a very risky business, because analogues invariably differ from each other in important ways that are often disguised by the similarities but are never-theless crucial. Granted, societies are not bodies. Nevertheless, both share an important quality—their identity and existence depend as much on a cooperative relationship among the parts as on the nature and identity of the parts themselves. This view is not new. Plato's *Republic,* which has had a defining influence on Western philosophy, was actually based on an analogy between the body and the state (hence the term "body politic"). Aristotle, in *Metaphysics,* refers quite explicitly to the whole as a sum greater than its aggregate parts. Thus this view is very ancient (and not only in Western society, but in Chinese and Indian societies as well).

The mechanistic and atomistic model, therefore, is not so much wrong as only partially right. For over two centuries, we have substituted a par-tial truth for the whole, with consequences that are only now becoming apparent in terms of both the mindless escalation of our weapons of mass destruction and the degrading impact of industrial processes on the en-vironment. So bear with me a bit longer. Even if you remain skeptical of my argument for balance in the way we look at the world, suspend your disbelief for now and follow my line of reasoning a couple more steps. Then, if you still disagree with me, so be it.

Take a plant or animal cell—any cell. It is constantly responding to changes in its environment—heat, light, moisture, etc.—by sending mil-lions of messages back and forth through its own channels of communica-tion. Then, through a process we might call "cognition," it mobilizes the requisite resources to maintain its own internal equilibrium and sustain the processes of life. The complexity of the interactions that take place even at that cellular level is quite astonishing. The human body, naturally, is vastly more complex. To be precise, each one of us is composed of about seventy-five trillion cells. Each cell is constantly responding to information of one kind or another. Some, indeed thousands, of those cells die in the time it takes for you, the reader, to read this sentence. Fortunately, however, an equal number of cells is being created to take their place. Your body is therefore in a state of constant and perpetual renewal from the moment you are born until you die. That renewal is itself the product of an incredible amount of information constantly circulating throughout the body both within and among its various systems: the endocrine system, the immune system, the respiratory system, and so on.

Let us further assume that all human institutions (social, economic, political), like the body, have qualities that are both organic and mechanistic. They have parts that can be studied by themselves, but they also participate in various levels of organization that can be usefully studied as interactive and mutually dependent wholes. Each level in nature is a whole with regard to the parts below it, and a part with regard to the whole above it. Just as any organism needs to renew itself at every moment of its existence—both to respond to changes in its internal environment and changes in its external environment—so also do human institutions need to respond to changes in both internal and external environments. Indeed, institutions come into existence precisely in order to respond to new challenges in the environment. How a given institution accommodates itself to those changes, in turn, depends on how accurately it comprehends the changes and how effectively it communicates that knowledge through its own channels of information.

As it is in the body, so is it also in human society. One of the best practical examples of this principle in Western history is the Renaissance. That "rebirth," in fact, was stimulated by the revival of classical Greek thought in Europe and sustained by the advent of printing, which greatly enhanced the flow of knowledge throughout the continent. Soon Europe was exploding with creative ideas (the Scientific Revolution) and entrepreneurial energy (the age of exploration), all because Europe was developing new institutions of both competition (the emerging nation-states) and cooperation (guilds, the Hanseatic League, banks, limited liability companies, and so forth).

It is through this very process of constant communication of information and transfer of energy, therefore, that all organisms in nature and all organizations in human society renew themselves. Our propensity to view the world in mechanistic terms, however, has prevented us from fully appreciating the significance of this dynamic interrelatedness of the world around us. By looking at society ecologically, that is, as an interconnected whole, we can better appreciate how central the process of constant renewal is to the well-being of the human community at every level from the local to the global. We have to understand the parts, but if we really believe in the fulfillment of the human potential, we have to understand the whole as well.

Why Moral?

At about the time that I sat down to write this chapter, my wife and I watched the marvelous film *March of the Penguins*. It portrays the astonishing pilgrimage taken by a colony of emperor penguins in Antarctica every year to their winter mating grounds. One segment of the film describes how the fathers sit on their mates' eggs for months, in subzero blizzard conditions, without eating, while the females head out to fatten up for their turn on the egg. This was my wife's favorite part. She has continued to remind me periodically how wonderful male penguins are in caring for the young. While I usually point out to her that she did not marry a penguin, and that I would not last long sitting on an egg in minus eighty degrees Fahrenheit, I do have to concede that these dads are a pretty responsible lot.

Or not. What, after all, does it mean to be "responsible"? Are the penguins being "moral" in any way recognizable to humans, or are they responding only to a genetic call of instinct that is essentially irresistible (and therefore irrelevant for our purposes here)? I do not know, and since this is not a treatise on penguins, I will not bother to go any further with this analogy. But it does serve to raise, at least for me, the interesting question of what exactly is meant by the term "moral."

For most readers, the word "moral" carries with it many connotations, some positive and some negative. Because much of what follows below depends on a shared definition of this complex term, it might be useful to clarify its meaning for this chapter. For the time being, let us set aside the question of defining morality in terms of standards of "right" versus "wrong." Those terms are, at least in the Western context, so closely associated with religious traditions that it is virtually impossible to discuss them without bringing theology into the conversation. That could be very profitable, but it tends to limit the terms of discourse only to those who share the same belief system. For the moment, it might be more helpful to broaden our scope to include definitions not affiliated with a specific religion. We can do that if we consider another common definition of the term "moral" as an attitude of "responsibility" or "obligation."

Those terms are, of course, not all that easy to explain either, particularly in a society based on a mechanistic view of the world. In such a society one would expect to find less emphasis on responsibility and more emphasis on individual freedom, since the latter by definition calls for the maximum latitude for individual choice unimpeded by the constraints of outside influences. So it is hardly surprising that America would be a textbook case of a country whose people communicate more readily in the language of rights than responsibility. (The Austrian psychiatrist Viktor Frankl, who believed that the exclusive focus on freedom and rights in the United States threatened to undermine the bonds that hold American society together, once proposed that America build a Statue of Responsibility in San Francisco Bay to counterbalance the Statue of Liberty in New York Harbor.)

Responsibility, which by definition requires a relationship, is therefore much easier to explain from an organic and ecological perspective than from a mechanistic perspective. Whereas those who have a mechanistic view of the world tend to see the relationship between freedom and responsibility as adversarial (the more of one, the less of the other), an organic or ecological view of the world would suggest a more complex and even complementary relationship between freedom and responsibility, to the point that individual freedom could not even exist without responsibility.

I once tried to explain this relationship to a class I was teaching. Nothing appeared to be making sense to the students. Eyes were glazing over. Heads were nodding. It just happened that there was a property rights initiative on the ballot at the time. At issue was a differing understanding of the role of rights and responsibilities conferred on the owners of private property. Some of those in favor of the ballot initiative argued that ownership implied complete freedom over the uses of that property. Ownership of property, they believed, was all about rights, not responsibilities. So I said to the class, "Let me show that such an assertion is unsupportable by its very definition, and that furthermore, without a balance of rights and responsibilities, even the concept of property itself would cease to exist." Instantly, I had everyone's attention. Eyes cleared. Heads snapped up.

I began with the assumption, for the sake of argument, that property ownership is only about rights and not responsibilities, or only about responsibilities and not rights. The former does not work for a simple reason—ownership itself requires formal title backed up by a legal system. Without a government, and all the responsibilities of contract law that flow from that institution, ownership itself would simply vanish, and with it any meaningful sense of the term "property." So it does not make sense to claim that ownership is only a matter of rights. But the opposite position does not work either, as all Marxist-Leninist societies in the twentieth century discovered to their dismay. They tried to abolish all rights to private property and ended up with economic stagnation and political tyranny.

The logical conclusion, then, is that rights and responsibilities are both necessary for each other.

I then went on to argue that, for every freedom we cherish, there have to be responsibilities, which are embodied in rules or laws (externally imposed) or moral habits (internally imposed), that protect that freedom. In this case, rules and laws are the tangible expression of intangible responsibility, the practical implementation of the theoretical commitment to a larger social whole. For every act of individual freedom by one person there has to be an equivalent act of social responsibility by another person. Neither, in fact, can be understood without the other. Put another way, they exist only in relationship to each other. The propensity to see them as unconnected and to see the world primarily in terms of freedom may, parenthetically, explain why American society seems to have drifted away from its commitment to equality. One of the manifestations of that phenomenon is the increasing perception of education as a private benefit and not a public good. Indeed, without a sense of ourselves as a community, it becomes difficult to justify almost any activity at all that requires individual sacrifice for the common good.

Back to the metaphor of the body. We have agreed on the principle that each organ of the body has to take responsibility for doing its job or the body as a whole suffers and potentially dies. If so, then the whole of a society can be seen, as we discussed above, as a body writ large—a complex interrelationship of parts, each of which performs a magic dance of responsibility and freedom. Energy flows from one part of society to another, information is constantly exchanged, goods are transported, rules are created to perform specific tasks and then enforced, the whole is protected by an immune system (known as the police and the military), etc. If the parts decide, in order to exert their freedom, to walk away from their responsibility, then the whole suffers—and potentially collapses. Instead of integration, there is dis-integration, a dissolution of the moral bonds linking the parts to the whole. On the other hand, if the whole suppresses the freedom of action necessary for the parts to respond effectively to the opportunities and challenges that confront them, then that very same whole will also suffer and eventually collapse (as the Soviet Union did for precisely that reason).

In this essay, therefore, the term "moral" is not derived from a specific religious tradition but from the observation of nature itself. To put it another way, when the religious traditions of the world use the term "love" or "compassion" or "kindness," they are grounding their understanding in a very simple truth that operates at all levels of the natural world. The whole, whether of an individual or a community, depends on the trust and communication and caring and integrity of the parts. By the same token, hatred and miscommunication and extreme self-absorption are corrosive, both to the individual and to the community at large. To have "integrity," on some level, is to be "integrated" in such a way that the pieces fit together into a single whole and work together for the common good. The centrality of this insight to both the religious and the secular systems' views of the world is revealed in the shared etymology of the terms "holy" and "whole." Thus by treating an individual as a whole person deserving of a special dignity, we acknowledge the sacredness of that wholeness. Alternatively, when we treat individuals only as parts, only as cogs in a larger machine, as commodities, we strip them of their full humanity. We dehumanize them. To be human, therefore, is to be both autonomous and integrated, both free and responsible simultaneously. Freedom and responsibility are not adversaries. They are indispensable partners in a moral world.

In the previous section, we saw how central renewal is to the flourishing of all life on earth. This section argues that all levels of the natural world live in relationships of obligation of one kind or another. In a sense, moral responsibility in human society performs the same role that instinct—or genetic code—performs in penguin society. Both societies, in order to survive and prosper, have to encourage cooperative and altruistic behavior. In penguins, the drive is genetic (or mostly so—there is still plenty of room for learning and individuality); in humans, it is moral (or mostly so—there is still plenty of room for genetic inheritance).

Why Education?

I wish I could say that I have always believed in education as the key to rebirth and renewal and that I have always favored a holistic, ecological worldview. In truth, I have taken a long and circuitous path to arrive at my present understanding of education as analogous in human society to the processes of communication and cognition that sustain all forms of organic life on the planet. Perhaps because my professional career began as a historian of China, I could not help absorbing some ideas from the traditional Chinese (and Indian, for that matter) worldview, which rests on an assumption that the world is made up of relationships. Chinese and Indian philosophers were what we would now call "systems" or "ecological" thinkers thousands of years ago.

But I did not arrive at this perspective by adopting the Chinese worldview at the very beginning—far from it. It was a very slow process. While I was buried in my own area of academic research, building abstract castles in the sky, I was also raising a family, teaching, and occasionally serving as an academic administrator in a complex university. Over time, I realized that all these activities were themselves interacting to give me a very different view of the world than I might otherwise have had.

I began to notice that good administrators were also systems thinkers, able to scan the horizon constantly and foresee problems before they arose or, when they did arise, address them in all their complex interrelationships, using wise judgment. The more I saw, the more appreciation I developed for the role of leadership in an organization—any organization—and the role that wisdom (a fortuitous marriage of knowledge and experience) plays in integrating the parts of an organization together so that they reinforce each other rather than undermine each other. I saw cases in which the parts might have been brilliant but, in the absence of leadership, led to a dysfunctional whole. And equally, I saw cases in which the parts were not individually outstanding but, through leadership, resulted in a highly effective whole. (At the risk of pointing out the obvious, successful athletic coaches and school principals are perfect examples of this phenomenon.) Above all, I noticed that good leadership is extremely rare, for the simple reason that the array of personal qualities needed to synchronize the parts is so large. Very few individuals possess that array, and fewer still make it to the top of the organizational food chain. For any organization to thrive, potential leaders need to be educated in a wide area of knowledge and experience and be put in constant communication with all their surroundings (hence the vital importance of transparency and accountability). The path for those potential leaders to advance, moreover, has to be open—not limited by class or race or gender or income or any other obstacle. The broader the pool of educated folks and the more open the access (one might even say "democratic" here), the more likely the organization will be well run.

On the one hand, what I am suggesting is not all that startling, namely that the more complex the tasks we confront in life, the greater the premium on communication and cognition. That process of the transmission and interpretation of knowledge we might well call "education." On the other hand, I am suggesting that the more conventional understanding of education—focusing on the transmission of discrete nuggets of knowledge we call disciplines or workplace skills—is only partially valid. We also need to understand the relationships among those nuggets of knowledge, and this understanding is a function of practical experience as well as theoretical reason, happens outside as well as inside the classroom, and involves the emotional as well as the rational faculties.

In the end our well-being as a society depends in large part on our ability to see the whole as more than the sum of its aggregate parts. That is what skilled leaders do, and that is what societies do if they wish to flourish. To the extent that we ignore that truth, we are preparing our children for failure. We cannot survive as a nation if we feed our children a steady diet of compartmentalized knowledge without teaching them how to put that knowledge into practice in ways that reflect the interdependent wholeness of the world around us and inside us.

Only through education can we learn how to reach a balance between the legitimate need for the continued autonomy of the nation-state with an equally legitimate need for international organizations of cooperation that transcend the nation-state. We need the nation-state to preserve our freedom, and we need some form of international governance to preserve our community. By the same token, only through education can we cultivate the level of appreciation for moral responsibility among our citizens that will be necessary for our global polity to thrive. So when someone like former vice president Al Gore travels the world giving speeches about global warming, he is educating the world in the moral responsibilities of global citizenship. He is performing the vital and life-sustaining role of communication and cognition that is at the heart of all life processes from the most basic to the most exalted. It is no coincidence that religious and educational institutions are among the most enduring of all institutions in human cultures. Without them we would lose sight of the whole and of our place in that whole.

Why Democracy?

For most of the twentieth century, education in the United States has been linked with democratic citizenship. John Dewey's influence here has been formative. An organic and ecological perspective of the kind articulated in this chapter further supports the strong complementarity between education and democracy first promoted by Dewey (and then sustained for the remainder of the twentieth century by educational leaders like John Goodlad). That ecological perspective, as I have discussed above, focuses on the complex relationship among the parts of any given environment, each responding to a constantly changing set of circumstances.

In discussing the role of moral responsibility, I suggested that it performs a function in human society analogous to that of instinct in penguin society. Let me expand on that theme here and apply it to democratic citizenship as well. The main proposition is that the more simple the organism, the more unconscious and instinctual the reaction. Humans, with the most sophisticated powers of consciousness and cognition, have developed their own mechanism—known as "culture"—for doing consciously and intentionally what all simpler forms of nature accomplish through a greater reliance on the vehicle of instinct. Just as the term "moral" is the human form of responsibility to the common good that takes place in penguin society largely through instinct, so is "education" the human form of a behavior of learning that occurs in nature through communication of information and then cognition. The cumulative knowledge we call culture in the human realm, in other words, replaces genetics and natural selection in the natural realm as the main engine of adaptation and response.

For human society to succeed, it first needs to be open to whatever information is relevant to its health and survival. Second, that information has to be accurate. Third, it must be communicated without interference. Fourth, it has to be understood. Fifth, it needs to be acted upon effectively, that is, by educated and responsible citizens and by wise leaders. Without freedom of speech, the various parts of society cannot respond to challenges effectively because they have been denied the knowledge and information they need to function. Without education, the information cannot be fully understood. Without democracy, a society lacks the freedom to act in its own best interests. Without a willingness to accept moral responsibility by an educated citizenry, a society cannot achieve synergy among the parts.

Here the major threads of this chapter are woven together to form a single fabric. From an ecological perspective, moral responsibility, education, and democracy each represent a quality or activity that is a consequence of our fundamental human identity as free agents and as beneficiaries of the cumulative cultural knowledge of the entire species. Because of our powers of conscious thought, we are endowed with the precious gift of freedom. But freedom alone is not enough to ensure the health and prosperity of a democratic community. It is a double-edged gift. In addition to choosing what is good for us, we also have, by definition, the capacity to choose what is not good for us, to make choices that are irresponsible, self-defeating, even suicidal. Wrong-headedness is thus a consequence of human freedom—an undesirable one, to be sure, but inescapable. We could, of course, try to force people to do what is right, in the name of some larger virtue such as equality. But in the process we would have to eliminate freedom. (Some would argue that the totalitarian states of the Soviet Union and China originally set out to do just that and paid a high price.)

The term "moral" thus encapsulates the profoundly tragic and potentially noble paradox of freedom. It is through democracy, moreover, that human beings compensate for and hope to mitigate the tragic consequences of this gift of moral freedom. Simpler organisms do not need democracy because they function, to a far greater degree than humans, according to the dictates of instinct. They do not need education or morality, either, for the same reason. But we are different. We need them all. Therein lies our capacity for both nobility and inhumanity, as well as our capacity to enhance the former and reduce the latter. That is presumably what the great Protestant theologian Reinhold Niebuhr meant when he wrote that the human capacity for good makes democracy possible, and the human capacity for evil makes democracy necessary. The former acknowledges our sense of moral responsibility, the latter our tendency to be corrupted by the desire for power, wealth, and fame. The simple fact is that without a developed sense of democratic responsibility and without a willingness on the part of everyday citizens to act in a responsible way in the service of others, the community will not endure. Democracy, based on a rule of law, committed to freedom of the press, open to the stimulus of diverse influences and information, and able to promote responsible leadership among its entire population, is not just one kind of governance among many, and not just a Western phenomenon, but a universal benefit for all humankind.

One fascinating recent development for both democracy and education, which further illustrates the applicability of an organic and ecological worldview to our present set of challenges, is the rise of the Internet—itself a complex web of relationships. It promises to make the sum total of human knowledge available to a far greater share of the human population, and at a far lower cost, than any breakthrough in communication technology since the advent of printing in Europe in the fifteenth century. At the same time, it "democratizes" that knowledge insofar as it bypasses the control of the government and prevents governments from monopolizing and therefore manipulating knowledge and information. This new development, on a global level, has enormous potential for education. It makes possible a level of integration and synergy that promises a renaissance—a fundamental renewal—of the human potential, just as printing was one of the indisputable catalysts to the Renaissance and the Scientific Revolution in Europe.

But, of course, the Internet—insofar as it is a tool of human freedom—will be a vehicle not only for the liberation of human knowledge but also for the increase of human suffering. As in all forms of technology from the invention of fire to the present, the Internet contains a potential for abuse and for reinforcing inequalities of condition and opportunity throughout the world. We must learn how to release its power to do good while simultaneously mitigating its power to do harm. Here, as in every realm of human existence, that trilogy of education, democracy, and moral responsibility becomes the essential tools for fully exploiting the positive

potential of human freedom and for bringing genuine equality of opportunity to every child in the world.

Conclusion

To renew America and to build a stable platform for world peace and environmental sustainability, we would do well to learn from the experience
of others. Civilizations and nations rise and flourish when the parts work
together in a mutually supportive way that produces an emergent whole
greater than the sum of its aggregate parts. They fall when the parts cease
to work together and instead undermine each other. To understand the
process, one has to look at the whole, not merely the parts. In all cultures
that flourish, the activity of education and the disposition to accept moral
responsibility are the means by which the parts are kept in a reasonable
state of cooperation and collaboration. A balance between an ecological
and mechanistic worldview, which includes a global as well as a national
perspective, is therefore necessary if we want to play the leadership role
that our gifts demand of us. Here the biblical passage "unto whomsoever
much is given, of him shall be much required" (Luke 12:48) seems particularly apt.

If we do not adapt rapidly to the challenges we face as Americans and as
citizens of the world, which require a strategy that balances cooperation and
the intense competition that we have followed for the past two centuries,
we will no longer be able to command our own destiny. Those who are
not willing to accept responsibility must be prepared to surrender their
freedom and abandon their equality. In other words, renewing America
requires that we rediscover the central role of education in a democracy,
of democracy in education, and of moral responsibility in sustaining them
both. Above all, we must never forget that education is not just one activity
among many in life. It is the identifying characteristic of our humanity—the
core of what it means to be human.

Chapter 3

Education Writ Large

Jane Roland Martin

In Plato's *The Republic,* when Socrates is asked to track down the nature of justice, he says that the search requires keen eyesight. Drawing an analogy to trying to read small letters at a distance and finding them easier to see when written large, he suggests that he and his companions look for justice in the city-state before attempting to observe it in the actions of individuals.[1] I propose that in order to grasp the nature of education in and for democracy we follow Socrates' lead: we should look at it first in society as a whole and only then try to discern it at the level of the individual.

Multiple Educational Agency

In the public mind, education and schooling are nearly synonymous. One opens a newspaper or magazine to its education section expecting to read about schools, colleges, and universities. The president appoints a new secretary of education, and we take it for granted that his or her domain is the nation's school system. When a scholar says that educational levels have risen, what he or she really means is that there has been an increase in years of schooling.

Take a hard look at society, however, and one will see education everywhere. It is, of course, discernible in schools. But in the United States, for example, one can also detect it in homes and neighborhoods; churches, mosques, and synagogues; zoos, parks, and playgrounds; the Boy Scouts, the Girl Scouts, and Little League; museums and libraries; symphony orchestras, ballet companies, and the recording industry; the print and electronic media; stores, banks, businesses, and corporations; the military, governmental agencies, and nonprofit organizations; hospitals, courthouses, and prisons.

The false equation between education and schooling has not gone unnoticed. Philosopher John Dewey rejected it in the very first pages of *Democracy and Education,* published in 1916.[2] In the 1960s historians Bernard Bailyn and Lawrence Cremin showed beyond a shadow of a doubt that, in the past, school was but one of many educational institutions in U.S. society and by no means the most important one.[3] And in his widely read 1972 volume *Deschooling Society,* Ivan Illich made it evident that the reduction of education to one of its many forms is untenable.[4] Yet, despite the whistle-blowers, the assumption that the word "education" means "schooling" is so deeply embedded in most people's consciousness that even those who explicitly acknowledge the mistake are apt to deny the existence of multiple educational agency in their next breaths.

When we examine the big picture, we discover that school is but one element of a vast educational system, and perhaps not the most powerful element at that.[5] We can see that education is not always a conscious, voluntary, intentional affair. To be sure, school's express purpose is to foster learning, and the designated task of schoolteachers is to figure out how best to do this. But home, church, neighborhood, the media, and all the rest teach countless lessons, many of which are not consciously intended. Furthermore, school itself produces a whole range of unintended learning outcomes.

Dewey had traditional schooling in mind when he asked in *Experience and Education,* "What avail is it to win prescribed amounts of information about geography and history, to win ability to read and write, if in the process the individual loses his own soul: loses his appreciation of things worth while, of the values to which these things are relative; if he loses desire to apply what he has learned and, above all, loses the ability to extract meaning from his future experiences as they occur?"[6] Deploring the kind of learning that in 1938 Dewey called "collateral," Illich and other school reformers of the 1960s and 1970s in their turn pinpointed what they labeled the "hidden curriculum" of schooling.

Here again the whistle-blowers have been forgotten and the educational version of the intentional fallacy prevails.[7] Nevertheless, whosoever looks unflinchingly at education writ large will find beliefs, attitudes, values, deep-seated feelings, emotions, and even worldviews being passed along by the vast array of educational agents in our midst. Perhaps some of this learning is consciously intended and publicly acknowledged and can therefore be said to belong to a formal, explicit curriculum. But much of it cannot pass this test.[8] Just as medical practices and procedures have unintended and often unanticipated side effects, the practices and procedures of our multiple educational agents produce unintended and often unanticipated learning.

Another feature that commands attention when education is writ large is its broad sweep. How often it is assumed that education is a strictly intellectual affair whose ultimate purpose is the development of the mind and whose main business, therefore, is the imparting of knowledge. When one takes into account education's myriad agents and all the unintended learning they produce, one realizes how misleading this cognitive bias is. For one then discovers that education is not a narrowly defined enterprise. On the contrary, it affects all aspects of our lives and our selves.

Finally, when education is written in big letters, one is able to see that education can shape our heads, our hands, and our hearts for the better or the worse. Think of the lessons in mendacity and greed that corporations and governmental agencies teach; the unhealthy eating habits that are daily passed down by the food, advertising, and television industries; and the self-indulgent attitudes toward the earth's resources that are inculcated by all of the above. Once the false equation, the intentional fallacy, and the cognitive bias are repudiated, it becomes apparent that education does not necessarily spell improvement. And once the myth of improvement is dissipated, it becomes crystal clear that if education in a democracy is to be a moral enterprise, it is up to all of us—"we the people"—to make it so.

Educative and Miseducative Societies

When he looked at justice writ large, Socrates saw that a state can be just or unjust. Similarly, one who looks at education written in big letters will see that a society can be educative or miseducative. Notice that to call a society educative is something quite different from saying that it is an educated or literate society. An educative society is one that shapes its members for the better, not the worse. As the case of Nazi Germany demonstrated, a society with a well-schooled, literate populace can be miseducative in the extreme. And so, for that matter, can a society whose every member has a Ph.D.

Another way to understand the educative/miseducative distinction is to think of the knowledge, skills, attitudes, values, worldviews, and so on that a nation or group or society passes down to the next generation as constituting that culture's stock. A large portion of this cultural stock can no doubt be counted as cultural wealth, but not all of it. Take, for example, poverty, slavery, terrorism, rape, torture, killing, greed, mendacity, and racism. These and other highly undesirable cultural practices and behaviors fall in the liabilities rather than the assets column. An educative society tends to transmit cultural assets—not liabilities. A miseducative society, in contrast, tends to transmit cultural liabilities rather than assets.[9]

Quite clearly, where educativeness is concerned, good intentions are not enough. A society whose educational agents attempt to transmit assets and block the transmission of liabilities but never actually succeed does not deserve the label "educative." This does not mean that a society's educational agents must only transmit cultural assets to be considered educative, for educativeness is a matter of degree rather than an all-or-nothing affair. Nonetheless, *trying* to be educative is not enough. If a society's educational agents are mainly transmitting cultural liabilities, even with the best intentions, that society must be considered miseducative.

The truth is, however, that most groups and institutions in U.S. society do not even try to pass along cultural assets rather than liabilities. And why would one expect them to when they do not think of themselves as educational agents, and neither does anyone else? To be sure, museums have education departments, newspapers and magazines have education editors, and television networks have some educational programming. Still, the very fact that an institution allocates one small portion of its resources to education serves as a reminder that it does not consider itself an educator in its own right. After all, schools do not have separate departments whose business is education, and school buildings do not have separate education corners. Indeed, it makes no sense for an institution that conceives of itself as an educational agent to have a special educational section or division.

Held captive by the false equation between education and schooling, it does not occur to us to make any educational agent other than school accountable for the miseducation it fosters. In good logic, an unacknowledged educator cannot be charged with contributing to the miseducation of the public.[10] Yet, in bombarding people daily with unwholesome, antisocial models of living and in making these appear fatally attractive, the print and electronic media are nonetheless guilty of doing precisely this. So are manufacturers of computer games when they send messages about the acceptability of violence and the cheapness of life. So are airlines, banks, and hotels when they hand down cultural prejudices toward, for example, people with disabilities. And so are businesses, governmental agencies, and the military when their representatives serve as role models for lying instead of truth telling and cheating instead of honesty.

Economists and other social analysts in the United States have often voiced their misgivings about the financial burdens the older generation is bequeathing to future ones by its military spending, its unwillingness to invest in social welfare, its degradation of the natural environment. The debt created by the miseducative tendencies of many unacknowledged educational agents in our midst is every bit as troubling.[11] Moreover, the problems they create for schooling can scarcely be exaggerated.

Democratic Miseducation

John Goodlad has called school "the only institution in our nation specifically charged with enculturating the young into a social and political democracy."[12] British philosopher of education Patricia White has said that school is "the obvious site for political education."[13] Even the most cursory inspection of the actions of our myriad educational agents reveals, however, that school is not the only site in which political education occurs.

Contemporary discussions of education for democratic citizenship often draw attention to the knowledge and skills needed for rational deliberation. But important as it is for the members of a democracy to be able to deliberate about the significant political issues of the day, deliberation is not the only aspect of democracy on which education bears. Indeed, the individual's relationship to the law is perhaps an even more basic respect in which democracy differs from authoritarian systems of government. In an authoritarian system, the individual is supposed to obey laws enacted by others, and that is that. In a democracy, the individual is both the subject and the author of the law. In other words, we are our own governors: the laws we obey are ones that we or our chosen representatives have written. Furthermore and very important, in a democracy as opposed to a dictatorship, everyone is subject to the law. No individual or group is above it.

Consider Elaine Mar, whose family immigrated to the United States from Hong Kong when she was a young child in the 1970s. In her memoir, *Paper Daughter,* she describes being taught authoritarian values by her mother. "A traditional Chinese," Mar's mother "saw herself in relation to family. She was a daughter, sister, and aunt. She spent her life waiting to become a mother." Mar recalls her mother once looking "down in shame" and saying, "How dare I question you?" after challenging something that Elaine's grandmother said. Mar writes about herself, "From birth I was expected to abide by the adults' rules." Her mother told her, "This is what it means to be an adult—you learn to be cautious and follow your elder's lead." On the subject of punishment Mar says, "I didn't think I had anything to worry about. Didn't everyone always say how clever I was? And didn't 'clever' mean the same as 'obedient'?"[14] Before long, however, Mar's mother was beating her whenever she spoke up or disobeyed.

Elaine Mar's memoir is a poignant reminder that the rule of law, a fundamental principle of democracy, cannot be taken for granted. People who are their own legislators are not unthinkingly and unquestioningly supposed to obey laws made by others; they are not supposed to act like sheep. On the contrary, they are expected to speak out when they do not approve of what their representatives are doing.

I do not mean to imply that the hidden curriculum of Mar's home was typical of the United States in the 1970s or that it is so today. On the other hand, it is rash to conclude that her home was unique in passing down undemocratic cultural stock. Consider, for example, this vignette in Frank McCourt's memoir *Teacher Man*:

> Augie was a nuisance in class, talking back, bothering the girls. I called his mother. Next day the door is thrown open and a man in a black T-shirt with the muscles of a weightlifter yells, Hey, Augie, come 'ere.
>
> You can hear Augie gasp.
>
> Talkin' a yeh, Augie. I haveta go in there you wish you was dead. Come 'ere.
>
> Augie yelps, I didn't do nothin'.
>
> The man lumbers into the room, down the aisle to Augie's seat, lifts Augie into the air, carries him over to the wall, bangs him repeatedly against the wall.
>
> I told you—*bang*—never—*bang*—never give your teacher—*bang*—no trouble—*bang*. I hear you give your teacher trouble—*bang*—I'm gonna tear your goddam head off—*bang*—an' stick it up your ass—*bang*. You heard me—*bang*? ...
>
> The man drags Augie back to his seat and turns to me. He gives you trouble again, mister, I kick his ass here to New Jersey. He was brought up to give respect.[15]

According to a newsletter of the Child Rights Information Network, "as part of their daily lives, children all over Europe are spanked, slapped, hit, smacked, shaken, kicked, pinched, punched, caned, flogged, belted, beaten and battered by adults—mainly by those whom they trust the most."[16] Even supposing that the United States is radically different from Europe in this regard, one must wonder in what percentage of homes the basic tenets of democracy are put into practice.

Let us not forget that homes with young children by their very nature are undemocratic institutions. Children do not choose their parents to be their representatives, and the rules parents make are not ones that the parents have to follow. Of course, just because parents and children are inherently unequal, it is not inevitable that the home is miseducative where democracy is concerned. An institution can be undemocratic in some very fundamental respects and yet promote democratic learning. But although it is possible to make homes the "breeding grounds" of democratic beliefs and practices, and many parents do just this, the unequal relationship can be—and often is—abused.

Home is not, of course, the only educational agent to pass down to the next generation cultural stock that is antithetical to democracy. The government, religious institutions, corporations, the military, the Boy Scouts, and neighborhood gangs all have hidden curricula that inculcate belief in the sanctity of hierarchical structures and unquestioning obedience to authority.

Nor is the individual's relationship to the law the only issue. Although it is by no means universally accepted as a goal of schooling, critical thinking appears on many lists of the qualities that the citizens of a democracy must possess. Accordingly, over the years, numerous educational theorists and practitioners in the United States have developed critical thinking programs for the nation's schools and colleges. At the same time, however, some of the most powerful educational agents in the United States are the custodians of cultural stock that impedes and may even prevent children from acquiring the skills and attitudes associated with critical thinking. Tacitly, but nonetheless systematically, they transmit uncritical modes of thought, unsubstantiated "facts" and theories, worldviews that equate critical thinking with treason or portray it as a sign of the devil, and the belief that it is wrong to question the written or spoken word being passed along to young and old alike.

Lest it be imagined that children are the only ones exposed to daily doses of democratic miseducation, think now of Enron. Here was an energy giant whose stated values were respect, integrity, communication, and excellence but whose culture increasingly fostered and rewarded greed, selfishness, arrogance, hypocrisy, deception, self-indulgence, ruthlessness, and disdain for the greater good.[17] To be sure, no single item in Enron's hidden curriculum except possibly disdain for the greater good can be considered undemocratic in and of itself. Still, the hidden curriculum of the Enron culture as a whole appears to have been inconsistent with the requirements of democracy.[18]

Think also about the more than thirty million full-time workers in the United States who have been laid off since the early 1980s. In *The Disposable American* Louis Uchitelle refers repeatedly to the loss of self-esteem these men and women have suffered. "Everything you think is important and do for your life's work, isn't. To have someone senior in the company say that so bluntly in public is terrible," says one executive.[19] Unfortunately, self-esteem happens to be a quality that looms as large as critical thinking on lists of the traits a democratic citizen must possess. Writes political theorist Michael Sandel, "In political debate in the public arena people have to have a certain economic security, otherwise they are likely to feel adrift, anxious and victims of circumstances beyond their control."[20]

It would require volumes to document all the sources and the full content of the political education and miseducation occurring in the United States today. For now, it suffices to note that with young children being exposed to political miseducation at home and in the community and with mature men and women developing traits at work that run counter to democracy, education for democratic citizenship is best thought of as a lifelong process.

Lifelong does not necessarily mean linear. An individual's self-esteem can go up and down, the skills of critical thinking can be turned on and off, democratic virtues can atrophy over time, and undemocratic attitudes and values can take root. Furthermore, the democratic miseducation of one group can rub off on another. In Uchitelle's book a psychiatrist who treated a number of patients for "laid-off related ailments" explained that layoffs are a trauma to the entire family:

> All of a sudden the parent sits at home and can't find a job and is depressed. And suddenly the child's role model sort of crumbles. Instead of feeling admiration for the parent, the child eventually begins to feel disrespect. Because the children identify with the parents, they begin to doubt that they can accomplish anything. They feel they won't be successful in life and their self-esteem plummets.[21]

School's Place in the Educational Firmament

The fact that education for democratic citizenship begins before children go to school, continues after they leave, and occurs outside school's walls while they are students does not release school from its duties as an educator in and for democracy. Rather, it means that school needs to keep education writ large in mind even as it concentrates on education writ small: that is, it needs to take multiple educational agency into account in decisions about the education of schoolchildren. Simple as this advice may sound, it requires a radical rethinking of school's place in the educational firmament.

In the United States and elsewhere the question of what schools should teach is hotly contested. The often radically different proposals have one thing in common, however: they tend to treat school as if it exists in an educational vacuum. Thus, subject matter is selected, objectives are set, learning activities are chosen, and methods of teaching are decided upon as if school were the only educational agent in children's lives.[22]

The aims of schooling are also contested, and once again the false equation and the intentional fallacy hold sway. Literacy, individual autonomy, appreciation of the arts, good health, responsible sexual behavior, or something else entirely: whatever the goal may be, the idea that other educational agents might be transmitting cultural stock that interferes with the achievement of school's aims is seldom entertained.

Discussions of education for democratic citizenship exemplify the tendency to think and act as if school is the one and only significant educator in children's lives. Political thinkers have distinguished many different forms of democracy,[23] and, on the basis of these, different lists have been compiled of the traits or dispositions that democratic citizens must possess. Yet, despite the very real disputes regarding the items on the lists and the weight given them, the various proposals are alike in paying scant attention to multiple educational agency. Not only is there agreement that it is school's job to educate citizens, but even those who acknowledge the existence of educational agents other than school stop short of asking if the lessons they transmit conflict with school's mission.[24]

Taking its cue from an old established theory of society, the resistance to acknowledging the educational role of home and family is particularly strong. "We don't want to deal with inequality in the private realm, because the only way you can deal with inequality in the private realm is to encroach on the private realm, order and regulate relations there in a totalitarian fashion, and create egalitarianism," says political theorist Benjamin Barber when discussing education for democracy.[25] "Families are appropriately protected from political regulation by rights of privacy" affirm political theorists Amy Gutmann and Dennis Thompson after stating, "If schools do not equip children to deliberate, other institutions are not likely to do so."[26]

In Western thought, it has long been standard practice to divide society into two separate "spheres" or "realms"—the public and the private—and to place home and family in the private sector and work, politics, and the professions in the public.[27] In this two-sphere ideology, education—which the false equation translates into schooling—is assigned the task of preparing children who grow up in the private world for membership in the public world. In view of school's designated function, one might expect that it would be represented as having a foothold in both worlds. But the two-sphere ideology posits a wall of separation between public and private that does not allow for this eventuality. And so it positions school squarely within the public world.[28] In consequence, the ideology tacitly regards the children who arrive in school as homeless individuals.[29]

In reality, there is no wall between home and family on the one hand and work, politics, and the professions on the other. Schoolchildren leave home each morning and return home each afternoon, and most adults also leave home to go to work. Where rules and regulations are concerned, the interaction between the two supposedly separate spheres is also continuous. Thus, for example, marriages are subject to civil law, births are publicly recorded, polygamy is outlawed, and abused children are removed from home and family by governmental agencies. In sum, the wall of separation posited by the two-sphere theory is not a historical necessity or a brute fact of nature. It is an ideological construct whose value must be demonstrated.

One mark against the wall of separation concept is its disconnect with political and social realities. Another is that in treating children as blank political slates on which home and community have never written, schoolteachers are forced to deny their own experience. And a third is that acceptance of the wall of separation makes it that much harder for school to fulfill its duty of creating democratic citizens.

"A popular Government, without popular information or the means of acquiring it, is but a Prologue to a Farce or a Tragedy or perhaps both," said James Madison after the U.S. Constitution was adopted. One might say the same of an educational agent that is assigned the task of creating democratic citizens yet denied knowledge or the means of acquiring it about democratic miseducation. "People who mean to be their own Governors, must arm themselves with the power knowledge gives," he added.[30] So too schools that mean to turn children into their own governors must arm themselves with the power that knowledge can give.

It goes without saying that education for democratic citizenship should not proceed in a totalitarian fashion or violate people's rights. Fortunately, schools do not have to make a forced choice between two evils: either act in a totalitarian manner or ignore the reality of multiple educational agency. There is nothing undemocratic about acknowledging that children experience one or another degree of democratic miseducation before they ever arrive at school and continue to do so throughout their years of schooling and beyond. There is nothing sinister about admitting that if school is to teach democratic citizenship successfully, it will have to counteract whatever democratic miseducation children are receiving at home. There is no risk of totalitarianism in school recognizing that home is also an educator of our young and that the education for democracy it provides can, as in school's case, be for the better or the worse.

I have singled out home for special discussion here because so many educational thinkers place it out of bounds. But for better or worse, church, mosque, synagogue, government, business, the media, and the myriad other institutions in a democratic society also contribute to the making—and in many instances the unmaking—of democratic citizens. If we the people do not take seriously the fact that school is but one of the many significant educational agents in the firmament, and if school itself does not acknowledge this and act on the belief as it focuses on education writ small, how can school possibly live up to its reputation as the preferred site of education for democracy?

Making Democratic Citizens

"A democracy is more than a form of government; it is primarily a mode of associated living," said Dewey in *Democracy and Education*.[31] Echoing this thesis, John Goodlad, Corinne Mantle-Bromley, and Stephen John Goodlad wrote in *Education for Everyone,* "Democracy, first and foremost, is a shared way of life."[32] Consider what these statements mean: a "mode of living" or a "way of life" is how anthropologists and sociologists define culture.

If we proceed on the assumption that democracy is a particular type of culture, we need to keep in mind that one becomes a member of a culture by being immersed in it. Two-day-old Henri does not learn to be a Frenchman by studying the history, geography, and governmental structure of France. He becomes French by breathing in the culture of France with the air.

Think what a simple matter the education of democratic citizens would be if children in the United States breathed democracy in with the air from day one: if their homes inducted them into a democratic mode of associated living and if the other educational agents in their lives did so as well. In that event, there would be no reason to single out school as the obvious or most appropriate site of citizenship education. Our educative society would do the bulk of the work, and school would only have to add the finishing touches. Because democratic miseducation is rife in the early twenty-first century both at home and in society at large, the claim that education for democracy is school's job takes on new meaning. Indeed, it all but entails that school become a site of democratic culture, for then children will be able to breathe in democracy with at least some degree of regularity.[33]

I speak of school *becoming* a site of democratic culture because the culture of many schools is at present undemocratic: governing structures are often hierarchical; rules are not always applied equally to children of different races, classes, genders, etc.; and many classroom practices deny children such fundamental democratic rights as freedom of speech and association. One does not have to agree with the sentiment that schools today "may conduct themselves as the least democratic institutions"[34] to believe that the culture of many schools would have to undergo significant change for them to make the grade.

The proposal that school's culture become democratic is also a tall order because it requires a ringing denunciation of the cognitive bias. When democracy is understood to be a way of life, education must be of the whole person: it must necessarily engage head, hands, and heart. You can teach Augie the three Rs; all the history, literature, science, and political philosophy you wish; and also the skills of critical thinking and political deliberation. But if in school he does not breathe in democracy's "middle way" between unquestioning submission to authority and rampant disobedience of the law; if he does not learn to respect both majority rule and minority rights; if he does not begin to act as if no one—not Augie and not Augie's father—is above the law; and if he does not also become disposed to protect his own rights and those of others, and to speak out when he sees democracy being subverted, he will not have learned to be a democratic citizen.[35]

Although it may not be easy to make school a site of democratic culture, it can be done. Because there is a fundamental inequality at the heart of schooling resembling the one that characterizes home—namely, that children do not stand in an equal relationship to their teachers—no school can be perfectly democratic. But perfection is not required. Being a democratic culture is a matter of degree, and in order to provide apprenticeships in democracy, the culture of schools needs only to approximate the ideal. Furthermore, the historical record shows that where there has been the will to overcome cognitive bias, there has been the way.[36]

When, overcoming all obstacles, school becomes a site of democratic culture, two long neglected aspects of education for democratic citizenship writ small will make themselves felt. One is that this education is not a mere matter of addition. Discussions of citizenship education often leave the impression that school only has to give children a bit of knowledge about democracy, a few democratic skills, and some new democratic behavioral patterns. Add these up, and, voilà, democracy will have new citizens! To the extent, however, that Augie, Elaine Mar, and their peers have absorbed the lessons of democratic miseducation, their education for democratic citizenship will have to involve addition, subtraction, and transformation. Yes, they will need to acquire some portion of the culture's democratic stock. But they will also have to let go of the undemocratic beliefs, attitudes, values, and patterns of behavior they have already made their own. And in so doing, they will, in effect, become brand new people.

A second neglected aspect of citizenship education writ small that will cry out for attention is the culture crossing made by those children who have become accustomed to living under authoritarian rule. Just as other kinds of culture crossings—for instance, Elaine Mar's from a Chinese child to an American schoolgirl—are apt to give rise to anger, guilt, alienation, and feelings of betrayal, so is this one.[37] Thus, for instance, home, religious institution, or neighborhood gang may object strenuously to the fact that school is teaching children to question the dictates of authority and to make up their own minds about significant issues of the day; the children may feel guilty about casting off the teachings of one or another educational agent; those who live in especially undemocratic homes and communities may find it increasingly difficult to switch back and forth each day between two opposite cultures and may end up feeling alienated from both.

Like it or not, when democracy is understood to be a form of culture and it is agreed that one of school's main functions is to create democratic citizens, the issue of school's relationship to the other educational agents in children's lives cannot be avoided. Goodlad and his colleagues have said that schools "cannot counteract the influence of parents, peers, media, and all that constitutes the social surround."[38] But this does not mean that those who care about education for democracy can in good conscience act as if these influences do not exist or that school can afford to ignore them.

Once it is understood that culture crossing can occasion pain and suffering, the question naturally arises as to whether it is morally acceptable to establish school as a site of democratic culture while disregarding the repercussions in the "social surround." In view of the Enron case and Uchitelle's study, the question also arises as to whether school's democratic lessons are for naught—if, in other words, whatever democratic cultural stock children do acquire in school is likely to disappear once they graduate. Given the degree and scope of the democratic miseducation that fills the "social surround," it is also necessary to ask if it is possible for school to become a site of democratic culture or, assuming that it can become one, how long school can survive as one.

Interestingly enough, Socrates' definition of justice is relevant here. Stating that justice is a matter of internal cooperation and overall health rather than the fair distribution of rewards and punishments, he argued that a just state is one in which the several parts of society work together for the good of the whole. By analogy he then determined that a just person is one in whom each part of the soul makes its own contribution to the well-being of the individual.

We have already seen that when education for democracy is writ small, it requires something akin to what Socrates envisioned in regard to justice, namely the full cooperation of head, hands, and heart. Writ large, education for democratic citizenship requires the cooperation of school, home, neighborhood, religious institutions, the media, the government, and all the other significant educational agents in children's lives.[39] To the extent that the nonschool educational agents undermine school's designated task of educating for citizenship, that society's well-being is surely in jeopardy.

Cooperation must not be confused with the suppression of disagreement or conformity of belief. A democratic society's educational agents can work together to foster democratic citizenship while disagreeing about matters large and small. Indeed, since freedom of thought is a basic tenet of democracy, it is imperative that differences of opinion are encouraged rather than stifled, whether they be about public policy issues or the nature of democracy itself. Thus, this plea for cooperation can be considered to be, among other things, a call for open-mindedness across the whole wide range of educational agents.

Counteracting Miseducation

What can we the people do to make education in and for democracy a moral enterprise? How can we create the kind of culture in which all our children breathe democracy in with the air?

Above all, we need to persuade the wide range of educational agents other than school, to acknowledge their status as educators and to agree that, like school, they therefore have an obligation to contribute to the making and maintaining of a democratic citizenry. But this is a long-term project. In the interim, we need to figure out how to counteract the democratic miseducation that is being purveyed here and now, and we also must remember that not a single one of us stands outside the educational process. Those myriad educational agents are not abstract philosophical entities. They are made up of flesh and blood human beings, and we are those people. Thus, in our everyday capacities as family members, churchgoers, breadwinners, sports fans, and all the rest, we need to be eternally vigilant that we and the educational agencies to which we belong are not undermining but making positive contributions to democratic living.

Notes

1. Plato, *The Republic,* trans. G. M. A. Grube (Indianapolis: Hackett, 1974), 368d, e. I thank Ann Diller, Susan Franzosa, John Goodlad, Barbara Houston, Michael Martin, Jennifer Radden, and Janet Farrell Smith for helpful comments on an earlier draft of this chapter.

2. John Dewey, *Democracy and Education: An Introduction to the Philosophy of Education* (New York: Macmillan, 1916), 4.

3. Bernard Bailyn, *Education in the Forming of American Society* (New York: Vintage, 1960); Lawrence Cremin, *The Genius of American Education* (New York: Vintage, 1965).

4. Ivan Illich, *Deschooling Society* (New York: Harrow Books, 1972).

5. For more on the false equation and the concept of multiple educational agency, see Jane Roland Martin, *Cultural Miseducation: In Search of a Democratic Solution* (New York: Teachers College Press, 2002).

6. John Dewey, *Experience and Education* (New York: Macmillan, 1963), 49.

7. The intentional fallacy is generally associated with the field of literary criticism and, more particularly, the New Critics; roughly, it is the belief that disputes regarding the meaning of a text are decided by appeal to the author's intentions. The concept is usually attributed to William K. Wimsatt and Monroe C. Beardsley, "The Intentional Fallacy," *Sewanee Review* 54 (1946): 468–88. Cf. William K. Wimsatt and Monroe C. Beardsley, *The Verbal Icon: Studies in the Meaning of Poetry* (Lexington: University of Kentucky Press, 1954). For an application of the concept to another discipline, see Steve W. Dykstra, "The Artist's Intentions and the Intentional Fallacy in Fine Arts Conservation," *Journal of the American Institute for Conservation* 35, no. 3 (1996): 197–218.

8. For an extended analysis of the concept of hidden curriculum, see Jane Roland Martin, *Changing the Educational Landscape: Philosophy, Women, and Curriculum* (New York: Routledge, 1994), chapter 8.

9. See Martin, *Cultural Miseducation.*

10. To be sure, the media are often criticized—for example, for showing too much sex and violence. My point is that if the critics are accusing the media of being miseducative, they are implicitly attributing to the media the status of educational agent. I suspect, however, that many of those concerned about the effects on the audience do not take the further step of conceptualizing what is occurring in educational terms.

11. For an interesting discussion of educational debt, see Gloria Ladson-

Billings, "From the Achievement Gap to the Education Debt: Understanding Achievement in U.S. Schools," *Educational Researcher* 35 (October 2006): 3–12.

12. John I. Goodlad, *Teachers for Our Nation's Schools* (San Francisco: Jossey-Bass, 1990), 48.

13. Patricia White, *Civic Virtues and Public Schooling: Educating Citizens for a Democratic Society* (New York: Teachers College Press, 1996), 23.

14. M. Elaine Mar, *Paper Daughter: A Memoir* (New York: HarperCollins, 1999), 8, 9, 23, 228.

15. Frank McCourt, *Teacher Man: A Memoir* (New York: Scribner, 2005), 91–92. Cf. the home life of "AP Frank" in Alexandra Robbins, *The Overachievers: The Secret Lives of Driven Kids* (New York: Hyperion, 2006).

16. Commissioner for Human Rights, Council of Europe, Child Rights Information Network, *Children and Corporal Punishment: "The Right Not to Be Hit, Also a Children's Right,"* http://www.crin.org/resources/infoDetail. asp?ID=8562.

17. Bethany McLean and Peter Elkind, *The Smartest Guys in the Room: The Amazing Rise and Scandalous Fall of Enron* (New York: Penguin, 2003).

18. This is not to say that a single individual who possesses the Enron package of traits poses a threat to democracy. My point is simply that from the standpoint of democracy, Enron's culture was seriously miseducative.

19. Louis Uchitelle, *The Disposable American: Layoffs and Their Consequences* (New York: Knopf, 2006), 101.

20. Quoted in ibid., 34.

21. Ibid., 187–88.

22. Schools do, of course, reach out and incorporate aspects of the environment into their planning. But for a school to bring, for example, television or computers into the classroom as an aid to teaching and learning is quite different from acknowledging that a TV network or the computer industry is an educational agent in its own right.

23. To identify the different types and determine how they are related to one another is a huge task that fortunately need not be undertaken here. For a discussion of a number of types, see, for example, Ian Shapiro, *The State of Democratic Theory* (Princeton, N.J.: Princeton University Press, 2003).

24. See, for example, the discussion of television in Amy Gutmann and Dennis Thompson, *Why Deliberative Democracy?* (Princeton, N.J.: Princeton University Press, 2004), 36.

25. Benjamin Barber, "Public Schooling: Education for Democracy," in John I. Goodlad and Timothy J. McMannon, eds., *The Public Purpose of Education and Schooling* (San Francisco: Jossey-Bass, 1997), 113.

26. Gutmann and Thompson, *Why Deliberative Democracy?,* 36.

27. It should be noted that, in the past, gender played a vital role in this ideology in that the world of the private home and family was considered to be women's domain and the world of work, politics, and the professions, men's domain. Although the ways in which the gendered aspect of the two-sphere

ideology has changed as more and more women have entered the workplace is an extremely important topic, it is not one that has to be addressed here.

28. Home schooling can be construed as an attempt to keep inside the wall that part of children's education that historically came to be located in school.

29. This is not to say that everyone views schoolchildren in this way. See, for example, the work of the Harvard Family Research Project: Heather Weiss, Margaret Caspe, and M. Elena Lopez, "Family Involvement in Early Childhood Education," *Family Involvement Makes a Difference* 1 (Spring 2006); and Lawrence Hernandez, *Families and Schools Together: Building Organizational Capacity for Family-School Partnerships* (Cambridge, Mass.: Harvard Family Research Project, 2000).

30. Quoted in John Nichols and Robert W. McChesney, *Tragedy and Farce: How the American Media Sell Wars, Spin Elections, and Destroy Democracy* (New York: New Press, 2005), 1.

31. Dewey, *Democracy and Education*, 87.

32. John I. Goodlad, Corinne Mantle-Bromley, and Stephen John Goodlad, *Education for Everyone: Agenda for Education in a Democracy* (San Francisco: Jossey-Bass, 2004), 82.

33. That is, children would be able to breathe in democracy unless their parents opt for a kind of home schooling that does not foster democratic living or for schools that perpetuate democratic miseducation.

34. Linda Darling-Hammond, "Education, Equity, and the Right to Learn," in Goodlad and McMannon, eds., *Public Purpose*, 111.

35. I am not ruling out here that some children may have learned all this at home or in their communities.

36. Consider the schools established by Johann Heinrich Pestalozzi and Maria Montessori, those modeled on the thought of John Dewey, A. S. Neill's Summerhill, and the open classrooms of the 1960s and 1970s. These are but a few instances of the education of head, hand, and heart.

37. For more on this subject, see Jane Roland Martin, *Educational Metamorphoses: Philosophical Reflections on Identity and Culture* (Lanham, Md.: Rowman & Littlefield, 2007).

38. Goodlad, Mantle-Bromley, and Goodlad, *Education for Everyone*, 86.

39. This does not mean that every single educational agent must cooperate. In a democracy there will always be room for some institutions that intentionally or unintentionally promote democratic miseducation. But when democratic miseducation becomes an obstacle to the achievement of education for democratic citizenship, it is time to be concerned.

Chapter 4

Elevating Education's
Public Purpose

Paul G. Theobald

The Interconnections of Education,
Politics, and Economics

The great error of would-be political and economic reformers of the past century is that they made their attempts without recognizing the degree to which their chances of success hinged on educational effort. Politics, economics, and education are deeply connected. To try to make changes in one without addressing the others is a kind of fool's errand. History has shown that some progress may be made on one front or another during times of duress—during economic depressions, for instance, or when the threat of military invasion seems imminent—but unless these times of duress are prolonged (as in the case of the Great Depression), little in the way of change can be expected. This is doubly true now that what gets

65

defined as "news" is essentially fixed for the public by multinational media corporations in a manner reminiscent of the way the feudal church–state connection once monitored topics acceptable for public discussion.

It is fairly easy to envision another period of duress. More than likely it would come—or perhaps it has already begun—as a result of overheating the atmosphere via unrestrained economic activity. Deadly storms resulting from altered climate conditions seem to be increasing. Or perhaps, like the Roman Empire centuries ago, our enemies will become too great in number, making a large-scale war inevitable. Or perhaps we will simply lose market share to new superpowers like India and China, dramatically reducing the standard of living in the United States—pushing two hundred million middle-class Americans into the ranks of the poor, and the forty million already there into the ranks of the utterly destitute. We can wait for any of these things to happen—that is, we can wait for them to inflict massive suffering—and then set about the business of making political, economic, and educational change. But a wiser course, it seems, would be to get started right away.

It is true, of course, that there is a chance that none of these scenarios is accurate. Maybe the earth's biophysical limits are greater than scientists presume. Maybe we can continue to embrace a growth economy without causing ecological disaster or military conflict, and without losing market share to emerging powers like China. If this proves to be the case, present trends will increase America's consumption of the world's resources to a proportion approaching half of what the earth has to offer for a mere 5 percent of the earth's population. The best-case scenario for the coming decades, then, is that consumption in the United States will create a global injustice so pronounced that the only logical outgrowth is global instability of the sort that breeds ever more terrorism. No wonder Jane Jacobs titled her most recent book *Dark Age Ahead*.[1]

There can be only two reasons to object to starting a drive for fundamental change in all three arenas NOW. The first reason is that the wealthiest 2 percent of Americans are growing ever richer by the circumstances that define the status quo. This rapidly accruing wealth is not reported to the general public for obvious reasons, but now and then one can get a glimpse into the world of America's financial aristocracy—the very aristocracy most Americans of the founding generation struggled to prevent. When the former CEO of General Electric (owner of NBC), Jack Welch, was divorced by his wife, his financial circumstances became public. "Mr. Welch, while still CEO of GE, received $16.7 million a year; access to the corporate aircraft; use of an $80,000 a month Manhattan apartment; with its expenses (including wine, food, laundry, toiletries, and newspapers) paid for by the company; along with floor-level seats to New York Knicks basketball games, VIP seating at Wimbledon tennis games, a box at Yankee Stadium and Boston Red Sox games, four country club fees, security and limousine service at all times, satellite TV in his four homes, and dining bills at a favorite restaurant."[2] Forty senior U.S. executives, the *New York Times* reported early in 2006, were set to receive $1 million a year for life in annual pension benefits. Citigroup's Sandy Weill was among the fortunate. He will be receiving a $1 million annual pension as well as a car and driver, secretarial support, and ten years' worth of free flights on Citigroup corporate jets, plus a $3,846-a-day consulting gig. Over his last ten years at Citigroup, Weill collected $1 billion in salary and benefits.[3] For those, like Welch and Weill, who profit from the status quo, change is not a particularly appealing prospect. Controlling what Americans see, hear, and discuss, as a consequence, is an enormous advantage in terms of trying to stave off change—and it is directly connected to the second reason one might oppose fundamental change.

The second reason is that the vast majority of Americans are simply unaware of how precarious our circumstances have become. Once again, leaders of democracies, no less than kings and dictators, crave the control of information. Because of the corporate-controlled development of mass media, today's democratic leaders can exercise a degree of control nearly as complete as that of kings during the feudal era. It is not in their interest to inform the American public of how dire conditions are becoming.

Americans, too, are not allowed to contemplate the wisdom or justice inherent in the dramatic upward distribution of wealth over the past several decades. As an example, the 109th Congress significantly altered the nation's estate tax laws, making it far easier for the top 2 percent of the population to pass their fortunes on to their children. Even though estate taxes affected a mere 2 percent of the population, a public relations campaign orchestrated with the complete complicity of the nation's news media called far and wide for the elimination of the "death tax." This campaign was so effective that a majority of Americans—as high as 77 percent in some polls—came to believe that they might have to pay such a tax unless Congress was able to eliminate it.[4] Here is an instance where 98 percent of the population gave $24 billion back to the wealthiest 2 percent and said, in effect, that they would make up that budget shortfall on their behalf. This is an example of a case in which Americans stood in desperate need of accurate information, but it was denied to them.

Still, an even greater concern has to do with yet another circumstance that has not been shared with the general public: an ever-growing economy is a biophysical impossibility. One day, if that day has not already passed, further effort at growth will only render the vast majority of the earth's inhabitants poorer, not richer. How so? Growth efforts—more buildings, more factories, more irrigation, more appliances, more roads—will speed up the depletion of the earth's finite resources and render the health of local ecosystems increasingly more tenuous. The classical economics tradition has great faith in the concept of growth—faith built up over a couple of centuries in which the world was sparsely populated by people—but that faith cannot change the fact that the earth is now filled with people (approaching seven billion) and the biosphere is finite. Commenting on the difficulty involved in changing human behavior in recognition of this fact, Herman Daly, an economist formerly with the World Bank, wrote:

> Because establishing and maintaining a sustainable economy entails an enor-
> mous change of mind and heart by economists, politicians, and voters, one
> might well be tempted to declare that such a project would be impossible.
> But the alternative to a sustainable economy, an ever growing economy, is
> biophysically impossible. In choosing between tackling a political impos-
> sibility and a biophysical impossibility, I would judge the latter to be more
> impossible and take my chances with the former.[5]

The truth of the matter, though, is that change is every bit as much an educational project as it is a political one. There are two large educational institutions in American society: the first is the public school, and the second is the print and broadcast news media that make up the corporate "school" and are dominated by a handful of multinational companies. The latter is not subject to much of anything in the way of democratic control. Citizens who are aware of this share the burden of trying to create media reform, but we should also recognize that the most direct path to that end may be through the other large educational institution—the public school. By comparison, for instance, a local school is much more amenable, or at least potentially much more amenable, to grassroots change efforts.

Our schools were originally created to enable citizens to shoulder the burden of democracy; that is, they initially had a distinctly public purpose. By 1918 that public purpose had been effectively buried in favor of elevating private purpose, in the process leaving matters of statecraft to the nation's elite. Or said another way, the goal of schooling was converted almost ex-clusively to outfitting the nation's youths for jobs. In recent decades, that goal has become cemented by educational policy that has greatly increased the amount of standardized testing in schools. Such policy is based on the dubious assumption that higher test scores would mean students are learning more of something with presumed value—or perhaps on the even more dubious assumption that higher test scores would increase our lead as the world's dominant economic and military power.

The truth of the matter is that performing well on exams is not a skill that lends itself particularly well even to the world of work, much less to more substantive goals, like the well-being of a democracy. The testing fetish that currently dominates the educational policy landscape will probably die a natural death in a fairly short time span, as numbers tell us so little of consequence—besides, even if we arrived at a point at which the exams resulted in steadily increasing scores, they cannot go up forever. There are certainly admirable uses to be made of standardized exams, but to convert them into the end goal of an educational system is to expose a kind of intellectual poverty, a general lack of real insight into the nature of the human condition—the natural result of allowing our educational system one hundred years' worth of institutional momentum moving away from any sophisticated definition of a true education.

Although, like political and economic reform, educational change is a monumental task, a couple of key differences may mean that it is in fact the arena most susceptible to citizen action. For one, the system is composed of local schools. For another, citizens are rightfully accorded a voice in the affairs of the local school since it so profoundly touches the deepest concern of parents—their children.

Ronald Reagan's Economic Recovery Act of 1981 was the start of an incredible boon to the wealthiest in America, and an incredible burden to the middle class—a group of Americans that has declined in numbers ever since. Those Americans who are aware of the way this law redistributed wealth upward tend to shake their heads and wonder how such a thing could happen. And a mere quarter century later came the totally unthinkable—drastic reductions in the estate tax. How does public policy that benefits so few see the light of day as a viable idea, let alone actually become law? The answer is that all eyes must be turned in the other direction. The wealthy must point across the room and say "What's that?" hoping the gaze of the American public will turn in a new direction long enough so that food may be taken from their plates. Those who do not fall for the ruse are bombarded with trickle-down theory: the superrich created by these policies will in turn create jobs, and so on. There are never any specifics tied to this argument—like where and when these jobs will appear and at what level these jobs will be compensated—and never any mandates that the rich must indeed invest in ways that actually do create jobs. This is something that will just magically happen, as the titles of so many economics texts contend.

The most effective "what's that" of the conservative ascendancy in America has been the educational crisis fashioned by the release of *A Nation at Risk*.[6] Since 1983, public education has been under a kind of political microscope. The think tanks that resulted from the incredible wealth created by Reagan's "economic recovery" routinely produce studies aimed at grabbing the attention of the American public. Pick up any issue of the periodical *Education Week* and you can read several stories of think tanks that just released another report on the ineffectiveness of America's public schools, or the ineffectiveness of teacher education, or on some such topic intended to raise the concern of Americans regarding the effectiveness of the nation's schools.

If there had been even an ounce of genuine concern over American schools in three decades of federal goals-oriented policy intended to fix public education, past presidents and other high-ranking officials might have asked educators to be involved in the search for solutions. But beyond involving teachers in the preparation of standards, educators have been left out of virtually all decision making. Look at the selection of presidential appointees to the office of secretary of education since Reagan took office. It is impossible to look at that list and say, with a straight face, that there was even a little presidential concern for the state of public education in America. Had there been such a concern, educators of world renown would have occupied that office. John Goodlad would have been there, and James Comer, Theodore Sizer, Nel Noddings; the list of highly qualified individuals could go on. Had this happened, we would be much better off than we are right now. Those who orchestrated the development of federal policy in education over the last thirty years exhibited no genuine concern for public education. Their efforts were merely a collective "What's that?"

An Example of Structural Reform

Shortly after Reagan's commission of noneducators released *A Nation at Risk*, John Goodlad published the results of a massive study of schooling in America in a book entitled *A Place Called School*.[7] He concluded with some fairly radical recommendations for public education—all of which, of course, we ignored. But had we moved quickly as a nation to implement the structural reforms he described, we would not labor today with a 40 percent high school dropout rate in our large cities, the teaching profession would not be paralyzed by straightjacket policies like No Child Left Behind, and in fact, improvement in the quality of American schooling and American culture would be well under way. As a consequence, it is worth a short digression to describe Goodlad's recommendations.

The essential thrust of his plan was to move the educational experience up by a couple of years in order to begin at age four and finish something analogous to the current K–12 curriculum by age sixteen. Under his plan, the school experiences of America's youths would unfold in roughly three four-year blocks. The primary block would begin on each child's fourth birthday, their first day in school. In this way, each child would start school with a birthday party and the warmest of welcomes into the world of formal education. According to Goodlad,

> The timing and rate of departure would approximate the timing and rate of entry—departure from the first phase at or near the eighth birthday, from the second near the twelfth, and from the third near the sixteenth. Children beginning a primary school would enter, more or less randomly, one of up to three or, at the most, four nongraded, four-year units of not more than 100 children each. For each unit this means the entry and departure every year of 25 children—two or three out and two or three in each month. The tumultuous business of socializing 25 or so beginners each September is completely eliminated. Schooling immediately takes on a highly individualized character.... Given maxima of four units and 100 children per unit, the maximum enrollment of a primary school is 400.[8]

The interested reader can find much more detail related to this plan in Goodlad's book. For now, it is merely important to get a glimpse of the many advantages Goodlad's proposal represents. Indeed, given all of the advantages, one cannot help but wonder why the U.S. never attempted a change of this kind. The few criticisms that were voiced regarding the plan had to do with what adolescents would do from age sixteen to age eighteen—and, predictably, how this might affect high school athletics.

But imagine what might be done with a civil service dimension to the educational endeavor in this country. Imagine community colleges everywhere orchestrating work experiences for those who avail themselves of civil service options in health clinics, in community neighborhood restoration projects, in pre-age-four child care, in after-school youth clubs, on newly created cooperative urban farms, and the list could go on and on. Military service and college, too, would be among the options for sixteen-year-olds. The opportunities are really quite endless, and the potential benefit for improving the quality and feel of America's public places is almost beyond calculation.

As far as school athletics are concerned, Goodlad's plan would go a long way toward muting the kind of feverish—and altogether unhealthy—athletic fanaticism that has followed in the wake of big-time and big-money collegiate and professional sports. Far too many children spurn academics assuming their futures will unfold on professional sports teams, when the reality is that only a small fraction of high school athletes will become professionals. Under Goodlad's plan high school extracurricular activities could remain relatively unchanged, but the pressure to perform at age fifteen at a level that might garner collegiate attention would be significantly reduced—though it could not be made to go away altogether.

Whether or not the nation ever chooses to implement something like the system Goodlad proposed, it is nevertheless possible to take a bold step to curb the unhealthy dimensions of athletic fanaticism in American culture. I believe the National Collegiate Athletic Association (NCAA) could make a huge contribution to this—and in the process cut its own violation investigation costs extensively—by merely stipulating that college athletes, whether they are in Division I or II can only perform on a college athletic squad if they were born in the state where the college is located. If a student was born in Detroit and wants to play college football, he could do it at Michigan State, or Central Michigan, or Hillsdale College—but he could not cross the border and play for Notre Dame. College, after all, is about academics, and while extracurricular activities are rightfully a part of the collegiate experience, they should never have been allowed to become the proverbial "tail that wags the dog." Years ago the president of the University of Oklahoma captured the sorry state of collegiate athletics when he remarked that he wanted to "build a university our football team can be proud of." If a Michigan-born student wants to attend Notre Dame, and he or she is accepted, by all means, he or she should go to Notre Dame. But if the goal is to go to college *and* participate in athletics, the student should pick and choose from the institutions his or her state has to offer.

Think about the problems this simple rule would solve. Recruitment abuses would diminish markedly, big-time gambling would be curbed to some degree, and enormous sums currently spent on travel to all corners of the country could be saved. On top of this, such a rule would likely improve the appeal of intercollegiate athletics as local communities could watch their star high school athletes compete close to home at the collegiate level. It is possible that a reform such as this might contribute to rebuilding community allegiance of the sort that revitalizes democratic traditions. The argument that it would somehow make collegiate sports less appealing for spectators is baseless. As well, the argument that less populated states would suffer is also baseless as the number of higher education institutions in a given state is a reflection, to a great degree, of the state's population.

Even this modest proposal for athletics reform and certainly John Goodlad's larger proposal for an educational system overhaul are examples of plans for structural change that could have moved American society into a far healthier position as a nation. They would positively affect lives that are currently chewed up by the educational system, and at the very same time they would infuse youthful energy into the restoration of public places and into the care of America's most helpless citizens. The first U.S. president to put a distinguished educational statesman in charge of the federal Department of Education stands at least a fighting chance of getting structural reforms of this magnitude under way. A parade of ex-governors or cronies of one sort or another into that cabinet position, with virtually no insight into the huge array of issues that come to bear on educational questions, will leave us mired in our current circumstances.

Beyond the suggestions already shared, *A Place Called School* included a startling research finding that has been systematically ignored as well. According to Goodlad's research, it turns out that good schools and poor schools do not look that different from one another—at least from a curricular or instructional standpoint. It is not uncommon to find the same series of textbooks used in good schools and poor schools, with lessons taught using similar, or the very same, methods. The difference, according to Goodlad and those who helped him conduct his massive study of schooling in America, was in the quality of the relationships between those who inhabited the school: the quality of the relationships between students, between teachers, and between administrators and also between students and teachers, teachers and administrators, etc. A school defined by healthy relationships is a pleasant place to be, a place where one will witness caring, courtesy, and a kind of earnestness in the way both adults and children go about their tasks.

Capitalizing on an obvious connection between relationships and community, Goodlad gradually began to weave the concept of community into his analysis of what is needed to dramatically improve the school experiences of American youths.[9] Community is a fundamental dimension of healthy human life; it provides the place where democracy can become real, and it is central to optimizing the educational opportunities afforded youths. Scholars have come to these conclusions in the past: Jefferson most notably, perhaps, but the list is much longer and includes such contemporary and near-contemporary figures as Mahatma Gandhi, Martin Luther King Jr., Wendell Berry, Aldo Leopold, David Orr, E. F. Schumacher, and many, many more.

What a genuine community will not countenance, of course, are imbalances of the sort that create inequity and injustice. When unfair policies are allowed to trump community well-being—for example, when the extremes of wealth and poverty grow ever greater or when one portion of society's population receives the best medical care available and another portion goes without it altogether—a sense of community diminishes. In such places, we should assume that disaffection, apathy, despair, drug use, and crime will become quite prominent. When imbalances grow to a global scale, as they clearly have done, antipathy, hatred, and violence are the imminently predictable result. The threat of terrorism in the twenty-first century is a perfect example of the outgrowth of politics, economics, and education unfettered from the standards created by healthy human communities. When one adds to that the development of impending environmental catastrophes from increasing global temperatures that have resulted from overexploiting the earth's store of Paleolithic sunlight (that is, coal and oil, of which there is a finite amount), the stakes premised on reinserting community as a value into political, economic, and educational reckoning are enormous—indeed, they have never been larger. We are literally at a moment when the phrase "daylight savings time" takes on a whole new meaning.

The stakes depending on a well-functioning public education system have never been higher. But our response has been to continue to hold the American public at arm's length related to educational questions. Indeed, the education policy arena has clamped down on schools with such vigor that the system actually performs poorly even for the most privileged in American society. The No Child Left Behind (NCLB) Act was built on the assumption that the establishment of learning standards was optimal education policy. But there is something embarrassingly childlike about the logic of standards, a logic that goes something like this: "Let's decide what all students should know. That way we can test them to see if they know it." The proponents of standards-based reform were apparently untroubled by questions related to the nature of knowledge, or the relationship of knowledge to the places where it is utilized, or the burden of seeing that knowledge is used well in the world, or any other kinds of questions that might confound the idea that all children in each state should learn the same things at roughly the same time in their lives. Or worse still, that all children in *every* state should learn the same things at the same time.

Beyond this shortcoming, there is a large, looming dark side to standards-based reform—though few like to talk about it. Standards undeniably shift the pedagogical focus of schools to right and wrong answers. The result is a kind of pedagogical tragedy as the development and nurturance of creativity becomes the first and most obvious casualty in the nation's schools. Yale's well-known creativity expert, Robert Sternberg, described this circumstance: "The increasingly massive and far-reaching use of conventional standardized tests is one of the most effective, if unintentional, vehicles this country has created for suppressing creativity."[10] At a time when the world has been declared metaphorically flat, creativity seems like a highly desirable characteristic for American youths to possess, but current educational policy might just as well overtly censor its development in the nation's schools.

The second tragic casualty of standards-based reform is a broad curriculum. Because of the design of NCLB, performance in math and reading, and to a slightly lesser degree science, has been the primary focus. Stories of elementary schools that limit the curriculum exclusively to math and reading abound. On top of this, governors meet frequently to collectively berate state departments of education for not doing enough to focus the high school curriculum on math and science—implicitly maintaining that dubious idea that widespread knowledge of math and science is the key to economic growth and development.[11]

The hubris behind the narrowing of America's school curriculum is nothing short of staggering. In over two thousand years of Western history, we have been exposed to countless sophisticated definitions of what constitutes an education, or an educated person, and none of these call for a curriculum built near-exclusively around math and science. In fact, it is fairly easy to make a good argument as to why such a narrow educational focus would be culturally and in other ways devastating to the United States. While math and science may be the wellspring of technological advances, they yield little intellectual leverage over how new technologies will interact with human society. It takes students who have studied literature, history, philosophy, or art to protect society from the unintended consequences of technological advancement—from the damage done by chlorofluorocarbons, for instance, or from CO_2 emissions. It takes students who have studied art, music, folklore, and so forth, to prevent mining companies from removing mountaintops in the search for coal deposits. In short, a healthy society needs citizens who are broadly educated and who only thereafter specialize across the spectrum of academic disciplines.

The third tragic casualty of standards-based reform is innovative, passionate instruction. The teaching act has two inescapable dimensions—one is curricular, the other instructional. The standards movement has had the effect of removing curricular judgment and curricular decision making from the professional lives of teachers. The result has been that a huge part of what makes the profession fulfilling was taken away—leaving only decisions about how to teach the material. And even this decision is far from sacred, as more and more school administrators demand a certain type of instruction in the foolish hope that *one* instructional approach will raise test scores for *all*. In point of fact, it is not just administrators who have begun to demand a kind of instructional uniformity. We have recently witnessed a totally new class of school personnel sometimes described as "textbook police." When a large district purchases a curriculum from a textbook publisher, they will send "police" out to schools to make sure teachers are teaching the right way, with the right amount of time, etc. Company profits increasingly depend on improving test scores in large districts, a circumstance that cannot be left to the idiosyncratic instructional practices of teachers. If these companies are going to make huge profits, teachers must be policed to see that they are doing their part, playing their role, toward that end.

The standards-based milieu in schools, flanked by a kind of "big brother" federal educational policy in NCLB, is slowly converting the teaching profession into a technical enterprise—sapping the passion and excitement teachers might otherwise bring to the classroom. It is ironic that this would happen in the face of clear research results that demonstrate that the teacher is the largest single variable affecting student achievement. Given this, you would think there would be a strong push to improve the professional lives of teachers rather than diminish them. And in this regard it would be fruitful to take heed of Antonio Damasio's research. A world-renowned neurobiologist, Damasio argued in his best-selling book *Descartes' Error* that human rational power can only be brought to its highest levels through the deployment of feeling, emotion, and passion.[12]

The federal government, thanks to the Constitution, has no official role to play in education. Many have viewed this circumstance as an indication of judicious wisdom among the Constitution's authors. I do not believe this was the case. Education, or citizen improvement, was simply not a part of the liberal project that the Constitution represents—and thus they did not condone or even make mention of the notion of public education. Those issues that went undiscussed in the Constitution by default became the province of the individual states. Again, that is our great good fortune, for it legitimates local and state efforts to turn away from federal education policies like NCLB. Regrettably, many states are just as much in the grip of powerful corporate interests as the federal government is. This means there may be little opportunity for those states to declare educational independence from the strictures of federal education policy. If that is the case, however, there is always the local school itself.

Local Reform for Those Who Will Not Wait

Talk to teachers. Talk to school administrators. While there are many professional educators who defer to the status quo, whatever that might be, most have the genuine interests of children at heart. Most will tell you that it is far easier to assess a child's progress via daily contact over the course of a school year than to make that attempt on the basis of one afternoon with a test booklet and a sheet full of bubbles. Most will tell you that if they had the opportunity, they could create exciting lessons for students, lessons that pique student interest and generate real enthusiasm for learning. Most will tell you that a classroom does not have to be a deadening, emotionally flat place where mandated "stuff" is covered and re-covered, taught and retaught. Most will tell you, however, that in order for these things to happen, the school must have a degree of curricular and instructional independence that it does not currently possess.

This can be changed locally, however, if the will is there to do so. Parents have the right to expect that their child's school will nurture creativity, will expose students to a broad curriculum, and will staff classrooms with teachers who exhibit passionate teaching. If you would like to see real change in the local school, build a coalition of parents intent on demanding these things. For those teachers and administrators fully committed to their profession, such a coalition of parents would constitute a breath of fresh air. Via school-community forums it may be possible to generate enough commitment to convince the local board of education to act courageously on behalf of the school's children. It might convince the local board of education, in fact, to openly embrace an act of civil disobedience of sorts by rejecting the mandate that they submit AYP (annual yearly progress on test scores) data.

It is important, though, that the rejection of NCLB be accompanied by a better plan for assessment, a better plan for demonstrating and documenting the academic achievement of all children who attend the local school. And it is equally important that such a plan be the product of joint school and community input. As John Goodlad argued in the first chapter, teachers and parents must begin to work as partners in the educational enterprise.

It is crucial that a school declaring curricular and instructional independence has the support of parents and community members that surround it. Citizens whose first passion might be the health of the environment, or media reform, or term limits, or campaign finance reform, or any other sort of political or economic reform need to recognize that a crucial first step to achieving those ends is genuine conversation about what goes on in the local school. Allow teachers to mine the curricular and instructional potential of the local community, the local neighborhood, and you have taken a major step toward raising the consciousness of the next generation with respect to the full range of circumstances—political, economic, social—affecting one's home, family, neighbors, and neighborhood.

It is impossible to overemphasize the need for an alternative plan for concerted, systematic assessment of student learning. Periodic standardized testing can certainly be a part of this, but it will not replace genuine oversight on the part of teachers *and* community members. In fact, one structural change that should probably occur at the state level is a demand that each school select a board of assessors by lot, that is, a group of adults charged with assessing student learning and monitoring the curricular decisions of teachers. Teachers, in fact, should make periodic curricular reports to such a board, in effect forcing them to think deeply about their curricular choices and how they might affect the subsequent achievement of students across the full range of school subjects, art and music no less than math and science. Inserting the public into the very core of the public school is a central part of John Goodlad's "nonnegotiable agenda."

Short of a state-level initiative mandating a board of assessors, however, those schools that garner the commitment of a sufficiently large group of community members, teachers, and administrators—enough to orchestrate an official act of curricular and instructional independence—may well wish to build a local board of assessors into their alternative assessment plans. It would be almost impossible for a state department of education to punish a school financially for declaring pedagogical independence when the declaration comes with the full support of the majority of the school's immediate community.

A school that frees itself from curricular and instructional shackles represented by policies like NCLB is free to take full advantage of what we know about learning and the development of human understanding. While the policymaking community seeks to entrench the status quo with an accountability movement that will effectively limit curricular or instructional creativity, research into the nature of learning and the development of understanding suggests that we need to promote an educational agenda that celebrates and expands what the current accountability movement limits and restricts. Human understanding is largely believed to be a constructive process.[13] It requires certain key elements such as new information, old information, and a kind of cognitive negotiation between the two in an attempt to appraise and exercise judgment regarding an evidential base. It is this last element that is widely neglected in America's schools but is a sine qua non with regard to the development of understanding.

One reason why so little attention is paid to the cultivation of judgment concerning evidence has to do with the purpose of schooling. If the enterprise is predominantly about occupational preparation, then the verdict, so to speak, is already in. We know what students need if they are going to be ready for the job market. Our best students, those clearly headed for the important and interesting jobs in society, are often afforded an education that includes the cultivation of reasoned judgment. They are the exception, however; most students are merely asked to acquire certain sets of facts and skills. Our stepped-up accountability efforts are designed to be sure that our students acquire them.

If we step out of our current milieu and into a community-oriented view of the world, however, it becomes apparent that at least one purpose of schools must be to attend to developing wherewithal for the political role youths will play as they move into adulthood. Given a communitarian interpretation of what makes us fully human, all children require the ability to look at problems from multiple perspectives, and all children require the ability to form reasoned judgments regarding evidence. The dignity of a life does not reside totally in an individual's ability to affect his or her economic condition; it also resides in the person's capacity as a citizen to affect the lives of others. In other words, there is a social or communal dimension to life that requires educational cultivation.

Mathematics, history, and virtually all of the traditional school subjects can be taught in such a way that students feel compelled to use them. What this suggests is that it is not enough for students to acquire facts; they must also acquire the ability to wield school subjects in an effort to shoulder the burden of community membership. This will do two things. One, it will provide practice at playing a political role, perhaps through local associations, thus invigorating democracy. And second, it will provide a catalyst for cognitive activity, the constructive process that results in the development of understanding. This is the essential thrust of what has become known as place-based education.

There is likely no better path to the development of disciplinary understanding and no better preparation for the political role democratic citizens should play. As student skills and abilities increase, the scope of the curriculum can broaden. For example, math students can be asked to use algebra, geometry, and statistics in ways that are beneficial to the policymakers in their community. They can examine a huge range of issues that dominate debate in the policy arena, including demographics, environmental concerns, income distribution, tax structures, the availability and cost of goods and services, safety concerns, housing patterns, employment opportunities, interest rate fluctuations, corporate citizenship, health care—the list could go on and on. Virtually every school subject could provide a viewpoint from which to examine these issues. All subjects could contribute to the development of wherewithal regarding the merits of evidence, for all children are political actors every bit as much as they are economic actors.

Moving the educational narrative in this country away from what the late Neil Postman called the "god of economic utility" toward a balanced approach that yields skills and knowledge of the sort necessary for the economic arena and the capacity for reasoned judgment necessary for the political arena is the great educational task that faces this nation.[14]

It should be noted that shifting the educational narrative in this way would constitute at least a partial return to the schooling purposes identified by the founders of the common school in the 1830s and 1840s, a period that marked the high point of community-oriented traditions in American consciousness.[15] I do not mean to suggest that the vision of Henry Barnard, Horace Mann, Caleb Mills, and the rest of the common school founders was not marred by dubious ulterior motives: assimilating immigrants, posturing for denominational hegemony, etc. But whatever else one might say about them, the idea that schools would exist to provide economic wherewithal for citizens, or to create a well-oiled economy, was a minor theme at the very best. In other words, preparation for democratic life is what public schools were created for in the first place. It is past time to put an end to our century-long amnesia related to what schools are for. Though the current policy context yields little reason to be optimistic that this might happen, the larger scholarly trends under way all point to a renewed interest in the role played by community in what it means to be human, a development that suggests that the insertion of community in public school curriculum may not be as far off as one might think.

One central theme of this chapter has to do with curricular and instructional liberation for teachers and schools. Teachers need to be free to frame lessons in light of neighborhood dynamics, the conditions that affect the real and everyday lives of students. The end result is that they will thereby educate citizens rather than self-interest pursuers—and we will have at last rid ourselves of the lingering vestiges of Social Darwinism in the public school experience. Students so educated will be far more likely to shoulder the burden of democracy and to interrogate sham public relations campaigns sponsored by corporate media.

This process has the additional benefit of resting on a completely new opportunity for civic engagement on the part of citizens: participation on a local board of assessors selected by lot. The curricular and instructional liberation of teachers must be monitored by the community so that the public can gradually feel greater and greater comfort with an educational system that minimizes the use of standardized exams. If we are unable to raise the social and political dimensions of life to at least an equal educational status with the economic dimension, there is little reason to hope that we will avoid what Jane Jacobs calls the Dark Age Ahead.

Create study groups composed of teachers, community members, administrators, and school board members. Read a book from a long list of those written to challenge Americans to revitalize communities and thereby invigorate democracy. Make a bold step. Create a board of assessors and liberate local teachers. Declare independence from educational policy ill-suited for local circumstances. Do these things as a commitment to a better future across the full range of dimensions to life that make it worth living. We need schools that specifically target new ends for education. Create those schools, and economic and political reform will unfold in their wake. As Wendell Berry observed many years before NCLB, local schools no longer serve the local community; instead, "they serve the government's economy and the economy's government."[16] In so doing, they destroy the promise of democracy. Find the courage to change the schools, and the doors to economic and political reform will be open once again.

Notes

1. Jane Jacobs, *Dark Age Ahead* (New York: Random House, 2004). Jacobs is not the only one to draw this parallel. See Morris Berman, *Dark Ages America: The Final Phase of Empire* (New York: Norton, 2006). Berman's account is quite pessimistic. According to his analysis, America has only two possible futures: (1) we fall into a kind of social and economic collapse quickly, or (2) we fall into a similar collapse slowly over time. Berman believes that the antidemocratic features inherent in our regnant political and economic theory condemn us to this future.

2. Ben H. Bagdikian, *The New Media Monopoly* (Boston: Beacon, 2004), 22.

3. Julie Cresswell and Eric Dash, "A Farewell to Citigroup: Weill Built a Giant, A Deal at a Time," *New York Times,* April 18, 2006, C-1.

4. Michael J. Graetz and Ian Shapiro, *Death by a Thousand Cuts: The Fight over Taxing Inherited Wealth* (Princeton, N.J.: Princeton University Press, 2005), 8.

5. Herman E. Daly, "Economics in a Full World," *Scientific American* (September 2005): 102.

6. National Commission on Excellence in Education, *A Nation at Risk: The Imperative for Educational Reform: A Report to the Nation and the Secretary of Education* (Washington, D.C.: U.S. Government Printing Office, 1983).

7. John I. Goodlad, *A Place Called School* (1984; repr., New York: McGraw-Hill, 2004).

8. Ibid., 328–29.

9. See, for example, "Education and Community," in John I. Goodlad, *In Praise of Education* (New York: Teachers College Press, 1997), 46–81.

10. Robert Sternberg, "Creativity Is a Habit," *Education Week,* February 22, 2006, 64.

11. See, for example, Michele McNeil, "NGA Kicks Off Push for 'Innovation' Agenda: Effort Stresses Math, Science Education to Keep Economic Edge," *Education Week,* December 13, 2006, 15.

12. Antonio R. Damasio, *Descartes' Error: Emotion, Reason, and the Human Brain* (New York: Putnam, 1994).

13. A sampling of literature related to constructivist theory includes Catherine Twomey Fosnot, *Constructivism: Theory, Perspectives, and Practice* (New York: Teachers College Press, 1996); Eleanor Duckworth, *The Having of Wonderful Ideas and Other Essays on Teaching and Learning* (New York: Teachers College Press, 1996); Jacqueline Grennon Brooks and Martin G. Brooks, *In Search of Understanding: The Case for Constructivist Classrooms,* rev. ed. (Washington, D.C.: Association for Supervision and Curriculum Development, 1999); and Maryellen Weimer, *Learner-Centered Teaching: Five Key Changes to Practice* (San Francisco: Jossey-Bass, 2002).

14. Neil Postman, *The End of Education: Redefining the Value of School* (New York: Vintage Books, 1995), 27.

15. The historian Christopher Clark has dubbed the 1840s as America's "communitarian moment." See his *The Communitarian Moment: The Radical Challenge of the Northampton Association* (Ithaca, N.Y.: Cornell University Press, 1995). Clark points out that at least fifty-nine separate community living experiments were begun during the 1840s, well more than the number established in any other decade of the nineteenth century (2).

16. Wendell Berry, *What Are People For? Essays* (San Francisco: North Point Press, 1990), 164.

Chapter 5

The Human Conversation

Bonnie McDaniel

The art of conversation has fallen on hard times. Instead of serious dialogue about the issues of our time, our national leaders give us sound bites and talking points. Conversation itself is sometimes considered to be a weakness among those people who favor bold, unwavering action. In times like these, readers may be skeptical of our claim that we can renew our democracy by engaging in community-wide conversations about the public purpose of our schools. Given all that we feel we must do to improve our schools, such conversations may seem like a time-intensive luxury we can ill afford.

But if democracy is what we want, there are no shortcuts. We must talk to one another. If we are not talking together, we are individuals with limited vision and private aims. We are easy to manipulate and control. When we start to engage each other in conversation about public issues something positive happens. Our vision improves as we learn to see the world through different eyes. We begin to think about more than our private pursuits. We set our aim higher and talk about the things we can only do together. We realize that things in our world are not as they should be. We should do better—we can do better. Participating in this sort of conversation can be enormously satisfying. Together we find a focus for our efforts; we build relationships that can sustain the cooperative work necessary to bringing our vision into being. We believe, and over time we come to know, that we can change the world. It starts with conversation.

Our schools are a natural subject for democratic conversation. Our school communities are not too big. Citizens can get together to talk about their local schools and expect that their voices will be heard and their actions will matter. Why should citizens get involved in conversations about their schools? Schools are places where we consciously shape the next generation. Our responsibility is to prepare the next generation both to preserve the aspects of our civilization that we hold most dear and to improve upon our shortcomings.[1] We all have a stake in what goes on in our schools.

Let us look at what is happening in one urban community in Ohio. In January 2007 a small group got together to talk about the challenges of democracy in America today and how those challenges are worked out in the daily life of their local school, Lakeside Elementary. The staff members at Lakeside are seriously engaged in the process of living democratically at their school and have learned to value opportunities to sit down and talk with members of the local community. Those who showed up for the conversation that evening came from different socioeconomic and racial backgrounds, a reflection of the diverse population served by the school. Seated at the table that night were three parents, Shawna, Carrie, and Bill; one community member, Joe; two of the school's teachers, Linda and Paula; one intervention specialist, Alison; the principal, Jo Ann; and Deborah, the facilitator for the conversation. Deborah began by asking the group to consider the role that citizens play in a democracy. The conversation heated up quickly, as the group took on some of the most serious issues we face as a nation. The challenges of democracy, as one parent concluded, cannot be separated from the challenges of education.

Democratic Ideal Versus Democratic Reality

DEBORAH: What do citizens do that makes a difference to the democratic process?

JOE: We give our voice. We give our opinions about issues of the day. I think that democracy allows for inclusion, and it allows for difference and, as a result, provides us with a forum and a platform to talk about issues. Sometimes those issues will be popular, and other times they will not be popular, but we are still able to give voice to them.

PAULA: Service—citizens in a democracy are called to serve.

ALISON: Democracy is a call to action. Citizens are called to act because our democracy is continually changing and evolving.

PAULA: It's also a responsibility.

CARRIE: As part of a democracy we are given rights. That's a very important part of our society. Democracy is a forum for discussion, like Joe said. You can have differences, and you can discuss those differences.

PAULA: I feel like there is a difference between our U.S. democracy and what democracy means ideally. Our U.S. democracy is not always democratic. I think that part of being a good citizen is knowing the difference between the two and promoting the spirit of democracy, not the bureaucracy.

DEBORAH: How do you understand the difference between our U.S. democracy and the democratic spirit?

JOE: The democratic spirit is that your voice is valued. In our democracy, your voice may be there, but often it is not acted upon. When you have people who are saying the same thing over and over again and people are still not hearing it, I believe that hurts democratic conversation. The point of democratic conversation is to act upon what you are hearing.

DEBORAH: What do you think it is that stops that from happening on a broader scale?

JOE: Sometimes we are tied so inextricably to what we believe that we don't have room to expand our thinking. Our experiences are such that they will not allow us to understand divergent ways of thinking. I think that we gain our experiences in several ways. But you have to act in order to change, and change is growth. Some folks think of change as unhealthy. It is almost like food. Because I eat food a lot, I'll use this analogy: if the only thing you eat every day is macaroni and cheese and someone tells you about asparagus, but you are really bent on just having macaroni and cheese, you are missing an opportunity. Some individuals aren't able to open their mind and say, golly that might be good for me, or at least let me try it. There are those who don't even want to try.

As Joe suggests, the democratic spirit is expressed by an attitude of openness to new ideas and a willingness to communicate with people who are unlike you. It takes courage to stand up and speak your mind in the presence of others who are likely to disagree with you. Those inspired by the ideal of democracy are willing to take the risk. They know that encounters with diverse viewpoints are stimulating: their own thinking becomes more sophisticated, more flexible, and more humane as a result. There are personal gains to be had by adopting a democratic attitude.

There are also social gains. When citizens from different walks of life meet together to deliberate on important issues, they typically walk away with a more nuanced understanding of the issue and more respect for those who hold opposing views. Authentic communication tends to have a depolarizing effect. It becomes possible for citizens to find common ground and build working relationships across differences. In the twenty-first century there are powerful forces pushing citizens away from each other. Democratic conversation can be a countervailing force bringing us back together. Our participants point out that there is a gap between the democratic ideal and the way we live today in America. They know that it is the work of citizens to close the gap.[2]

DEBORAH: Where else is the democratic process not evident, when we look at the country as a whole?

PAULA: The government is such a big bureaucracy. It takes so much effort to get through the steps to have your voice heard. Locally it is different. If you are talking federally, though, the lack of money keeps people's voices from being heard. Just writing a letter campaign probably is not going to have much effect. If you are not a lobbyist, your idea may not get through. That is part of the reason why the democratic spirit is not so evident. It is a massive bureaucracy, and money talks.

CARRIE: Another problem is that young people are not involved in the process. Young people do not have a big voice because they do not go out and vote. Why not? Maybe because they were never encouraged to be part of that process.

BILL: Participation is an inconvenience for young people. It takes some energy and some effort. But for many young people, that's low on the totem pole. I don't think we see activity among young people the way we did in the 1960s. I don't think the political climate is the same.

DEBORAH: What interests me is that these children we say are apathetic are our children. We gave birth to them. So why don't they have that same fire that we had in the 1960s?

CARRIE: Older generations have felt the bite of war. We have lost uncles and brothers and cousins in battle. People in their fifties, sixties, or older know someone, or know of someone, who fought in a war. I think that that brings the importance home. And I don't think the younger generation has truly felt that. I think that is a big difference.

BILL: Why were people so passionate in the 1960s? Vested interest. There were a whole lot of black people saying, this is it. Either I get something, or I don't. And there were a whole lot of young people saying, either I stay here, or I get to go to Vietnam and die. That's the way they saw it. Does anyone really sit around fearing that they're going to get sent off to Iraq? No. It is almost a completely volunteer army. So unless you happened to sign up as a reservist, it doesn't really affect your life a whole lot. People would be a lot more passionate about it if their sons and daughters were being shipped out.

SHAWNA: Why hasn't the younger generation felt that passion? Because they're not being taught that. They start off with a seed of hope in kindergarten, and by the time they get to middle school or high school, that little voice has been stifled. Unless it is opened back up, or nurtured at home, or in church, or in the community, it is not going to come about. I try to encourage that with my own children. I want them to be in a learning environment that nurtures that little voice. Right now, for my oldest child, that voice is being stifled. And I'm trying to bring it back. I'm trying to show him avenues that are going to nurture it. Our public schools are doing a great job of stifling it in our young people. Then we wonder why the eighteen-to twenty-five-year-olds don't want to vote. If that passion, that voice, is not being encouraged at home, in their community, in their churches, where are they getting it from? Because it is not being encouraged at school. That is the sad reality. But we want to encourage it. That is why we are here.

There is silence in the room for a few moments as the group considers what this woman has said. The group is moved by the passionate appeal of a mother on behalf of her child. If she had not been in the room, the conversation might have taken a different turn. The other participants might have continued their abstract analysis of the problems of adolescents in a fast-paced consumer society. But the urgency in this woman's voice changes the tenor of the conversation. We feel the tragic dimensions of what is happening to her child. Those of us who have children or grandchildren are gripped by her plea. I want my child's spirit to be nourished, she tells us. I know I cannot hold on to him forever. I have to let him go out into the world. My hope is that the world will nurture my child's spirit as I have. But that is not happening. My child's voice is being stifled. It is happening right now. The problem is no longer one that calls for abstract theorizing. It is our problem together, and it calls for immediate action.

Antidemocratic Lessons Learned at School

It may be difficult for some of us to see tragedy in the silencing of a child's voice at school. For so many of us, that was our experience too. We learned how to get along by blending in. We learned not to rock the boat. Looking back, it does not seem so bad. Could it really be any other way? The participants in this conversation were all able to laugh about the antidemocratic lessons they were taught in school. But perhaps the laughter hides a sense of loss. What has been the cost to us of a schooling experience that shut us down? How might things have been different for us if our schools had truly seen us and heard us? Don't we want something more, something better, for our children?

DEBORAH: How does public education in a democracy differ from education in a country that is not a democracy?

CARRIE: We are supposed to be taught to stand up for what we believe in and let our voices be heard. I'm sure that's not the case in many other countries in the world.

DEBORAH: How many of you were taught to stand up for what you believe in when you were in school?

(Silence. Nervous laughter.)

LINDA: I particularly know I wasn't.

SHAWNA: I wouldn't say that I was taught that in school per se. I was taught that at home.

JO ANN: I was taught that in church.

LINDA: Right.

ALISON: I was taught the opposite in school. I was taught to listen, to trust, and to conform.

LINDA: When I think back to my school, even if they did teach U.S. government and democracy, they told us, "This is how it is, and this is how change happens. But you are not going to do that in my classroom. You are going to follow my rules." It was kind of a mixed message.

CARRIE: You can see it, but you cannot have it.

PAULA: I remember when I was at a particularly rebellious age, probably fifteen or sixteen, I said in class that the pledge of allegiance was not accurate because there was not justice for all, and I was not going to stand for it. Guess what happened to me?

JO ANN: You got expelled?

PAULA: I didn't get expelled. But I got sent to the office. My father, who was a car salesman at the time, had to leave his office and come in to school. I got in huge trouble. Huge trouble. Now, I was a fifteen-year-old, remember. I was very idealistic. I'm not saying that this was such a good thing to do. I'm just saying that was the reaction. There wasn't a discussion.

DEBORAH: What do you think you learned from that?

PAULA: Be quiet. Conform. You are not supposed to rock the boat.

SHAWNA: Mmmm. Hmmm. (Heads nod in agreement.)

Those of us who had school experiences like these might stop to think about what we really learned about democracy as a result: That democracy is not something to be taken too seriously? That democracy is something that was secured for us in the hazy past, something that asks nothing of us now, except perhaps to pay lip service to the ideal, while denouncing other forms of government? Is that what democracy requires from its citizens?

Living Democracy at School

Educators who are serious about forming future democratic citizens know otherwise. They know that textbook lessons on democracy are never enough. They know that students have to live democracy if they are going to learn democracy. Our schools must be places that cultivate our children's agency and voice. Our schools must be places where the values of liberty, equality, and justice are living principles governing how we relate to one another at school. If they live it, they will learn it. So why have we not insisted that our schools place the values of democracy at the center of everything they do?

Perhaps we are afraid that real democracy takes us dangerously close to anarchy. If so, we are in good company. Great thinkers throughout history,[3] beginning with Plato and Aristotle, have been skeptical about democracy for precisely that reason. What would happen if we gave students meaningful choices at school? Would the entire system come crashing down? One envisions sixth graders voting to eliminate home-work, or doing away with school entirely for that matter. But teaching democracy does not mean letting students do whatever they want, any more than democratic citizenship means that we adults get to do whatever we want. Children can be taught liberty in developmentally appropriate ways. They can talk together about the meaning of social justice, and they can be supported to take action in the face of injustice. Under the guidance of wise teachers, students learn that with freedom comes re-sponsibility. Arguably, it is only if we provide an education in citizenship to our children that we can reasonably expect our democracy to amount to something more than mob rule.

Educators who are trying to live democracy at school every day know that we do not need to be afraid of it. As it turns out, our children can handle it. The adults working at school can handle it too. The values of liberty and justice are remarkably robust. As long as they pervade the system, as long as the conversation about what they mean is kept alive and remains open to all, a developmentally appropriate democratic order can be maintained at school. It is all in a day's work at Lakeside Elementary.

LINDA: I'm thinking back to something Paula was saying. Democracy is not tangible. It is not something that you can go to the store and pick up quickly and digest it and then walk away with it and say, "I'm part of the democratic process. I did my part today." It has to be something that is active in my life daily.

JO ANN: I also think that many people have not had an opportunity to truly be a part of democracy. So if I've never been in a situation where participation has been something that has worked for me and where I've gotten some sort of response from it, why in the world would I try? I wonder how much that contributes to the problem of apathy among young people that Bill was talking about.

BILL: You make the argument that you have to teach people how to be citizens of a democracy. But very rarely do we run the household as a full-fledged democracy.

DEBORAH: That would be scary.

BILL: Contrary to what your son might tell you, you don't let the twelve-year-olds vote on what you get for dinner every night. You probably don't need an experience with democracy every day, but you need one or two experiences in life where you can say, "My voice was heard, and it made a difference." But you also have to be provided with an environment where that is possible. At some point, people have to be taught. The classic example is the failure in Iraq. That failure is probably at least partly related to the fact that these people don't know what a democracy is. They haven't seen how it is any good for them. Why would they lay down their swords and try to get along with one another? How is that going to pay the bills at the end of the day? What they know is: grease the palms that make the wheels turn.

JO ANN: I was listening to the radio the other day and they were interviewing the new head of state in Iraq. They asked him how he would define a successful democratic transition in Iraq. He answered that in a democratic

Iraq we wouldn't have these disagreements. Now, I don't think that democracy is about putting your disagreements aside. I tried to put myself in his shoes. I think he meant that in a democratic Iraq we'll stop shooting and killing each other. I'd have to agree with that. But I don't think that democracy is about putting your differences to the side. It is about putting them in the middle. It's about discussing and examining them and learning how to have civil discourse and then growing from what comes about as you listen to someone who disagrees with you.

ALISON: If all that happens is that you talk about democracy, or if you sit and listen to a teacher and read a book about it, then it is really abstract. You have to apply democracy if you are going to teach it to children. They have to see the effects in order for them to understand it.

LINDA: You have to have a staff and teachers that are on board, or it is never going to be implemented. Even if children want to be democratic, they're going to be shot down. You cannot teach democracy as a scripted lesson plan. You have to have a person who believes in it to spearhead it and get it moving.

BILL: You can't teach passion. But you can teach the skills of civil discourse.

LINDA: I don't think it is always taught. Most adults say, "Oh, don't talk politics. That's taboo." It's not encouraged. There isn't that respect for different perspectives because adults won't talk about it.

BILL: Right.

CARRIE: That is why it is important to teach our children to have a voice: to hear and to be heard and to be part of the process. It is much easier to have your voice heard in a smaller arena. If our children can learn that they can make a difference here at school, then maybe they can make a difference in high school. Maybe they can make a difference in the community, or in the state. As they get older and their ideas grow, so can their ambition. But if they're not given that little seed of hope in the beginning and taught, then those ideals are never going to grow and bloom.

LINDA: Passions change and interests change throughout adolescence. But there are common denominators that are not going to change. They are the same, whether you are in an educational environment or in the broader society. There are human needs that are not going to change. For example, when we began our school year, we had our town hall meeting, and we came up with the values of our school. The common conversations you heard when you walked around were phenomenal. What was important to the core of these students didn't change from one age group to the next.

DEBORAH: It probably would be about the same in society generally.

LINDA: Passion changes, but the root wants and needs of individuals are strikingly similar.

DEBORAH: How have your ongoing conversations about democracy influenced what you do in the classroom? What have you learned about democracy by putting it into practice in the classroom?

PAULA: If you go where the children lead you, you don't know where you are going to end up. That is choice. It is a little scary. But that's good. Let me give you an example. A while back, we were studying government. Our local government was in an upheaval at the time. The students' assignment was to find out about our city council. While we were learning about the council, some people on the council resigned. I kept my students up to date on current events. Then I read in the paper that they were going to appoint new council members. How much better could that be? I asked the students to read the bios and come to a consensus about who they would select for the positions and to give me the reasons. They voted for two women, one of whom was African American. They did not vote for any white men. Later, I had to go back to them and tell them what really happened. Their candidates were not selected. They were upset. So I asked them how they wanted to handle that. What are the avenues open to you? They decided they wanted to write a letter to the editor, and they wanted to do a PowerPoint presentation for city council.

CARRIE: Let me say that this whole lesson has been very, very effective. My husband and I have been very involved in politics. I know a lot of politicians. And my child knows *more*. He knows more people, he knows more issues, and he has more PowerPoint presentations to make about city council than any other person I know. So ... (She gives the teacher applause.)

JO ANN: I tried to write this story up for our newsletter. The theme for the newsletter was about how we honor differences and different cultures in our classes. I remember that some of the students doing this project talked about whether or not they would pick a candidate who was black because they were black.

PAULA: We had that conversation.

JO ANN: What the students came up with was, "No, but if you have two people who are equally qualified and there are no blacks on the council, then, yes, we would pick a black person because there needs to be representation."

PAULA: That is in their PowerPoint.

JO ANN: I didn't have the details for the newsletter piece. So I went to class thinking that I'd grab Paula and she'd give me the details. Well, Paula was on the other side of the room with a small group of students. So I went over to one of her students, "Sam—psssst! Sam!"

(Laughter.)

JO ANN: "Sam, I'm trying to write about what you guys did. Can you tell me the details of city council?" Not only does Sam get passionate telling me about it, soon a bunch of other students are jumping in on top of each other: "Then such and such happened, and then so and so resigned. . . ." There were several things that were refreshing about this. The first was the degree to which they were passionate. They were clearly involved. The other was the degree of knowledge, and third was the degree of comfort with which they automatically talked about race and racial relations. It was part of the story, so it wasn't a case of "I guess I can't talk about that." It had to be a part of the story. It was incredible. It really was.

PAULA: What better place, what other place are you going to have that diverse a group of people but a public school?

JOE: What do you mean by diverse?

PAULA: I mean diverse in every way: boys, girls, race, socioeconomic status, and religious background. That's the place to stir it up and teach the students how to handle conflicts, how we resolve issues, and how we have our voice heard. What better place to do it?

Democracy as the End and Means of Change

What better place indeed. Why is it not more common? One reason is that deeply entrenched structures of schooling that took shape over one hundred years ago militate against it. Our schools reflect the mechanistic worldview that Alan Wood describes in chapter 2. The way we organize time and space in our schools conveys the message that the whole is nothing more than the sum of the parts. We divide the school day into equal segments to study discrete subjects. We sort students by age and ability and then place them with a teacher in an isolated compartment for the day. A premium is placed on standardization throughout the system in the name of efficiency. The many at the bottom of the hierarchy follow directions from the few at the top.

This may have been a good way to organize factories for the industrial era, but it is not a good way to organize schools to nurture democratic citizens. It values compliance more than critical thinking and responsible action. It rewards form instead of substance. It prefers to distribute disconnected facts rather than promote meaningful individual experience. It perpetuates the myth that we are all the same instead of allowing us to recognize and respect our differences.

Of course, these charges against the structure of schooling are not new. John Dewey recognized the dangers that these structures posed to democracy even as the present system was taking shape.[4] Reformers throughout the twentieth century tried to change the system to make it more capable of providing an authentic education fit for a free people. But the system has proved to be remarkably difficult to change. Over the years, we have adapted to this system; it is familiar and predictable. Many of us spent the years of our childhood habituating ourselves to it. We know what a real school is supposed to look and feel like. When reform proposals deviate too far from our internalized image of a real school, we resist. As our conversation participants point out, change is scary. Even when educators manage to embrace a new vision for their schools, the powerful pull of community expectations can undermine their efforts. Before long the schools again resemble our internalized image of them, even though we know we can do better.

There is hope for meaningful change, but it does not lie in another round of reforms imposed from the top down. There is hope if communities start talking about what education is and what they want their schools to be. The power of conversation should not be underestimated. Through conversation, the community educates itself. Communities talking together can build a new vision of what our schools should be. They can learn to let go of models that have outlived their usefulness. The educators at Lakeside Elementary know that their school is part of a broader community that influences what it can do. While they are indebted to the handful of visionary school leaders who recognize and support their efforts, they consider the education community in general to be at best indifferent and at worst openly hostile to their mission to live democracy at school.

DEBORAH: Has the world outside the walls of this school been supportive of what you are doing?
(Silence. Nervous laughter.)
SHAWNA: I don't see it.
BILL: I see it in the extreme opposite. I think the educational community, both locally and nationwide, is almost in opposition to this kind of school.
CARRIE: They do not understand. They have not done the research. They do not know, and what you do not know scares you. Change scares

people. This school is definitely a change from the norm. Explaining to my in-laws that my child doesn't get a report card is an issue every grading period. It really is.

ALISON: It is a constant conversation; it needs to be a constant conversation.

JOE: The level of understanding of what happens in here simply does not exist out there. That is why it is critical to put Lakeside out there front and center. People need to see what happens here on a regular basis. Part of the challenge is that there are not enough people who really understand what happens here, so the perceptions of us are not aligned with what Lakeside really does. There is an opportunity here to develop ways to bring people in and change the stereotypes. We can either say, "Oh, well, that's the way it is, and let's just keep paddling upstream," or we can say, "This is the way it is, and let's change the paradigm. Let's change the thinking. Let's bring people in so they can see what happens here."

LINDA: We are a very transparent community. I walk down the halls in the afternoons, and I love it. I get excited about where I work. I see the children going in and out. I see parents coming in and out. At different times of the year we have community members here. We are a transparent staff because we have the conversations with the parents. We want the active involvement.

DEBORAH: Would you say that this is an outstanding school?

JOE: To my mind, yes.

DEBORAH: So what is your proficiency test score? That's going to be the first question that many people ask.

JO ANN: We are in continuous improvement.

DEBORAH: How can you say you are an excellent school when you are in continuous improvement?

JOE: I think that the argument could be made that life is more than a standardized test. (Applause from the group.) Somewhere along the line that message has to be first and foremost. To my mind, it is better to graduate a literate person who has self-confidence and aspiration, as opposed to one who passes all the tests but whose demeanor and persona are stunted because he's been stifled in this box. The message that has to come out is that this is not just about proficiency tests. This is about preparing young people for life. It is about preparing them for their experiences and making them whole. It's about making them feel valued and valuable.

DEBORAH: You realize that what you just said is completely opposite of what the national drumbeat is.

JOE: But, my friend, that is what democracy is. Democracy is giving voice to issues that may not be popular, you see? This country was not founded on the idea of being popular.

CARRIE: Somehow that idea lost popularity.

DEBORAH: Why did you send your child to this school?

CARRIE: Thinking back, I knew several other children who had come through this school, and I really liked the people they were when they left this school. That was a big reason why I sent my child here. I think that proving to the community that we are a good school has a lot to do with the students that we turn out. You know, the proof is in the pudding, and they are the product that is produced here.

LINDA: I really wish that we had the data on that, because in this district, data talks. Where did our students end up? Were they leaders? What activities were they involved in when they left this school?

DEBORAH: What do the other schools think about your school?

JOE: My response as a layperson is that schools here are in competition with one another. This whole testing deal has folks biting at each other's heels. When you say that our school is really doing well in this area or that school is really doing well in that area, folks don't want to hear that. That's where the environment comes in. You've got to create an environment that says, "We're in the same gumbo. You may be a sausage, I may be a pepper, but we're still in the pot."

SHAWNA: We all make it taste good.

JOE: When you are test conscious, you are not really concerned too much with citizenship. You are not too concerned about how a person behaves or how a person acts. You are not trying to reach a child's core. You're worried about whether or not she's done the third grade right and whether she's done all of the tests correctly. Then maybe you worry about the whole person. But you see, the whole person is better than the test. You've got to create the whole person.

SHAWNA: But that is not where society is leading us. Unfortunately.

ALISON: But these are the people who are going to come back to your community. You want them to come to your community. You want them to stay in your community. You want them to be the next leaders of your community. That's not happening in our community.

JOE: You want them to come back, and you want them to stay. But you don't give them the whole-person feeling. Yes, they passed the test, but you treated them so shabbily that they want to get their hat and get out. If you treated them better, even though they might not have scored the greatest on the test, they can come back to this community. You see, this whole treatment of people is important. The callous way we engage with one another is coming back to haunt us. We are behaving badly.

DEBORAH: To put it mildly.

This is the sort of realization that human beings can come to in conversation with each other. When Joe tells us that, "the callous way we engage with one another is coming back to haunt us," he refers to a collective body that is essentially moral in character. Does it really exist? It does when individuals recognize themselves to be part of the "we" who are behaving badly and are moved to join in the conversation and then take action to make things better.

Sometimes it is difficult to get started. There are many ways to jump in and get involved. The first step is to start talking. Talk to your neighbors about the purpose of schools. Invite someone you think will disagree with you to join in the conversation. If one does not already exist, form a conversation group of citizens and educators interested in improving your local school. Read this book together. Invite your local school principal or school board member to join the conversation. Talk about the issues that matter most to you. Decide together what can be done to improve your local school, and then do it. Form an online community with other active civic groups working to improve education. Share stories, suggestions, and resources. You may still feel that you are paddling upstream, as Joe put it, but it is encouraging to talk to other folks out there with their oars in the water.

We have followed the path of just one conversation. Can you imagine how your voice might add to the conversation? Do you see things differently? There is room for all in the larger conversation about who we are as a people and how we want to live together. The more voices that join in the conversation, the richer it becomes. In Shawna's words, "We all make it taste better."

We are all members of the human family, and the human conversation is how we tell our story. When asked to list their core values, Lakeside students gave remarkably similar responses across classrooms. Indeed, members of the human family hold a significant number of concerns in common: we want to live good, purposeful lives; we care about the health and well-being of ourselves, our families, and our environment; we want the freedom to develop our potential as individuals; we want strong, stable communities. These issues make up much of the substance of the human conversation. Our commonalities allow us to understand one another and make conversation possible.

Of course, human beings differ greatly in their answers to life's big questions. Sometimes we agree on the ends but disagree on how to get there. We disagree about how to balance worthwhile values when they conflict. We disagree about who should have the authority to make the decisions. Our differences make conversation necessary. How else are we to figure out how to live together happily? Although we might wish it otherwise, many of these issues cannot be settled once and for all. The world changes. New problems emerge. We interpret old problems in new ways. Each generation must take on the big questions for itself, in light of present circumstances.

We have become impatient with difficult questions that yield no final answers. It is tempting to stop asking difficult questions and to ask only the ones that can be answered by experts with hard data. We tell ourselves we are being practical and tough-minded by doing so, but something is lost in the process. Some of the value in asking the big questions lies not in the answers yielded, but in who we become as a people by tackling them together. We are defined to some extent by the questions we ask. When we ask big, searching questions, we become more expansive, more humane people. When we stop asking such questions, the human conversation is diminished. And the ends of our shared life are left to be determined by those with the wealth and power to get what they want. If we want our democracy to thrive, we must not let that happen. It is our privilege and our responsibility to join in the conversation and to work together to shape the future. Our schools should be places where we are welcomed into the ongoing human conversation about who we are and who we wish to become.

Notes

1. Philosopher Jane Roland Martin has devoted considerable attention to the critically important problem of carefully selecting what we should preserve in and let go from our culture. See her *Cultural Miseducation: In Search of a Democratic Solution* (New York: Teachers College Press, 2002).

2. For a diverse array of writings on the critical issues confronting democracy in the twenty-first century, see Stephen John Goodlad, ed., *The Last Best Hope: A Democracy Reader* (San Francisco: Jossey-Bass, 2001).

3. For a critical analysis of our democracy and comparison with the Athenian, see the book by Paul Woodruff, a professor in ethics and American society, *First Democracy: The Challenge of an Ancient Idea* (New York: Oxford University Press, 2005).

4. Dewey wrote a great deal about democracy. See, for example, John Dewey, *Democracy and Education: An Introduction to the Philosophy of Education* (New York: Macmillan, 1916).

Chapter 6

Making Moral Systems of Education

Gary Daynes

The Role of Hope

In the American system of education, beneath the students, the teachers and administrators, the curricula and assessments, the buildings, and school boards, resides a set of hopes. Hope is a fragile thing—less formidable than fact, more gently held than belief, harder to come by than conviction. But hope endures when facts change, when beliefs bend, when convictions crumble. Hope describes our aspirations. Hope looks better when life looks darker.

Here are our hopes. We hope that all young people become educated, that they not only learn the basics and train for employment but also enter into the human conversation. We hope that education is a moral act, one that lifts students closer to what is good even while it equips them for success in a morally ambiguous world. We hope that schools are moral places, where rules and relationships together lead to deeper learning and fairer play. And we hope that the other institutions in society—families, churches, governments, businesses—will support, or at least not destroy, the hope for our children's moral well-being.

These hopes are, today, imperiled. Many children do not learn; fewer become educated. Much education does not lead to moral ends; many schools are not moral places. And even when education happens, when the classroom is good and students learn and the school supports them, the institutions of our society often undercut that education, teaching young people to trade moral education for an amoral world.

And so to the list of hopes must be added one more: that somehow the entire culture that educates can work for the good of each of its parts. Teacher Herbert Kohl puts it this way: "This is the very source of hope—that we can create places where young people can dare to dream without being brought down by the realities of their terrible experiences in schools and by an adult world that dares them to succeed rather than welcoming their energy, love, and contributions."[1]

There have long been places of the sort that Kohl desires. Anyone interested in building a moral educational system, one that includes schools, churches, businesses, and families working together to help students flourish in American democracy, must attend to both schools and the rest of the public sphere.

What Is a Moral Educational System?

A moral educational system is three things. First, it is composed of schools and the other institutions that, purposefully or not, educate people. Too often American public conversations talk about education as if it only takes place in schools. But there is no reason to think that this is the case. School, after all, runs for 180 or so days a year, but students learn from the media and their families every day. And as much as we might sometimes wish that students derived their habits and beliefs from school, the data show that peers, home life, and standards of living all have more influence on children than do schools.

Second, the system of education has to be considered as a system, that is, as a group of organizations whose policies, purposes, and activities interact with each other, even as they have an influence on students. Historian of education Lawrence Cremin has noted that the United States has rarely thought in terms of educational systems.[2] Instead, policymakers and educators have together placed primary responsibility for education with the schools. Further, they have passed on to schools tasks that might naturally reside with other institutions in society. Cremin traces this history, noting how in the early decades of the twentieth century schools gained responsibility for vocational training. Since then, they have added responsibility for training drivers, discussing reproduction, and responding to America's competitiveness gap, among other things. This is not to say that sex education and civics classes are unimportant, only to observe that schools have an increasing burden of mandated obligations. Cremin, writing in 1990, argued that the real challenge facing schools was not "the crisis of putative mediocrity and decline," but instead, "the crisis inherent in balancing this tremendous variety of demands Americans have made on their schools and colleges."[3] Though Cremin does not note it, the increased responsibilities of schools have come at a time when other major educative institutions—churches, clubs, and political parties among them—draw ever smaller portions of Americans' time and attention. Families are widely perceived to be under threat (though the nature and direction of that threat varies with the commentator). Only the entertainment media, which must include television and the Internet, have won a larger portion of Americans' time.[4]

Third, a moral educational system must have a visible and publicly beneficial morality, one committed both to the good of individual students and to fostering the common good. The problems in creating such a morality are immense, especially if we are concerned about education rather than schooling. It is difficult to get educative institutions to agree on moral purposes when they have no actual obligation to each other. A school and a church may wish to teach honesty, but their efforts are diffused because not all students go to the same church and because notions of honesty differ in religious and schooling contexts. It is of course conceivable that, over time, a school and a church might figure out how to work together, but only if they consider that they are both parts of the same system, a consideration that is rare indeed today.

Creating a moral system of education is difficult also because institutions have both explicit and implicit curricula. Many are the schools that talk about fairness but are perceived as unfair by students and teachers alike. Many are the corporations that talk of being good citizens but sell destructive products. Many are the parents who simultaneously love and fail their children.

If we assume this definition of moral educational systems and diagnosis of their difficulties, there are obvious lessons to be learned. The first, for parents, educators, politicians, and citizens, is that there must be room in the United States for a wide variety of educational systems, for only such variety makes it possible for people to find the system that is best for them and their communities. The second, for reformers, is that any effort to reinvigorate our educational hopes must be systematic. One may wish to fix a school, but as Sara Lawrence Lightfoot argues, the good school is good in its context.[5] The third, for all of us, is that the shortest path to creating a moral system of education is to reinvigorate the public purposes of education. This is both a formidable task and a possible one, since the histories of education and of public life contain resources that we can use to this end. But by beginning with a reinvigoration of the public purposes of education, we can develop the conversations and relationships that create and sustain moral systems of education. What follows is an effort to bring to light the public traditions of education and show how a concern with what is public has led, in some cases, to moral systems of education.

The Public Traditions of Education

> The business of education has acquired a new complexion by the independence of our country. The form of government we have assumed has created a new class of duties to every American. It becomes us, therefore, to examine our former habits upon this subject, and in laying the foundations for nurseries of wise and good men, to adapt our modes of teaching to the peculiar form of our government.
> —*Benjamin Rush, "Thoughts Upon the Mode of Education Proper in a Republic," 1786*[6]

Benjamin Rush was a physician and writer, a friend of Tom Paine and a signer of the Declaration of Independence, an educator and the leader of a remarkable group of people—including Thomas Jefferson, Noah Webster, Judith Sargent Murray, and George Washington—who called for the creation of a system of education that would serve the public purposes of the new American nation.

The nation has done at best an uneven job of achieving the aspirations of the founders. Perhaps most obviously, our definition of "public" has nearly always excluded huge portions of the populace, and our public schools have nearly always had a narrow definition of those who deserved to be educated.[7] Further, our schools, public or private, have not done a good job of educating their students to be effective participants in public life. In the most recent National Assessment of Educational Progress civics results, 75 percent of fourth graders, 76 percent of eighth graders, and 70 percent of twelfth graders were at or below basic skill level—meaning only about one-fourth of students were proficient in civic knowledge.[8] A recent study sponsored by the Intercollegiate Studies Institute found that the average score for seniors at fifty top colleges was 53 percent on a civics test. At sixteen of the fifty colleges, students' civic knowledge actually declined while they were in college.[9] Whatever you may think of the No Child Left Behind Act, the absence of civics, history, or social studies from its areas of emphasis suggests that impetus to improve civic knowledge is unlikely to come from federal policy. The lack of a meaningful core in the general education programs of our colleges and universities suggests that they, too, might not be a place to reinvigorate the public purposes of education.

The problem is not just a lack of knowledge about public life. Our schools are also failing in giving students the opportunity to be involved in the real stuff of democracy. It is worth recalling that both K-12 and higher education were born in the United States with the goal of developing students into citizens, and this was not because it would be good for them but because it was necessary for the endurance of our republic and for the good of their education. It is reasonable to ask if this is still the case and, if so, whether our system of education achieves that goal. Education's definition of "citizenship"—a grade based on behaving oneself in K-12; committee in higher education—suggests that it is not, and that the system does not.

I think people would agree that this lack of knowledge and skill matters for democracy. After all, one would be hard-pressed to argue that uninformed and uninvolved citizens are good for a democracy. But I want to argue that civic knowledge and skills are also essential for student learning; in other words, they make education better. This is a good thing, if only because the main purpose of education is education. But it is good also because civic knowledge and skills are key to reinvigorating the rest of the public sphere in a way that makes systems of education more likely to be moral.

If the public component of education has long been and remains in danger and if it is essential for student learning and for moral systems of education, then what do we do? I would like to suggest a few steps. None of them is radical; in fact, the thrust of my argument is that we attend to a civic tradition in American education and that we do it proudly and publicly. To make this point, I will first examine the way we generally talk about the "public" components of education. Then I will describe the civic tradition in American education by telling stories of schools that successfully blended civic knowledge and skills with learning in a way that created moral systems of education. From those stories emerge both a list

of the outcomes that must result from good public education and a set of
actions that can help us create moral systems of education.

What We Mean When We Say "Public"

Well over two hundred years ago, American intellectuals began debating
the meaning of the word "public." One stream of that debate revolved
around the question of whether the public (or "the people" or "the masses")
was intellectually and morally capable of self-government. The debate is
enshrined in the nation's bicameral legislature—a House of Representatives
to represent the voice of the people and a Senate to blunt its force.[10] It is
also, in part, the impetus for creating a system of public schools, since such
schools could be charged with teaching the public how to govern itself.[11]

In the past two decades, American thinkers have again turned to the
meaning of "public," especially in the context of public schooling. That
turn has been influenced by three trends. First, a decline in civic engagement has forced educators to look again at their role as the trainers of
citizens. Second, the gap in performance between the rich and the poor
and disparity among ethnic groups has provoked a conversation about
whether the public schools do, in fact, serve the whole public. And third,
the private purposes of education—job training, personal advancement,
the accumulation of prestige—have overtaken schooling's public purposes
in many places.[12]

If most of what we do in public education is attend to education, what
do we mean by the "public" part of that phrase? It seems we mean two
things. Schools are public, we say, first because the state controls them, and
second because they are, when taken as a whole, open to all. That is, the
public part of public education is either about politics or simply a euphemism
for "people of one sort or another." These are certainly public things. But
imagine how diminished our public life would be if it included only politics and people. Gone would be the associations—churches, clubs, service
organizations, nonprofits—that have formed the backbone of American
democracy since before there was America and are key to moral systems
of education. Gone would be civic knowledge—understanding how to
change policy or organize your community—and civic behavior. Gone
would the spontaneous acts of countless Good Samaritans. Gone would
be social capital. Gone would be the vision that places schools in service
of the common good—our nation's most important contribution to the
worldwide discussion of education. In short, gone would be the American
tradition of democratic self-government. What I mean to say, then, is that

the public part of education is an enormously important thing and something we overlook at our peril.

At this point, I need to hazard my own definition of the word "public." I will do it by referring to something less complex and less dignified than schools—bathrooms. Think about "public" restrooms. They are sponsored by institutions, like stores. They are accessible to the public. They are used for private ends. Let us assume that these things—sponsorship, accessibility, and ends—are the components of something that is public and that these components can be used to think about education as well as about restrooms.

In the United States today, much of our discussion about the public part of education relates to sponsorship: Are charter schools public? Should public funds be spent for vouchers to attend private schools? What role should the legislature play in setting curricula? It also attends to accessibility: How should school boundaries be drawn? Is it okay to limit who attends a school? Give up control over who attends? On what grounds? Is a class of thirty-five students too big? Do students from poor neighborhoods and rich neighborhoods get equal educations? When we talk about ends, we often talk about private things—the ability of individual students to pass tests or graduate or get good jobs. But it is the public ends that are key to improving both education and the quality of public life, or at least so believe the educators who have done the most to improve the civic component of public education.

The Public Ends of American Education— Two Traditions

Schools in America have taken two pathways (two means) to get to the end of a better public life. The first, and most common, has been to teach about civics as part of the curriculum. This was the pathway that Benjamin Rush had in mind in another essay, "Plan of a Federal University," which he penned in 1788. In it, Rush argued that the republic would fail "unless the people are prepared for our new form of government by an education adapted to the new and peculiar situation of our country." To preserve the nation, Rush proposed the creation of a federal university that would train all bureaucrats serving in national government. He wrote, "In this university, let those branches of literature only be taught, which are calculated to prepare our youth for civic and public life. These branches should be taught by means of *lectures,* and the following arts and sciences should be the subjects of them."[13] He then outlined a curriculum including government, history, agriculture, manufacturing, business, mathematics, natural philosophy, chemistry, natural history, philology, German, French, and "athletic and manly exercises."[14] (Elsewhere he added religion and vocal music to the list.[15])

Rush's vision of a lecture-based civic curriculum today seems both odd (how might chemistry support civic life?) and luxurious, given the ways in which civics has shrunk into a corner of the curriculum over the past hundred years and the courses that Rush saw as serving public ends now do not. Nonetheless, nearly every adult has taken a civics or American institutions class in school or college, often taught, as Rush envisioned, through lectures. Evidence suggests that these courses have a modest positive impact on students' civic knowledge and civic behavior.[16] It also appears that such courses are becoming less common in the schools (though some of their work is picked up in history courses) and positively rare in higher education, where they have been eclipsed by courses that introduce political science as an academic discipline, not civics as a public obligation. The other institutions in our systems of education have made some effort toward civic knowledge, but it is certainly not the main purpose of, say, businesses, churches, or most nonprofit organizations.

The second tradition, which I will call civically engaged education, is nearly as old as Rush's vision of civic education. It has never been as common, though, and its home in the system of schools has never been sure. On the other hand, it has consistently transformed schools, improved communities, and trained students for active citizenship while simultaneously deepening their understanding of other disciplines—all achievements beyond the scope of most courses in civics.

Educating for the Public Good: Four Stories

We can pick up the story of the tradition of civically engaged schools in the 1830s, at the moment when the movement for free, compulsory, public education emerged in New England and its cultural region. That movement was not just an effort to increase literacy or regularize education. It was wrapped intimately with other reform movements, including the movement to abolish slavery and the religious revival that swallowed up great sections of the Midwest and New England in the 1820s and 1830s.

Today when we think of the public school movement, we usually think of Horace Mann and the schools of Massachusetts. But while Mann was a great organizer, teacher, and politician, his works were preceded and surpassed by the school makers of Ohio. This group, centered on

Cincinnati, created an education system in the state because they saw it as the necessary foundation for freedom. The people in this circle were also a who's who of abolitionists in America. Arthur Tappan, a wealthy New York textile merchant, provided money for education in Ohio. Tappan and Charles Grandison Finney, the evangelist credited with starting the religious revival, also founded Oberlin College, one of the first colleges in America to educate women and blacks alongside white men. Tappan convinced Lyman Beecher to move to Cincinnati to found Lane Theological Seminary and later to teach at Oberlin. Three of Beecher's children would have a profound influence on America—Henry Ward Beecher, through his preaching; Harriet Beecher Stowe, through her book *Uncle Tom's Cabin*; and, less famously, Catharine Beecher, through her effort to train teachers and her work, with William Holmes McGuffey, to create materials that would support civically engaged education.

Many Americans know of McGuffey through the *McGuffey Readers,* the textbooks that did more to establish American schooling than any other work. But McGuffey was more than the compiler of the *Readers.* McGuffey was also an educator, a college president, and one who believed that the measure of education was in the ability of students to create a good society through acts of service to each other and in their ability to publicly and clearly declaim their views. The *Readers* are filled with stories meant to teach reading, public speaking, and the nature of good relationships in community. Their contents are all the more remarkable when one considers the context in which they were written. The *Readers* make no distinction on the basis of race, and their users among the abolitionist community in Ohio certainly understood them as textbooks of freedom. But Cincinnati, McGuffey's home in Ohio, stood on the border between freedom and slavery. It was home to riots, beatings, and more anger than we can imagine. In the midst of this chaos, McGuffey's readers sold widely both North and South, something that no doubt pleased McGuffey, who saw education as the pathway to freedom.

One can long for McGuffey's vision even now—that people in his adopted hometown would simultaneously be able to serve each other generously and argue with each other clearly. The writer Marilynne Robinson, from whose essay much of this story comes, sums up the aspirations of McGuffey, his *Readers,* and the public schools of Ohio in these words: "What did they [McGuffey and his contemporaries] hope for? The universalization of literacy and of modest prosperity . . . and the normalization of democratic attitudes and manners, which were a novelty in the world at that time. We have not ourselves achieved these things, nor do we [even] hope for them."[17]

Eventually the Republican Party emerged from the work of abolitionists and political reformers. The first president elected from the Republican Party, Abraham Lincoln, counted John Huy Addams among his Illinois friends and supporters. Addams was a Republican state senator, a mill owner, and father to Jane Addams, whom he loved and educated. After her father's death, Jane Addams traveled to Europe and, having confronted urban poverty there, returned to Chicago, where she and her friends established Hull House.

Hull House was a social settlement, a place dedicated to empowering Chicago's immigrants and urban poor to escape from poverty, and was open to all of the people in the neighborhood. Many immigrants spoke no English, most worked in the nearby meatpacking plants, and nearly all had children. Those children played a special role at Hull House. Addams and her supporters from the University of Chicago cared for the children during the day, taught them in kindergarten, established a theater, created a museum, built a playground, and sponsored dozens of classes for children and their parents, with subjects ranging from Plato to Shakespeare to acquiring American citizenship.

Hull House soon became what Addams called "a protest against a restricted view of education."[18] Perhaps the clearest evidence of what Addams meant by this came from the way that the children and women of Hull House, together with sociology students from the University of Chicago, studied and solved the problems of garbage in the streets around Hull House. In the years before automobiles, Chicago's streets were filled with animal leavings and tons of trash dropped by their human owners. The trash was a source of illness, foul odors, and danger for children. Hull House went about solving the problem first by examining the source and composition of the trash (eighteen compacted inches in some places). Then they investigated what the city was supposed to be doing. They found a corrupt city government in which friends of the local alderman were paid to collect the trash whether they did or not. Addams, the children, and the parents organized a political campaign to replace the alderman, which resulted in the election of a Hull House supporter and the collection of the trash. Addams, for her part, was appointed to the Chicago school board. But perhaps more importantly, immigrant children in the city learned both how the political system worked and how to do social science, a skill that they later applied to studies of truancy, typhoid fever, the use of cocaine, children's reading, newsboys, tuberculosis, midwifery, infant mortality, and the social value of the saloon.[19]

Chicago's reputation for government corruption continues to the present. But less well known is the ongoing commitment of college students in the city to the commonweal. In the late 1940s, black and white students at the

University of Chicago united to protest racial segregation in the city. College students from Chicago, along with hundreds of others from across the North and South, later committed themselves to the civil rights movement.

Portrayals of the movement today tend to focus on Martin Luther King Jr., major protests, the success or failure of nonviolence, or the enduring appeal of "the dream." But we must remember that the movement was also about education. Participants took classes in nonviolence before taking part in sit-ins at segregated lunch counters or marching through the streets of Montgomery or Selma. College students and schoolteachers provided local support for nearly every major action. And in summer 1964, in the midst of the violence and promise of Mississippi's Freedom Summer, hundreds of college students met with thousands of young Mississippians in Freedom Schools.

The Freedom Schools set out to provide both a civic and an academic education to Mississippi children whose educational needs were going unmet by the state. Their curricula were based on two key considerations. First, questions form the basis of learning. The course outlines from Freedom Summer did not contain the content that students were to learn but the questions that might help them learn what they needed to learn.[20] Second, students were to begin where they were. That is, since most of them lived in rural Mississippi, it was rural Mississippi that formed the core of the course of study.

Within this structure, children and their teachers (students themselves, remember) spent the summer learning. Their coursework included a citizenship curriculum as well as approaches to reading, mathematics, history, and in some instances sciences and theater. And their learning paralleled the experiences of their parents. As their parents worked to obtain the vote, the children studied what it meant to vote. On Election Day in August, the children ran a parallel convention, selecting their own delegates. The children's convention, though, was not solely about politics. It was also about the improvement of their own schools.

This last point is perhaps the most stunning result from the Freedom Schools. In the diaries and letters left by their teachers, it is clear that the students came to be owners of their own education. This is something that we hope college students will do, but this civic tradition seems to make it possible for such a thing to happen much earlier. It is certainly the case at Hawthorne Elementary in Salt Lake City, where over the past fifteen years fourth, fifth, and sixth graders of all academic levels have joined together in an organization called KOPE (Kids Organized to Protect the Environment), led by teacher Sheri Sohm.[21]

KOPE started as an activity for students identified as gifted and talented. Their first activities were basic ones—trash pickups and recycling. But one day while picking up trash in the Sugar House neighborhood of Salt Lake City, they came across a piece of open land filled with garbage and construction debris right in the middle of town. That piece of open space also had a stream running through it—one of the only sections of Parley's Creek to remain uncovered in the city.

At that point KOPE kids turned their efforts into something much larger than a class activity. The children, with their teachers, began to study the open piece of land, investigating its history, its ecosystem (the plot contained a surprisingly large assortment of native plants, something missing from much of the rest of the city), and its prospects. They found that the place, which they named Hidden Hollow, was likely to be developed, and they set out to get it preserved instead. Their work drew together a remarkable coalition of people—Sugar House residents who had some memory of the place when it was a park, local environmentalists, neighborhood activists, members of the community and city councils, and students and faculty from the University of Utah, Brigham Young University, and Westminster College, where I work.

This coalition studied Hidden Hollow in much the way that Jane Addams and the residents of Hull House studied garbage in Chicago. And they acted in much the same way as well, eventually figuring out how the political system worked, putting together a proposal and a coalition to protect the Hollow, winning the political battles, and then proudly opening the place to the public.

Hidden Hollow is today a key part of the renaissance of Sugar House. It continues to bring together that coalition of people, who are now working to invigorate Sugar House culture and develop a system of trails and open space that would link Hidden Hollow to the public spaces of the rest of the city. And it continues to educate students, from fourth grade to graduate school, in history, science, math, and politics.

Learning from Tradition:
Civic Outcomes and Moral Systems

These four stories—of the origins of public schools in Ohio, Chicago's Hull House, the Freedom Schools, and KOPE—contain both a set of outcomes that can be measured if you are interested in reasserting the public purposes of education and a set of lessons for those wishing to build moral systems of education. Here are some of the things students can learn and we can assess:

1. Education based on developing civically engaged students deepens those students' understanding of their course contents, whether mathematics, history, science, or English. Remember, in none of these instances was the purpose of civic activities solely civics. In each the purpose was to provide what we would call active learning and authentic assessment. The evidence of learning is quite clear—active, hands-on education is the most powerful way to help students gain, retain, and apply knowledge.

2. Public-minded education also leads to the development of civic knowledge, skills, and behaviors in students and the community. In each instance students did not just learn about the political system; they experienced it, developing the habits that would allow them to be active, informed citizens in their own communities. They also learned to work in what we call today "diverse settings" across the boundaries of difference. In short, they developed bonding and bridging social capital. And the organizations that were drawn into their learning developed those same skills and orientations as well. That is, attending to the public ends of education in each case created a coalition of organizations dedicated to participating in a moral system of education as well.

3. Public learning projects help all of the institutions in the system of education solve problems in a democratic fashion. Problem solving is of course a key component of active learning. The children and their teachers in these stories all faced complex, real-world problems, not hypotheticals, not simple problems with a single possible answer. And they solved them publicly, in a way that shared and developed leadership. But problem solving also helped the other parts of the system learn how to resolve difficulties as well. In a democracy these sorts of skills are necessary if systems hope to come to some sort of working agreement about what is good—that is, what is moral.

4. Civically engaged education ultimately adds to the civic infrastructure—the network of organizations, friends, and citizens who ensure that education serves both private and public ends. In each instance students not only learned but also improved their communities and their schools in obvious, powerful ways.

Learning from Tradition: Schools as Catalysts for Moral Systems of Education

If it is possible to describe the outcomes of civically engaged education, it is possible also to define a set of steps that we might follow if we wish our schools to achieve the public ends of education and reinvigorate moral systems of education. Here are a few:

1. Higher education and K–12 schools must jointly be examples of civic engagement. If our colleges and universities cannot describe and defend their contributions to the commonweal, then it is unlikely that new teachers will, and it makes it much more difficult for primary and secondary schools to do the same.
2. Schools must be examples of reciprocal relationships, for it is in their relationships with other institutions that schools are catalysts for moral systems of education. Too often schools and other educating institutions forget that their actions influence other institutions. Reciprocal relationships are based on the assumption that civic acts—teaching freedom, improving public health, preserving open space—benefit both the actors and the other organizations connected to them in the educational system. Reciprocal relationships, then, provide the structure for moral systems of education.
3. Leaders must defend the public ends of their activities—they must publicly name what they are doing as being for the public good. It is not enough for legislators to talk about test scores, or churches to focus on religious instruction, or business owners to talk about profits. And it is not enough for those same leaders to permit civically engaged education. Leaders must lead here, in the same ways that McGuffey, Addams, and others did.
4. Teachers and administrators must remember the public ends of their work and allow for others to pursue it. Teachers especially must focus on their courses and content but recall also that civic learning can come in any discipline and without seeming like an add-on to their work. And people who work in the other parts of the systems of education—shopkeepers and volunteers, church leaders and legislators—must recall that they too are teachers and that their actions instruct as much as their words.
5. Students must experience civically engaged education. Talking about civics does not teach civics, but being involved in civically engaged

education helps students learn to defend the public ends of education and to participate in rebuilding moral systems of education.

6. The final measurement of the power of civically engaged education is to be found in the community, in the broader system of organizations that make up a moral society.

A Real Education in Civics

There are many ways in which I might have been wrong in what I have written. I may have chosen inappropriate examples or drawn the wrong conclusions. I may have misunderstood the current educational landscape. But one thing is not, I believe, disputable: from the founding of the nation, schools, regardless of their sponsorship, student body, or place in the continuum—from kindergarten to graduate school—have had a public purpose. That purpose is not just to talk about the public realm or to offer a class or two in civics. It is to provide students with a combination of civic knowledge and skill.

This training is, of course, supposed to be good for the students. After all, it gives them the ability to participate more fully in public life and to negotiate their way through the challenges that face them. But helping students develop civic skills should not be seen so narrowly as another action to help an individual. It is instead an activity that, done well, requires the support of teachers and principals, parents and coaches, churches, businesses, clubs, and government. And out of that support emerges a moral system of education, one made up of more organizations than schools, one that understands itself as a system, one that has a visible and publicly beneficial morality. It is only in such a system that our most basic hopes—that all students can be educated and that such an education can be *good*—are sustained.

Notes

1. Herbert Kohl, *The Discipline of Hope: Learning from a Lifetime of Teaching* (New York: Simon & Schuster, 1998), 330.

2. Lawrence Cremin, *Popular Education and Its Discontents* (New York: Harper & Row, 1990), viii, 37.

3. Ibid., 43.

4. There is a huge literature on the decline of civic institutions. The best summary work remains Robert D. Putnam, *Bowling Alone: The Collapse and Revival*

of American Community (New York: Simon & Schuster, 2000). See especially section II, "Trends in Civic Engagement and Social Capital," and section III, "Why?"

5. See Sara Lawrence Lightfoot, *The Good High School: Portraits of Character and Culture* (New York: Basic Books, 1983), 23–26.

6. Benjamin Rush, "Thoughts Upon the Mode of Education Proper in a Republic," in Eve Kornfeld, *Creating an American Culture, 1775–1800: A Brief History with Documents* (Boston: Bedford/St. Martin's, 2001), 110.

7. See, for example, Deidre Cobb-Roberts, Sherman Dorn, and Barbara J. Shircliffe, eds., *Schools as Imagined Communities: The Creation of Identity, Meaning, and Conflict in U.S. History* (New York: Palgrave Macmillan, 2006).

8. National Assessment of Educational Progress Civics, "Percentage of Students At or Above the Civics Achievement Levels," http://nces.ed.gov/nationsreportcard/civics/findachlvls.asp.

9. Intercollegiate Studies Institute, "The Coming Crisis in Civic Literacy: Civic Literacy Report," http://www.americancivicliteracy.org.

10. See Federalist 62 and 63 in Alexander Hamilton, James Madison, and John Jay, *The Federalist Papers,* Garry Wills, ed. (New York: Bantam, 1982), and the very helpful discussion of "separated powers" in that volume's introduction by Garry Wills, xvi–xviii.

11. On the question of the possibility that schools could create an informed public, see the debate between Walter Lippmann and John Dewey that took place in the 1920s. Lippmann, arguing against the possibility that education could create a public able to govern the nation, made his point in Walter Lippmann, *The Phantom Public* (New York: Harcourt, 1925). Dewey's more optimistic response can be found in John Dewey, *The Public and Its Problems* (New York: Henry Holt, 1927).

12. The classic work on the decline in civic engagement is Putnam, *Bowling Alone.* The best thinking on the meaning of public and private in schooling is represented in a series of works emerging from the Institute for Educational Inquiry. See, for example, John I. Goodlad and Timothy J. McMannon, eds., *The Public Purpose of Education and Schooling* (San Francisco: Jossey-Bass, 1997), and Roger Soder, John I. Goodlad, and Timothy J. McMannon, eds., *Developing Democratic Character in the Young* (San Francisco: Jossey-Bass, 2001).

13. Benjamin Rush, "Plan of a Federal University," in Kornfeld, *Creating an American Culture,* 120.

14. Ibid., 122.

15. Rush, "Thoughts Upon the Mode of Education," 113.

16. Melissa K. Comber, "Civics Curriculum and Civic Skills: Recent Evidence, November 2003," http://www.civicyouth.org/PopUps/FactSheets/FS_Civics_Curriculum_Skills.pdf.

17. See Marilynne Robinson's essay, "McGuffey and the Abolitionists," in *The Death of Adam: Essays on Modern Thought* (New York: Picador, 2005), 148–49.

18. Quoted in Gary Daynes and Nick Longo, "Jane Addams and the Origins

of Service-Learning Practice in the United States," *Michigan Journal of Community Service-Learning* 11 (Fall 2004): 5.

19. Jean Bethke Elshtain, *Jane Addams and the Dream of American Democracy* (New York: Basic Books, 2002), 168–72, xix.

20. The documents making up the Freedom Summer curriculum have been collected and are available at http://www.educationanddemocracy.org.

21. Documents relating to the history and structure of KOPE are in the author's possession.

Chapter 7

Toward Democratic Schools

Jim Strickland and Dianne Suiter

Why should educators responsible for the daily operations of classrooms concern themselves with something as seemingly remote as the problems of democracy? One reason is that we are losing our students, as indicated by our staggering national dropout rates. What if we created democratic school cultures where all students belonged? What if students believed that their ideas and their work really made a difference because they *actually did* make a difference? As the authors of this chapter know firsthand, democratic school cultures can help our young people find meaning and direction in a rapidly changing world. Another reason that educators should concern themselves with the problems of democracy is that our democracy is in danger. Widening economic and social divisions in America threaten our ability to understand each other and to govern our collective lives together. Now more than ever, we need to prepare young people for the responsibilities of citizenship.

In this chapter Jim Strickland, community-based educator in Marysville, Washington, and Dianne Suiter, elementary school principal in Middletown, Ohio, tell us what they are doing to live democracy in their schools. Both work in public schools with diverse student bodies. Strickland shares his belief that youngsters are hungry for meaning and that too many are disconnected from school because schools are not meeting this need. Suiter tells us stories that reveal the multiple sites where the challenges of democracy are worked out at her school, Central Academy. Teaching democracy goes far beyond the formal curriculum: democratic values inform the way her school organizes time and space, and they govern relationships between members of the school community. Keeping democratic structures alive and well requires a great deal of behind-the-scenes work, Suiter tells us. The rewards for individuals, and ultimately for society, make living democracy at school worth the time and effort.

Jim's Story: Something Worth Doing

Meet Zach Luton

At age two Zach Luton was found wandering the busy streets of Everett, Washington. Miraculously unharmed, he was removed by the state from his drug-addicted mother and placed in the care of Terry Luton, who was already serving as the foster parent for Zach's two older siblings.

Even in Terry's stable home, Zach very quickly began exhibiting serious learning and behavioral problems. He was prescribed medication for Attention-Deficit/Hyperactivity Disorder (ADHD) at age four and declared eligible for special education services at school. Terry found the support available at the elementary level sufficient for Zach to make steady progress, but things really began falling apart when he started middle school. With a schedule that included numerous teachers, higher academic demands, and inadequate communication from the school, Zach's behavioral and academic troubles sharply escalated. He started to fail his classes and become increasingly disconnected from school.

I first met Zach when I became his special education case manager at Marysville Junior High School. I saw him often when he was removed from classes for disruptive behavior or refusal to work. At the end of his eighth-grade year, it was determined that Zach would be a good candidate for a new program I developed called Something Worth Doing (SWD). SWD is a project-based, experiential learning program that uses community engagement to facilitate students' progress toward learning goals.

Observing Zach as he began SWD was something akin to watching a racehorse being released from the starting gate. When given responsibility for making class decisions and freedom to follow his most passionate interests, Zach immediately began exhibiting leadership and self-direction. It was a challenge for me to keep up with him.

Zach's gifts were most apparent in our community service-learning projects. His natural sociability, a liability in many of his traditional classes, was an invaluable asset in working with others in our community. Zach became a shining star in his work at our local senior center and in a preschool class for children with developmental disabilities at a nearby elementary school. In these settings Zach was described by others as responsible, competent, and enthusiastic.

Outside SWD Zach excelled in technology education, where he demonstrated advanced skills in woodworking, welding, and computer-assisted drafting. At the end of the year Zach was singled out for a schoolwide award for achievement in Tech Ed, making him the envy of many of his peers outside special education.

After completing the ninth grade, Zach left SWD and started tenth grade at Marysville-Pilchuck High School, a large, comprehensive high school of about 2,600 students. While Zach was initially excited about being involved in the school ROTC program, performance in his other classes quickly began deteriorating. As of this writing, six weeks into the new school year, Zach is regularly skipping classes and producing failing grades. Terry, who is now Zach's adoptive mother, is in the process of filing an At-Risk Youth petition with the courts to help her manage Zach's behavior and provide legal leverage to keep him in school. All available evidence indicates that this is going to be a challenging year for Zach and the Luton family.

In reflecting on Zach's story, one has to wonder about the stark differences between his ninth and tenth grade years so far. Are Zach's current troubles a result of his being lazy, unmotivated, or incompetent—labels often applied to kids in his situation? Or could it be that SWD somehow tapped into Zach's natural motivations, his yearning for real responsibility and opportunities for self-direction, and his hunger for work that meant something to him and made sense in his world?

For better or worse, there are many Zachs out there in our communities. Some of them have intense needs, but they also have amazing strengths, dreams, and unique gifts to give. They need and deserve lives worth living and work worth doing, and the quality of their lives will have a direct impact on the quality of our own lives, our communities, and our democracy. The question we must ask is: Do we have the vision and the courage to meet them where they are?[1]

What Do We Want for Our Children and Youths?

In the workshops he conducts for parents, educator Alfie Kohn likes to start off by asking, "What are your *long-term* objectives for your children? What word or phrase comes to mind to describe how you would like them to turn out, what you want them to be like once they are grown?"[2] In response, parents typically say that they want their children to be happy, balanced, independent, fulfilled, productive, self-reliant, responsible, functioning, kind, thoughtful, loving, inquisitive, and confident.

When parents and educators engage in the process of defining goals, we are challenged to question whether what we are doing—how we are raising and educating our children—is likely to produce the results we say we really want. In other words, are the *means* we are presently using actually going to lead to the *ends* we say we are aiming for? It is in the discrepancies we find among our current practices, our professed values, and the long-term goals we have for our children that we find the work that truly needs to be done.

I became a teacher not because I wanted to teach, but because I was, and continue to be, consumed with the following question: What is the best way to help a young person develop into a human being who is passionate, life-loving, competent, creative, empathetic, compassionate, engaged, thoughtful, generous, intelligent, aware, and self-directed?

These personal characteristics and social capacities are foundational to the development of both healthy *individuals* and responsible *citizens* capable of effective participation in our democratic society. My work is based on long-held beliefs that people must always come before institutions and that it takes good, whole, healthy people to create a good, whole, healthy society. Because institutions shape behavior, we must take care to ensure that our schools are serving human beings, and not vice versa.

Something Worth Doing

When I started teaching children with special needs seventeen years ago, it did not take me long to realize that schools not only were failing in this primary task of nurturing holistic human development but were often its largest obstacles. As the saying goes, "If you are not part of the solution, you are part of the problem." For too many of my students, school was, at best, *not* part of the solution to the problem that was *their lives*—Who am I? How do I live my life? What work out there is really worth doing?

Like most of my students (and most human beings), I have a hard time putting much effort into things I do not find personally meaningful. For me as a teacher, this burning *drive for meaning* meant that I had to be able to clearly see that what I was doing was actually helping my students grow as thinking, caring, engaged human beings. For students with disabilities, school seemed unable or unwilling to meet even the bare minimum required by the physician's familiar maxim to "first, do no harm." Well, doing no harm is a great place to start, but I do not know any teacher who wants to stop there.

As I grappled with the purpose of my work in public schools, I was struck by philosopher John Dewey's understanding of education as *growth*. In *Popular Education and Its Discontents* historian Lawrence Cremin wrote:

> John Dewey liked to define the aim of education as growth, and when he was asked growth toward what, he liked to reply, growth leading to more growth. This was his way of saying that education is subordinate to no end beyond itself, that the aim of education is ... ultimately to make human beings who will live life to the fullest, who will continually add to the quality and meaning of their experience and to their ability to direct that experience, and who will participate actively with their fellow human beings in the building of a good society.[3]

So what kinds of schools and classrooms are required to nurture this continuous growth toward quality, meaningful lives lived to their fullest? And how do we make sure that such schools and classrooms are the norm rather than the exception?

Let us start with human nature. Since the drive for meaning is such a foundational part of who we are as human beings, this seems a reasonable place to start in our efforts to create schools that are humane places to live and grow. But aren't there as many different ways of finding meaning in what we do as there are people out there searching? And is *meaning* something that can be given, or does it have to arise from within as we engage in a continuous give-and-take with others and the world around us?

While many young people seem capable of postponing present meaning for the sake of some hypothetical payoff in the future, students who for various reasons are considered "at risk" have a much harder time doing this. If a young person is unable to make that leap across the chasm of disconnect between what schools say is important and what is truly meaningful in their own minds and lives, what are we to do? Is it helpful to continue berating students because they do not respond to the light we are so "helpfully" shining in their eyes?

An old adage tells us that you cannot get where you are going unless you start where you are. Herein lies the shift in thinking that must take place if our classrooms and schools are to become the truly engaging, growth-producing places they need to be for all of our students.

The fact is that young people are quite capable of determining what is meaningful to them, but they tend to check their interests and passions at the door when entering our classrooms. Why? Because we indirectly, or even directly, ask them to. Hey, we are the teachers, right? We are older and wiser, and we know what is important, right? Isn't it our job to get students to do the important things we tell them to do so they will learn the important things we want them to learn?

Well, yes and no. The problem with this mentality is that our interests and passions are direct expressions of who we are as human beings. When we ask students to leave these outside our classrooms, we are asking that they leave *themselves* outside as well. Then we wind up with what we all too often find in our schools today—bodies without souls, motion without meaning, a depressing lack of authenticity, and destructive rebellion.

In *How Children Learn,* John Holt articulates the fundamental paradigm shift that I believe would completely revolutionize our understanding and practice of education: "We do things backwards. We think in terms of getting a skill first, and then finding useful and interesting things to do with it. The sensible way, the best way, is to start with something worth doing, and then, moved by a strong desire to do it, get whatever skills are needed."[4] Something worth doing—what could be more motivating and inherently meaningful than that? *Worthiness* implies that this something, whatever it is, is *real* work that needs to be done for *real* reasons. This is work that challenges, that engages, that connects—it is work that feeds the soul and produces healthy pride and a sustaining sense of accomplishment that comes from contributing to something greater than oneself.

And what better place than our schools to experience this powerful learning? How tragic that we quarantine our young people in isolated islands of academia, where the prescribed work is justified solely by some hypothetical future need. We are losing our young people because of the artificial gulf separating them from the world that so desperately needs them and that they so desperately need.

I started Something Worth Doing as a way to bridge this gap and create a classroom that was more akin to the hub of a larger wheel than to a disconnected island or the lonely crowd of an academic shopping mall. Something Worth Doing is the fruit of my ongoing examination of the relationship between democracy and education and my continuous exploration of ways to more effectively teach and practice democracy in our schools and classrooms. It is based on the premises that one size does *not* fit all when it comes to education, that some students need a more experiential approach to learning, and that people learn best when engaged in real work that is related to their personal interests and goals. Also, the kind of thoughtful engagement that democracy requires is not best learned from a textbook, but from active immersion in an environment of democratic values and practices.

The staff at Marysville Junior High School started in spring 2005 by acknowledging that the learning support services we were providing were not working for a significant number of our special education students. In spite of our efforts to help them build basic skills and successfully access the general education curriculum, many were becoming increasingly disconnected from our academic program. As attendance problems also became more widespread, the writing was on the wall—we were losing these students. They were not going to make it through school unless we provided a more radical alternative.

Our Learning Support Department, responsible for making our school programs work for students with special needs, got together and chose ten upcoming ninth-grade students with disabilities who were clearly not making it in school. Their academic skill levels ranged from a couple who were virtually nonreaders to some who were functioning at or just below grade level. Their disabilities included specific learning disabilities, health impairments, behavior disorders, and mild mental retardation. The one thing these students had in common was that they had mentally "checked out" of school.

These students and their families were invited to participate in Something Worth Doing. SWD spans a three-period block making up the second half of the six-period school day. A major goal is to remove artificial barriers that separate learning from the rest of life to promote a natural integration of learning and living. SWD is about doing whatever it takes to help youngsters grow into good human beings, engaged citizens, and lifelong learners.

In SWD students use our surrounding community as their primary classroom and object of study. Project- and inquiry-based learning activities are collaboratively planned to both reflect student interest and meet personal and state academic objectives. SWD allows students to meet and learn directly from the individuals, organizations, and institutions that make our community work and to develop a sophisticated awareness of the interdependent components of a healthy, functioning community. Since one best learns democracy by living democracy, a primary emphasis of SWD is to incorporate the practice of democracy as a way of living and working together characterized by, among other things, compassion, mutual respect, open and ongoing dialogue, shared power, cooperative decision making, and responsible self-direction.

We hope that, through our activities, students will develop a powerful sense of their place in the larger community and a greater understanding of how their active participation makes a difference. We also want students to learn how to work toward their own personal goals while simultaneously acknowledging and respecting the needs and interests of others. Ultimately, we want students to leave the SWD program with the knowledge, experience, and community connections needed to successfully take on the challenges of adulthood in our democratic society.

Our program themes are *action* (finding things worth doing and doing them), *connection* (building meaningful relationships with other people and organizations in our larger community), and *self-direction* (taking control of our learning and our lives). Our motto is "Find something worth doing and *do it!*"

Over the course of our first year, individual projects chosen by students have ranged from raising and breeding various animals (hamsters, bearded dragons, parakeets, and fish) to exploring the history of all the buildings ever to exist on our particular school site and then presenting a PowerPoint exhibition at our local historical society. One of our nonreaders followed his interest in basketball to research the origin and evolution of the slam dunk, while another created a slide show examining graffiti as the artistic voice of the powerless in our society.

Collaboratively planned group projects have included volunteering at our local senior center, working with preschoolers with disabilities at a local elementary school, and developing and operating an Italian soda business that raised money for our program. Community-based learning excursions have included meeting and interviewing our mayor, visiting our local wastewater treatment facility, and touring a historical fort that once guarded the entrance to Puget Sound. Students have also been able to plan and participate in mini-apprenticeships at local businesses, such as a beauty salon, an espresso stand, and an automotive shop. As for assessment, students exhibit their work before real audiences and in real work settings, where they are evaluated by the standards appropriate to that particular environment.

The beauty of the way SWD works is that students play an active role in planning the curriculum, thereby ensuring their commitment to the success of the work. As for academic skills, these are determined and developed as they are needed to successfully complete our various projects. Does it work? In *The Big Picture* revolutionary educator Dennis Littky writes:

> I have enough faith in the interconnectedness of what we call "subjects" to trust that a student could study only one thing (say, music, if that's what he's passionate about) for all four years of high school and still get enough of the other skills and knowledge he needs to be successful. If you go for depth over breadth, you are allowing the learning to really take hold inside that kid. If it's something that's real to students, and if it matters to them, and if we respect their desire and ability to learn it, they will learn it. And they will keep learning it beyond our influence, because learning will have become a way of life for them.[5]

Programs like Something Worth Doing may not be for everyone, but it is working for these students in this place at this time in ways that our traditional program was not.

Something Worth Doing is a specific program developed in a specific context to meet specific needs. The practical characteristics that make it unique also make it impossible to transplant it to a different setting. As is the case with all successful programs, they must be organically grown by the blood, sweat, and tears of those who need them, in the particular plot of soil where they are needed. Our efforts have not been random, however. They have been guided by a core set of democratic values that can be used by any community to grow programs that work for them. Let me offer a few guiding questions that can be used to evaluate specific programs:

1. Does it build meaningful connections to the larger community?
2. Is it in line with what we know about human nature and basic human needs?
3. Does it produce the desire and capacity for further learning?
4. Does it produce the desire and capacity for creativity, critical thinking, responsible self-direction, and genuine human empathy?
5. Does it balance self-development with opportunities to connect, identify with, and relate to the rest of humanity?
6. Is it unambiguously worth doing?

Whatever questions or criteria we use to guide us, they must encompass shared values that are discovered and refined in the forge of ongoing democratic dialogue. It is out of these powerful, unifying values that our actions arise, and it is by these values that they are continuously judged.

This never-ending process is at the heart of all human endeavors that can rightly be called *moral,* and it is this process that will produce the value-driven, purposeful classrooms and schools that alone can justify our efforts in public education. That is something worth doing.

Dianne's Story: Living Democracy at Central Academy

Democracy Is for Everyone

Sitting in the small circle in our music room, Marcia, one of the sixteen parents attending Principal's Coffee, suddenly leaned forward in her seat, listening intently. At Central Academy we hold Principal's Coffees frequently. These meetings run about an hour and a half and give small groups of parents time to have a cup of coffee with me and talk about progressive education generally and Central Academy specifically. We talk about our philosophy and why we do things the way we do, and then the parents break into small groups and observe students and teachers in our classrooms. When they have finished, they come back to our coffee circle and ask questions or make comments on things that they saw.

We were discussing the importance of everyone finding their sense of voice and power in a democracy—and how that is blended into our day-to-day operations at Central. Marcia and her husband, both working professionals in our town, have a daughter with Down syndrome who has attended our school since kindergarten. It was clear that this part of our philosophy and structure was important to her for her daughter. They also have two sons, both of whom perform well above grade level. Her sons at that point attended a private school in town. As I noticed her change in intensity, I also had a hunch that she was seeing the importance of this experience not only for her daughter but also for her sons.

Central Academy's underlying philosophy and belief in working together as a part of a democracy seems to strike a deep chord in many parents. A large number of these parents are like Marcia and her husband, people who take active roles in our small town. These parents are active in their churches and other community groups. They serve on the Board of Education, sell hot dogs on Friday evenings at the football stadium to earn money for the band, work in the community theater organization, and serve on various church and civic committees.

I suspect that these parents want their children to understand and experience this kind of active involvement in community life at an early age, realizing the sense of fulfillment their own activities have given them. They also know that it will take citizens willing to give hours of their time to keep our small town alive as a community (resisting the encroaching spread of bedroom suburbia).

There is another phenomenon that happens when I talk with parents about our school. As we sit and talk about the importance of our students finding their sense of voice and power as community members, I frequently see our African American and biracial families connecting strongly with this concept. As I explain why we have children making daily decisions about their learning, or encourage students to initiate various activities in or outside school to help others, African American mothers and fathers nod their heads in agreement. For them and their children, even more is at stake.

Those who have experienced injustice or marginalization can see immediately the need for their children to find their voice and power. To have the opportunity to send their children to a school that lives this challenge daily, and is constantly open to deepening our understanding of others, is a gift.

There is an important difference between these two groups of parents. The realities of our society are such that some children are more at risk than others. It is likely that Marcia and Will's sons will be successful and active citizens. For their daughter, however, the future is less secure. The same could be said of our African American and biracial students and for our students, both black and white, living below the poverty line. The opportunity to lead others, to have their ideas heard, and to make a difference in the community is far less likely for some of these students. With every lost opportunity comes an increased risk that some will never even try to become full members of society or will simply give up at some point along the way.

For our families who have been marginalized, our school provides an opportunity to give their children a vitally important experience. And for all of our families, the fact that they are part of a very diverse school community gives them the opportunity to learn with and from each other, both as adults and children, on a daily basis—to grow in appreciation for each person's innate abilities and contributions to the whole. We offer an experience to become committed to the democratic ideal that brings all kinds of people together—living and working in community.

After the Principal's Coffee Marcia stayed to ask me more questions about the democratic structures and activities at Central. By the end of the year, she had enrolled her sons in our school for the following year.

With educational debates currently bogged down across our country in the minutia of standardized test results and how to "lower the achievement gap," these conversations about broader and deeper learning for all of our students are critical not only to the survival of schools like ours but also to the survival of a thriving and productive democracy in our country. It is important not only that we continue *doing* this daily for our students but that we also help to increase our families' understanding of the importance of it. How do we go about this? In many ways. It is woven into how we do education day by day, minute by minute.

Working Together

When visitors come to our school, they inevitably remark on the way we use space. Not only are students working both individually and in small groups in classrooms, but our common areas are also constantly in use, with small groups of students working and learning together. In fact, one of the students' favorite places in the school is actually underneath the landing of a stairway. Because this stairway has massive windows, sunlight floods the spot.

Our classes are multiaged, with students of approximately two years' difference working together. A student stays with the same teacher for two years, once as a "younger" or "rookie" and again as an "older" or "pro." We also take great pains each spring, as our staff works collaboratively to place our olders in classes for the next year, to make certain that classes are heterogeneously grouped in terms of gender, race, socioeconomic status, and ability level.

While each of our students has individual goals developed quarterly with his or her teacher, all but our youngest students work from learning contracts, which indicate work needing to be accomplished in specific periods of time. Some of the work on these contracts is defined by the teacher; other work leaves more room for the student to bring individual interests and choices to the assignments. The selection of work and the order in which it is to be accomplished is left to the students. In some cases, students also determine whether they would like to work alone or with others.

In addition to being heterogeneously mixed, our classrooms are also fully inclusive. When one of our teachers with expertise in assisting students with special needs comes into a classroom, he or she frequently works with students at all ability levels. (We have no special pullout classes for students needing specific assistance.) Anyone needing help is welcome to seek teacher assistance or join a small-group lesson that a teacher is giving.

This incredible mix of collaborative work and help spills over outside individual classrooms, bringing students from different levels together. Any student who wishes to tutor or help a younger student is invited to do so. Our common areas are crowded with olders working with youngers on reading, math, special research projects or even tutoring in a specific skill, such as the violin.

Of course, in all collaborative work there always comes that moment when the parties working on the project disagree. This becomes a teachable moment, as students struggle to come to an agreement. Last year, for example, a group of three girls in a late primary class had to overcome conflicts as they worked together on a presentation about the life of Rosa Parks. The incident spoke powerfully to me because two of the three girls were white and one was African American, reflecting almost exactly the racial mix of our school.

The excitement and rigor of their work on the project was equaled only by the intensity of the arguments that unfolded as different opinions arose about how various parts of the presentation should look. Group projects can be messy business, as we learn how to work together. We had several impromptu problem-solving sessions in my office. Typically, two of the girls agreed on an idea and were angry with the third girl for disagreeing with the idea. What the students had to discover through dialogue was a way to represent all ideas equally or, failing that, to find a new approach to the conflict that would be satisfying to all. This is tough work for students of this age—and frequently tough work for us as adults. I found myself thinking about the challenges of these three girls in completing their group project as I watched the advertisements for various political campaigns this fall. To their credit, the girls kept their arguments focused on the concepts, never letting the disagreements sink into personal character attacks on each other. I cannot say the same for the political advertisements.

The girls learned about Rosa Parks and her remarkable life, and, just as importantly, they learned about how we live and work together, making communal decisions that not only feel good for us individually but are also best for the group as a whole. My primary role was as questioner, not peacemaker. I refused to make any of the decisions, instead asking what I hoped were questions that might deepen their thinking. The entire project taxed the patience of all of us at times, but it certainly increased my understanding of group dynamics. When the project was complete and had been successfully presented at our all-school celebration, we met again to reflect on what we had each learned.

I was amazed at the depth of understanding and the insights that each of them had developed about themselves and each other. Each girl was able to tell me the specific contributions that the others had made to the project. What was more, they were also able to tell me the specific skills and abilities that had helped to make the project a success. Finally, when I asked them what they had learned from the project, one of the girls summed it up this way: "We need to stop fighting so much and get down to figuring out how to do it better."

Will the girls be able to continue this newly found understanding of group dynamics? Will all of their work in the future be blessed with a deep understanding of the importance of compromise and consensus? Probably not. They are, after all, people, and young ones at that. But will the deeper understanding of others gained though this experience be reflected in their work on future projects? I am quite certain of that. My hope is that they will bring their hard-won understanding to bear on issues they confront later in life. What difference would it make if experiences like this became commonplace for children? For starters, we might see far better political advertisements!

Balancing Freedom and Responsibility

Democratic educators constantly walk many very narrow lines. Teaching and leading in a progressive, democratic school is much like being the proverbial fiddler on the roof, struggling to keep our balance each day with various pulls coming from many different directions.

One of the most difficult struggles, particularly for those teachers new to our school, involves to what degree the teacher is "in charge" of his or her classroom. At the heart of learning, we want students to be responsible for their work and their classroom. They need the freedom to make decisions about their activities, their time, and their interactions with others.

Rather than decreasing the responsibilities for the adults in our school, this increased freedom for students actually increases our work and responsibilities. Students come to recognize that the inverse of freedom of choice and thought is actually responsibility. But this awakening comes at various times and paces for individual students. And once a student has recognized this concept, there is no guarantee that he or she will automatically reflect that understanding in all of his or her future actions and decisions—anymore than we, as adults, can guarantee that in our own behavior!

We address this conundrum with students in many ways. At the beginning of each year the adults in our community all agree to accept the African concept that it takes a village to raise a child. We agree that we will be a village. With three hundred students, the school is small enough for all of us to know each other. If any adult sees a student making bad choices, he or she takes a minute to talk to the child right then. Of course, our older students are doubly accountable by virtue of having teachers who worked with them in two-year spans previously, making the relationships between our oldest students and past teachers remarkably strong. This agreement calls for an important professional recognition on our part. If another adult corrects one of your students, it is in no way a reflection upon you as a teacher. It is all of us working together to surround our students with love and support—and high expectations.

Another way that we address this balancing is through meetings in each classroom. Each day, students gather with the adults in the room. We sit in a circle so that everyone is on the same level and we can all look at each other eye to eye. Some classes gather on the floor, others circle their chairs. The rules of the circle are simple. You must actively listen (no sidebar conversations allowed). We go around the circle one at a time to speak, and no one may jump turns. When your turn arrives, you may choose to speak or pass. All are expected to show respect to others (no eye-rolling or other nonverbal cues of disrespect or disagreement). The rules apply to all—even the adults!

The structure of our daily circle serves us well when we have to take on tough social issues. Bullying has become a serious problem nationally in our schools today, and we at Central are not beyond the influence of this destructive societal problem. After addressing it individually in small groups and in each classroom for most of the year, we decided the time had come to take more serious measures. We called a town hall meeting. Every student attended this meeting, sitting in a large circle around our gym floor. Likewise, every adult in our school, including the custodian and the school secretary, came and sat in the circle. With a traveling microphone, I served as a facilitator, asking questions and then taking the microphone to various students who wanted to speak. It is important to note that this was not a time for adults to speak to or lecture students about their behavior. It was a time for us to gather as a community to address a problem together, and for students to see the importance of their own voices and actions.

Several weeks after the town hall meeting, we found that a student named Tyrone had continued to use a racial slur on the bus when refer- ring to another student, Amy. Since Tyrone had been involved in several other name-calling and bullying incidents over the course of the year, and several other intervention strategies had not worked, I met with Amy's class during circle time and asked them how they would like to handle it. They decided to invite the offender to come to their room for a meeting.

Tyrone came reluctantly. I assured him that I would go with him to the meeting so that he would have an advocate. We sat in our circle, and Kim, the teacher, asked the children to share how they felt knowing that Amy had been called this name. Some students chose to pass when their turn came, but no one phrased anything in hurtful terms. Tyrone looked down at the floor throughout this part of the meeting, and my heart went out to him several times. It cannot be easy hearing that your peers feel sad, angry, or frustrated by your actions. But more importantly, he was hearing from his peers that his actions were not acceptable to them. When the circle was completed, Kim and I exchanged looks. The students had done an incredible job of sharing their feelings without accusing or belittling Tyrone.

Kim then asked that they go around the circle again. This time, she asked that they share how they would feel if they saw anyone saying something hurtful to Tyrone. Interestingly, not only did the students once again do a remarkable job in sharing their feelings, but every student also chose to share this time around. Every one of them expressed that they would be upset in various ways if someone called him names. Perhaps even more telling, this time Tyrone looked at every student as each spoke. He was hearing many voices earnestly coming to his defense should he ever be the victim.

When that question was addressed, we then turned to possible solutions for the problem. After a round of suggested options, the students decided that Tyrone should come to their classroom for a day so they could all get to know each other better. Further, during that day, he and Amy should be special friends, doing much of their work and play together so they could better understand and know each other. Student solutions can be remarkable in their simplicity and wisdom.

Developing Routines That Help Advance Democratic Learning

As educator George Wood has often pointed out, in traditional schools we teach reading by having children read. We teach math by having them do math. But we teach about democracy by having them read about it. We at Central Academy view the task of teaching democracy differently. We ask how we would structure our day to reflect the living of democracy, thereby giving our students a chance to experience and learn it from within, as a part of the way we work together. This kind of intrinsic, gut-level understanding of how to be a member of a community then becomes a habit—in both mind and heart.

Many of the structures already described lend themselves to this kind of thinking. Our circles, problem-solving strategies, and student choice and responsibility in work all communicate democratic principles. Structuring our classrooms so that all materials are out and available for student use, for example, decreases student dependency on adults.

We talk a lot about the importance of students (and adults!) finding their voices and power as members of a democracy. Our voice is that intrinsic barometer that causes us to speak up when we think something is or is not taking place for the good of the community as a whole or an individual within it. Our power is defined by those times when we are moved beyond talking into action. And because we talk about this not only among ourselves but also with our students, they too are beginning to see the importance of it.

During one early primary class discussion about how students wanted to be treated socially, Sam, a highly verbal younger in the class, did an excellent job of waiting for his turn to talk. When his turn finally arrived (which for six-year-olds can seem an interminable wait), he earnestly spoke out, "I need for my voice to be heard!" We all have this need—no matter our age.

I am constantly reminded of the importance of thoughtfully approaching school structures in order to support the mission of our school. If structures are implemented or repeated thoughtlessly, we risk the chance that the very enacting of the structure will actually work against our desired outcomes. Conversely, thoughtfully structuring situations throughout the day and year can lead to layered support for student goals.

Jalen's story illustrates the point. At one of our assemblies our early primary students were invited to share research reports they had written about people who played an important part in the civil rights movement. Jalen, who is a truly precocious artist but struggles with reading and writing, worked feverishly on a report. After a couple of days, his teacher found that his report was two pages copied word for word from a book. She sat down with him to explain what plagiarism is and why we cannot do it. She suggested that he still had time to begin again, using his own words. But at this point Jalen shut down and stated that he no longer wanted to give the presentation at the assembly.

Our structure of students staying with their teachers for more than one year helps to ensure that teachers really know their students well. In this case Jalen had been with his teacher for three years. She knew very well his sense of perfectionism. She also knew the role that perfectionism can play in inhibiting risk taking and how that had sometimes hindered Jalen's development in reading and writing. She also knew how to read his nonverbal cues and demeanor. And she knew from all of these that Jalen was hurting, very much wanting to give the report, but afraid to take the risk of writing and delivering an imperfect report.

She talked with him about this several times, and he remained adamant. Then she came to me to see if I would offer to help him. She thought that might motivate him to begin the work again. I asked Jalen that same day if I could scribe his report for him, explaining that I very much wanted him to be able to present at our assembly. To no avail. His teacher and I knew that time was running out. There were only two more school days left before the assembly.

Finally, on the last day before the assembly, Jalen came to me asking if I could help him with the report. I followed him to his room, where we sat together and worked. I told him to just tell me what he knew about Martin Luther King Jr. As he talked, I wrote. Soon his face became animated as he spurted information that I had never known. Every now and then, if I was unsure of the accuracy or if he faltered on a specific date or place, he would tell me to wait a minute, dash across the classroom to root through stacks of books until he found just the right one, then come back to me triumphantly with the book.

After an amazing hour in which he found information and recalled details with no help at all, we were finished. He had two and a half pages, which I had printed on his lined paper to help him with reading it later. We high-fived and hugged, and I moved the discussion into his need to practice reading the report now. He agreed and said that he could practice over the weekend with his mother and sister.

Jalen completed the project on time and read it perfectly at the school assembly the following week. After the assembly, his older sister and his mother confided to his teacher that he had nearly driven them crazy over the weekend asking them to listen to him practice reading the report until he had it perfect. Our classroom structures helped Jalen achieve his goals and grow not only in reading and writing skills but also in self-confidence. The very success of this story also raises some serious questions about larger structures that push against us every day.

There are several realities for Jalen. Despite many targeted interventions with specialists and his regular classroom teacher, he still reads well below grade level, particularly as it will be measured next year on the timed, standardized state tests. We will increase support for him in this area, and we are quite confident that he will continue to make true progress. And while we are all hoping that he will suddenly put the reading and writing pieces together next year, the reality is that even if he makes a year's worth of progress or more, there is a strong possibility that he will not be able to score as proficient on those timed tests.

When we speak of walking a narrow line at our school, this is perhaps the most concerning of any of those balancing feats. This artificial means of determining what any child can do academically seems at rigid odds with our daily process of collaborative work and individual achievement. I cannot help but wonder how the entire generation of children who have been raised with these tests will view themselves and their own abilities in the future. Will Jalen's hard-won self-confidence from his daily victories remain if he finds he has not "passed" the reading and writing tests?

In our state we begin to label children at the third-grade level as advanced, accelerated, or proficient based on these tests. Those falling below the proficient level are labeled as basic or limited. Whether we like it or not, and no matter how much we downplay it at school, students, particularly those who are on the losing side of these tests, know which category they fall into. I wonder what the ramifications will be for individual children. I wonder what the ramifications will be for us nationally. And I wonder how all of this will affect Jalen's prospects for living a happy, successful life.

Deepening Adult Understanding of Democracy

If we are to be a truly democratic school, then every aspect of our operations must reflect this value. We must "walk the talk"—not just the students but the adults too. Our structures at Central must encourage adults to live democratically with one another.

One of the clearest barometers of this democratic process lies in our governance procedures. Rather than utilizing traditional hierarchical styles of operation, we work together collaboratively, utilizing what is called shared leadership. This structure removes the top-down procedures and places all of us into a web of leadership. As the principal I am located more at the center of our work, rather than at the top. Teachers are complete professionals who contribute to the larger professional conversation of the school, beyond their own individual classrooms. Rather than needing to move through rungs of a hierarchy, which can greatly hinder the production of new ideas, this democratic, shared leadership gives each one of us the ability to create new practices as needed to accomplish our goals.

Working together in this way takes more time. Many times at district principal meetings, we are asked to decide what or how our school will handle a specific task. I am always the odd-person-out: I have to say that I will get back to them after the staff discusses it and decides. It also calls for a good bit of risk taking on the part of the principal, since no matter how decisions are made, at the end of the day, the principal is held totally accountable.

What this process clearly does, though, is to empower every adult to bring ideas forward, to become an active and contributing part of the community. I have also found over the years that several people sitting down together to problem solve can inevitably come up with better ideas than any one person. Perhaps most importantly, we take the time and energy to do what we ask our students to do. No one can simply sit back, wait for a decision, and then complain. Everyone has the opportunity, and the responsibility, to speak up and help the community.

An interesting consequence of all of this work is that our adults, just like our students, develop a very strong sense of voice and power. They readily question, offer ideas, and sometimes take action if they feel it is needed. We see this as helping to produce a stronger democracy for all. But those who speak up are sometimes not appreciated. Not everyone values others' voices and power.

Several years ago, an extreme budgetary problem left our school district in the uncomfortable position of needing to pass a $13 million operating levy in order to sustain current programs. Unfortunately, our school was one of the programs that was on the brink of being eliminated if the levy did not pass. In an effort to bring the community together, the Board of Education held a series of four public forums in which community members were asked to share their reactions and ideas with the superintendent and board members.

Our parents were by far the most active in attendance at all four of these meetings. Wearing bright red scarves so they could clearly be identified, they filled each forum, representing from 60 to 80 percent of those in attendance at each. While I did not always agree with everything that every parent said, they clearly were involved with the process and were willing to express their opinions about it. Beyond that, they were committed to doing the hard work that went into campaigning in our town for the levy.

While not everyone appreciated the extent to which our parents got involved, that also is a part of this messy collaborative concept of democracy. Once someone has found his or her voice—no matter how old or young—he or she will inevitably use it. Our parents, teachers, and students are frequently known throughout the district as those who speak up. That is something that can make some people uncomfortable. We, on the other hand, see it as a sign of a healthy democratic community.

Engaging Schools

Democracy as a political system produces opportunities for engagement, but democracy as a *way of life* is defined by it. And this is not just, or even primarily, political action. It starts where we live in how we relate to our families, our neighbors, and our coworkers.

In this chapter we have provided examples of how particular people in their own unique contexts have sought to create, nurture, and sustain cultures of engagement. And true engagement is not to be confused with compliance. It is, in fact, its very opposite. Compliance is mindless, while engagement is mindful. Engagement is an investment of heart, mind, and soul in meaningful action that produces growth, connects us with others, and taps our creative potential as human beings.

Current legislation forces our schools to start from the top with an imposed, predetermined agenda. Democracy requires that we start from the bottom with each other and where we live. Our schools should not be primarily about conforming to rigid standards or even about "passing" classes. School should be about becoming part of a community—a community where everyone is valued for the gifts they bring, a community relentlessly dedicated to the continuous growth of all, a community that both expects and produces personal engagement, a community where failure is not an option.

The future of democracy is a future of engagement in such communities. Our schools play a vital role in creating this future by engaging students in the present. What does it take to engage so many wonderfully diverse students? Well, it takes whatever it takes. This is our call and our challenge.

Notes

1. Since this writing, Marysville-Pilchuck High School has reorganized into smaller learning communities to create more personalized learning environments for all their students.

2. Alfie Kohn, *Unconditional Parenting: Moving from Rewards and Punishments to Love and Reason* (New York: Atria Books, 2005), 3.

3. Lawrence Cremin, *Popular Education and Its Discontents* (New York: Harper & Row, 1990), 125.

4. John Holt, *How Children Learn,* rev. ed. (New York: Delacorte/Seymour Lawrence, 1983), 164.

5. Dennis Littky, *The Big Picture: Education Is Everyone's Business* (Alexandria, Va.: Association of Supervision and Curriculum Development, 2004), 102.

Chapter 8

A Tale of Two Districts

James R. Lowham and William Mester
as Told to Barbara A. Lippke and Eugene B. Edgar

In a democracy public schools have the moral mandate to educate all students to high levels of individual competency and to prepare the next generation of citizens for our society. This is the mandate of the Agenda for Education in a Democracy, and it was clearly articulated by the work of John Goodlad and his colleagues over the past thirty years. To accomplish these lofty outcomes, schools also need to be centers of democratic action in the communities they serve. The schools need to develop a public for the public schools, a public that believes in democracy and the role of the schools in realizing its ideals.

As the leader in a school district, the superintendent has many issues to address and many constituents to please. Superintendents oversee the development and balancing of budgets, the proposal and passage of bonds, the hiring and training of bus drivers, the selection and alignment of curricula, and the organization and training of custodians. They must attend to the everyday running of the schools and to the moral compass of the schools. They have a big job. Superintendents' core values allow them to address big ideas, such as forming democratic character and developing a public for the public schools, and guide them in the mundane but crucial everyday tasks that must be accomplished.

This chapter tells the stories of two superintendents who are working to promote democracy in their districts. Jim Lowham tells the story of how wary stakeholders in his district of Natrona County, Wyoming, intentionally created a Compact of Trust to enable democratic participation in decision making there. Next, Bill Mester shares his experience building community support for his schools in Snohomish, Washington. Both agree that, by modeling democratic principles, the school district can provide powerful experiences in democratic participation for adults working inside the district and in the broader community. They tell their stories to a district administrator of a third district, Barbara Lippke, and a teacher educator from a university, Gene Edgar.

Jim Lowham, Wyoming

GENE: Jim, tell us the theory of action you use as a superintendent, and give special attention to your notions of democratic practices and how this might address developing a more democratic public.

JIM: What does democracy in a school district look like? Is a democratic organization preferred, feasible, or even possible? Easy questions with simple answers, but not simple in terms of action. Political scientist William Hudson identifies four types of democracy: the protective democracy with the goal to protect liberty, the developmental democracy with the goal to nurture citizenship, the pluralist democracy with the goal of protecting and promoting diversity, and the participatory democracy with the goal of fostering public participation.[1] My actions as superintendent have been shaped by the ideas of the developmental and participatory models. Both are based on the belief that citizens have the ability to evaluate public issues in terms of the interests of the public, to act upon the evaluation, and to rise above pure self-interest. By participating in the democracy, both the individual and the culture are enriched.

GENE: Do you, or did you, use these words in talking about your theory of action to those you work with? Did you early on get into developing an understanding of what democracy is?

JIM: Democracy is a broad concept that needs to be unpacked. There are many ideas about democracy. For many people it means voting. That is *not* what I mean; I mean participation, being engaged in decision making and doing the decision making in a democratic manner—with full listening and working toward a broad consensus. In school districts, the relationships among administration, the school board, and the union are often adversarial. Trying to use democratic decision making is a way of deliberating and acting.

GENE: This is a challenging route to go. How did this play out in your district?

JIM: This is the story of a school district's wishing to increase the level of democracy practiced in the district—a level of democracy in which the participation of all stakeholders is valued. Of Hudson's four models of democracy, the district has been moving toward developmental and participatory democracies—developmental because of the desire to involve more individuals in decision making and participatory because the stakeholders are becoming involved in decisions that were previously restricted to elected leaders of the district.

GENE: This appears to me to be a sharp departure from the norm. How did you convince the others to get involved in the decision-making process?

JIM: Roger Soder's notion of persuasive speech helped me in this regard.[2] Educator Soder talks a lot about how people do not need to become persuaded but rather need to come to believe in some idea. People are busy and do not want to take the time to be involved in decision making. Nurturing democracy takes time and energy. The easy way is for everybody to be told what to do. Then we can argue about it or silently agree. Many times we prefer being told what to do; top-down seems easier than engaging in deliberation. The more diverse the participants are, the more diverse the interests and opinions and, therefore, the possible solutions will be. I have found that a nurtured democracy is a nurturing democracy.

I believe that humans are capable of civic virtue and that citizens should be active participants in a democracy—a democracy in the sense of self-rule by the people. This being the case, it is necessary for schools to enculturate the youths and, indeed, the entire community into this form of democracy. Hence, it is desirable to have classrooms, schools, and a school district model participatory democracy and in doing so move the entire community closer to participation in democracy.

BARBARA: Jim, would you tell us a little bit about the Natrona County School District?

JIM: The Natrona County School District is located in central Wyoming. In round numbers, the population of the county is approximately sixty thousand persons distributed over some six thousand square miles, with fifty thousand people living within a radius of approximately five miles. About twelve thousand students attend public schools in which approximately two thousand employees work. The board of education is composed of nine elected residents, called trustees, who serve terms of four years.

BARBARA: Now for your story. Tell us what has been going on in the Natrona County School District over the past several years. And tell us the bad as well as the good news.

JIM: I have been involved in the Natrona County schools since 1972, as a teacher, a building administrator, an assistant superintendent, and now as superintendent, and so I have lots of stories. A professional negotiations agreement was developed between the teachers and the district in the late 1960s. The relationship between the teachers and the district ebbed and flowed for the next thirty years. Various forms of negotiations were attempted. In one of the early years, the board contracted with a professional negotiator who favored positional tactics—largely from the top down. In the late 1980s, after twenty years of positional negotiations, the district and the teachers moved to the interest-based negotiation (IBN) process.[3] By the late 1990s, the IBN process was used only when both sides agreed that it was acceptable for the topic being discussed. For the important issues, the teams used positional processes once more.

By the late 1990s, a great deal of energy and time was consumed by the maintenance of a formal agreement. While everyone may have thought that they were there for the children, many in leadership roles were spending large amounts of time and energy arguing over where the commas should go or what was intended by this or that word in the document. Impasses in renewing the agreement were the norm, and negotiations were nearly year-round activities. Trust was low, and frustration was extremely high. It became commonplace for individuals to be categorized as "good" or "bad," with few in between. Day-to-day activities frequently became entangled with maintenance of contract issues. People were combatants rather than colleagues.

BARBARA: The picture you present is depressing, to say the least. It sounds like a mess! What happened to change it?

JIM: In June 2001 the school board voted to terminate the professional negotiations agreement. What little trust was left was dissolved. Relationships that were tenuous prior to the termination became nonexistent.

We hit bottom, and then things began to change. In August the newly installed president of the teachers' association and the vice chairperson of the board had coffee and dessert with a handful of other leaders of the association and trustees. It may have been important for progress that all the participants in the meeting were women. There are no records of the meeting, but when the story is recounted, it is clear that no business was conducted. Rather, these leaders began to find out that each person at the gathering was human. Each found that the others had a past—a past that connected them to each other through common experiences of life. The seeds of relationships were planted.

GENE: Can you tell me a little bit more about who was there and why they met and what happened? This part of the story will be very helpful to others.

JIM: As I said, they had dessert and coffee, then told stories to each other, and through this experience, discovered their common humanity and common desire to work together to help the school district. By mid-August the chair of the school board had been contacted by representatives of the National Education Association (NEA). It was the desire at all levels (local, state, and national) of the NEA to reestablish the formal written agreement between the board and the teachers. Wyoming is a right-to-work state; only a handful of districts had a negotiated agreement, and now one was lost. The board members were not opposed to an agreement, but they did not want to consume resources and time with negotiations.

By early September, school had started without major problems, and the leadership of the district and of the local teachers' association had agreed to meet with two facilitators at the end of September. The teachers' association and the district each chose a facilitator. Both of the facilitators had been involved in the collaborative work of the NEA and the National Association of Educational Negotiators (NAEN). The goal for the weekend was to provide training related to interest-based negotiations, and the expectation was for the parties to talk to each other instead of about each other. Unfortunately, the attitude of "been there, done that" was evident among many of the participants. By the middle of the second day of this meeting, through critical conversations, the parties had agreed that children should be at the center of decisions and that the people involved in the situation were human rather than the embodiment of Satan or selfish curmudgeons.

BARBARA: It sounds as though you had uncommon success in getting feelings and values into the open. How did this happen?

JIM: The large group was divided into two smaller job-alike groups of administrators, community representatives, and teachers. They told stories about themselves and the hopes they had for the schools. Both groups came up with a focus on the children. This may sound trite, but through the stories there appeared a common understanding that they discovered for themselves and shared. The process and the stories allowed the participants to focus on commonalities rather than old feuds. At the end of the two-day workshop, one of the teachers' association leaders turned to the board chair, who had been depicted in an editorial cartoon in the newspaper as a demon, and said, "I know now you are not a demon but are a real person who cares about children."

BARBARA: Getting closure in meetings like this is exceedingly difficult. How do you explain what happened in those meetings? Do one or two things stand out as significant?

JIM: Winston Churchill said, "We shape our buildings; thereafter they shape us." Until one stops to examine the impact of the building, one is rarely aware of its power to shape behavior. This is equally true for the structures and practices of organizations we develop. The structures, processes, and practices an organization adopts and adapts also shape the behavior of the participants in the organization.

GENE: Wait—I don't get this Churchill quote. It sounds abstract and remote from the substance of our discussion.

JIM: This intriguing observation comes from a speech Churchill made in the House of Commons on October 28, 1944. Churchill made the speech during the rebuilding of the House of Commons, which had sustained heavy bombing damage during the Battle of Britain. Embedded in the observation is a profound architectural truth that applies to all buildings, public and private. In the beginning, buildings reflect the qualities of the people who design and construct them. Once they are built, the people who live and work in them take on qualities of the buildings they inhabit.

These meetings were the beginning of the compact we formed in the Natrona County school district. This compact, and especially the process we used to develop it, became a structure that shaped the way we wanted to work together. The compact was the building that shaped our lives and ways of being with one another.

Our culture began to change as a result of our compact and the process of developing it. The document titled "Compact of Trust," referred to as "the compact," was developed and adopted by the board of trustees, the teachers' association, and all other employee groups in December 2001. The compact that was developed by approximately fifty individuals shapes our thinking. It addresses characteristics of a democracy that must be continually renewed so that all the participants understand how to be with one another.

The compact shaped the culture just as buildings often shape the culture. It became the container in which the culture thrived. This new culture was based on collaboration, shared ownership, and the outcomes the children achieved. This could only happen after trust was developed, and the initial meetings were the beginning point in building that trust. The compact and the process of developing the compact changed the culture from that of individualism and fighting for individual rights to trust, collaboration, and deliberation.

GENE: Tell us a little bit more about how this happened and what you think the key events were that caused this change from individualism to a more collaborative way of being. It is an impressive metamorphosis.

JIM: Because of a loss of organizational memory about why the organization had attempted interest-based negotiations and because of the recollection that it had failed, the facilitators and the groups working to resolve the situation knew that staying focused on the IBN process would not be acceptable. These people had to find a common bond. As easy as it now seems, it was difficult to do. To admit that the "other side" had redeeming value was not easy and was even more difficult to say openly. Telling stories, getting to know one another as human beings who shared dreams and hopes, and focusing on the common goal of working for the children proved to be a strong bonding experience. That common bond is not unique to this group or any other group of people deeply involved with education. Yet the simple private and public acknowledgment that children should be the focus of our decisions proved to be pivotal. The level of dissonance was high; one could not be a demon and a person with a strong calling to be deeply involved with schooling and children. A healthy relationship was being created and nurtured.

BARBARA: The devil is always in the details. Can you share some of the specific actions that created this healthy relationship?

JIM: We did this through interest-based decision making. The first step was for each participant to tell personal stories about the topic. The rule was that you could not challenge another person's story but could add to it or give your own perception. The second step was for the participants to share the perceived interests they had in the topic. The third step was to develop options that were as inclusive as possible for all the interests that were expressed in the discussions. Everyone was asked to focus on listening to the content of the stories and the interests involved.

Not only were healthy relationships developed, but there also was a purpose for them—the renewal of the schools. The key seemed to be that agreement was reached on the "why" of the entire work—to make schools better for the young. A serious effort to better identify commonly held foundational beliefs was undertaken along with the interest to expand the IBN process into all critical decisions so that the process would become ingrained in the culture. At the core of these interests was a desire to be more collaborative. There was widespread agreement that the culture needed to change to one with children and learning at the center.

GENE: The word "culture" means different things to different people. Please explain to us what you mean by culture.

JIM: My definition of culture would be the unwritten rules and assumptions that we hold about how to be with one another and the motives we assign to others. In this case, the process of developing the compact allowed us to make these assumptions explicit. We chose to be collaborative with one another, and we chose to view the other as a person with positive motives. The storytelling and the entire process helped these assumptions come to light and, in so doing, changed the culture.

BARBARA: Can you be more specific about your thoughts and actions during this time?

JIM: Well, I started out by thinking to myself, "Can a classroom, school, or school district be democratic?" If one believes a democracy is where everybody does his or her own thing, my answer is no. If one considers a dictionary definition of democracy—"the political orientation of those who favor government by the people or by their elected representatives"[4]—the answer may be yes.

However, for me at least, the definition that Roger Soder uses is most enlightening: "a political regime that is characterized by freedom, constitutionality, and democracy (in the sense of self-rule by the people rather than by the one or the few) in a republican state (in the sense of elected representatives chosen from parties presenting viable and significant alternative philosophies and programs)."[5] Soder goes on to identify several conditions necessary for a democracy. Consideration of three of these conditions—trust, respect for civil discourse, and ecological understanding—played a significant role in the development of the compact. I selected these three because of their particular importance in the emergence of participatory and developing democracies.

BARBARA: Give us some more detail about what you mean by these ideas of trust, respect for civil discourse, and ecological understanding and about how these ideas found their way into the compact. People often promote these concepts at the very time they are abusing them.

JIM: It is hard to conceive of situations in which democracy is present or emerging and trust among the participants is nonexistent. It is equally difficult to conceive of an organization in which the amount of trust does not ebb and flow among situations and actors. What reverses a long downward spiral? What builds trust, encourages exchange, or builds social capital? For this district, it was a crisis and a recognition, through the development of the compact, that each party was dependent on the others. Especially visible was the linkage between teachers and management. One could not exist without the other. Both could make the situation miserable or much better. The parties came to understand the reality of mutually assured destruction, and none preferred that option.

President Reagan's farewell address captured the situation in which trust is low but hope is building when he spoke of President Gorbachev of the Soviet Union:

> We must keep up our guard, but we must also continue to work together to lessen and eliminate tension and mistrust.... What it all boils down to is this. I want the new closeness to continue. And it will, as long as we make it clear that we will continue to act in a certain way as long as they continue to act in a helpful manner. If and when they don't, at first pull your punches. If they persist, pull the plug. It's still trust, but verify.[6]

In the Natrona County School District, the relationships were personal and daily. "Trust, but verify" seemed to be an ever-present perspective. Having an agreement in writing was important to satisfy this end.

The compact addressed trust in several places, including the following as a statement of philosophical understanding:

> Relationship of Value and Trust—The recognized employee organizations and Board are committed to a relationship of trust and respect between each other and among teachers, District and site-level administrators and other employees. We will strive for understanding, dialogue and honesty.[7]

GENE: I understand this to mean that the group pledged to focus on dialogue, deeply listening to one another and trying to understand what others believe and why they believe that way. These conditions are not easily sustained.

JIM: Yes. I think that captures it and also leads into the next notion, that of respect for civil discourse. Soder states that as a condition for democracy, people must be willing to "entertain propositions, consider evidence, and accept ambiguity."[8] Besides being a necessary condition, such willingness may be an assessment of several factors, including trust and respect. The compact stated that "valuing includes: (1) demonstrating a commitment to the success of faculty, staff, administrators and partners; (2) recognition that goes beyond financial compensation; (3) development and progression within the district; (4) sharing knowledge so faculty, staff, administrators, and partners can better serve the students and stakeholders and contribute to achieving the strategic objectives; and (5) creating an environment that encourages creativity."[9]

The climate prior to the development of the compact left little time and no desire for civil discourse. All the energies were on the contract, either wordsmithing it, arguing over commas, or preparing for the next contract. It was a never-ending annual cycle. But with the compact the board wanted everyone, including each board member, to be able to focus on teaching and learning and not the contract. One was extremely cautious to "think out loud." Nearly every discussion, even those within stakeholder groups, involved talking around the elephant in the room that no one would mention.

GENE: Wait a minute. What was the elephant in the room?

JIM: Lack of trust. We are "nice people," and no one would say it out loud, but everyone knew it was there: no trust. Everyone wanted everything written down, in great detail. There was no faith that deliberation would lead us anywhere. Remnants of this condition existed after the development of the compact. But the willingness to recognize the elephant has encouraged the recognition that there are multiple perspectives regarding both the elephant and difficult problems. Additionally, more people feel sufficiently secure to seek clarification of their thoughts through dialogue with other stakeholders and other stakeholder groups. Civil discourse is entered into much more quickly and much more deeply than ever before.

GENE: The discourse you talk about is often claimed to be for the students, but frequently it is not. Did you involve the students in all the decision-making events?

JIM: Students have been engaged in decision making and do a good job. Students in grades seven and up have been included on large decision-making teams, such as the superintendent search and the closure of the junior high school. In the junior high closure the parents and staff wanted the students to stick together at the new schools. Students argued that they wanted to become students of the new school, not visitors from their old school. The students prevailed.

BARBARA: You have referred to "ecological understanding." What is this, and how did it play a role in the compact?

JIM: It is this aspect that may differentiate between the developmental and the participatory democracies. The representatives of the developmental democracy may be perceived as knowing more facts and, therefore, better able to make decisions. Those who adhere to the participatory model of democracy value the ability to know the connectedness of the context, to know the entity as an organization of organisms rather than a collection of facts. Those best suited to govern the entity are those who perceive the value of the living, breathing, evolving, and connected nature of the beast—the ecology of the total context of the ongoing work. They are aware of the whole.

This is a significant change for any organization. Those who sought positions so they could have the power to make decisions had to learn to share the power. Those who avoided decision making, for whatever reason, found themselves in the position of being responsible for making decisions. Finding levels of management to blame became more difficult, as did finding groups of employees to blame for problems of implementation. Everyone must practice leadership behaviors, rather than delegating leadership to a few. The organization had seen the elephant, and it was us.

BARBARA: The story of educational change usually is one of optimism followed by regression. How are things going now?

JIM: Operating the district remains a challenge from day to day. Trust remains dynamic, rather than static and linear, as organizational leaders change and grow. In the old days the teachers saw that what the association did for them was to fight with the board over specific issues. Now, with the compact, what the association does for teachers is less obvious. Getting everyone committed to the process remains a problem. The group has not been good at keeping a written record, and the oral history becomes forgotten. Board members have changed, as have teacher leaders and administrators. There is constant need to renew the process, which is sort of the developmental nature of democracy. It is not linear but progresses through starts and stops, turns and loops, with the process needing to be repeated; training, storytelling, and trust building are ongoing activities. It is sort of like renewing the vows of the organization and creating new ones on an ongoing basis. The descriptive word for it is "renewal." Operating an organization that is evolving from being controlled by fear and distrust to a climate of openness and sharing of information continues to be a challenge. This is the condition to work toward and achieve for public school districts that have as their responsibility the enculturation of the young to be participants in the social and political democracy in which we yearn to live.

Bill Mester, Washington

BARBARA: Bill, tell us the theory of action that you use as superintendent, and give special attention to your notions of practices that might address the work of developing a more democratic public.

BILL: The schooling of children in classrooms and the life of children within the confines of a school provide common examples of the inextricable link between public schooling and our democracy. But the larger context of school systems and the communities they serve can provide a different vantage point for viewing the connection between public schooling and democracy. A school district signals its underlying values by how it conducts its business and by the conditions it creates for the formation of relationships within the community. Schools, through their representations and relationships, can serve as models and exemplars of democratic practice. Just as teachers can create democratic conditions within classrooms that serve as catalysts for children's growth, district practices can provide the context for the adults within the system to experience and grow in their own understanding of democratic ideals or values. Aligning organizational practices around such values creates a culture that enables the adults to experience democratic practice more directly in their work life. The connection at its simplest is this: If we want classrooms to be places where students can learn through experience about democracy and citizenship, then the adult organizational culture should be guided by those same democratic principles. Districts themselves should operate in a manner consistent with democratic values.

BARBARA: Let me try to summarize what you said. Schools need to focus on teaching the students to be citizens in a democracy and also need to model democratic principles for the larger community. Now will you explain your theory of action as a superintendent?

BILL: If a school district is aligned around the ideals of democratic practice, its influence extends beyond the employees and students within the system. The larger communities of parents, nonparents, businesses, churches, and public agencies are also affected by these values and practices. A district, through its practices, has an opportunity to further educate the community at large about participatory democracy. It can invite the diverse members of the broader community to gather and then deliberate on matters of importance to both the community and the district.

GENE: Jim has given us a vivid picture of some of the challenges faced by his district and community in trying to effect deliberation that leads to actions in his community and school district. What are some of the guiding ideas that you use for involving the community?

BILL: Much of the literature on democracy and schooling has as its focus the life of the child in school. Civility and character education are very relevant and important matters in education. The district, as a leader in democratic practice within the organization and with the larger community, provides an important means by which people may be further educated about participatory democracy. From this vantage point, it is possible to examine the effects such practices can have on the overall culture of both the schools and the community. It is evident to me that when the adults in a community experience greater democratic conditions in their work relationships, they are better able to support similar conditions in classrooms with students and also in their continuing relationships with one another in the community. Attending to the creation of these conditions becomes vitally important to the overall well-being of both the schools and the community. School leaders, through their practices, can be seen as conveners of the diverse sectors of the community that they serve.

If school leaders are to see their role as conveners of community, then it is important that they are intentional and clear about what attributes or characteristics need to be present for democratic involvement to take place. The attributes of these practices must be viewed from the perspective of how they influence the nature and quality of the relationships within the community. It seems that for a community to thrive and be democratic in character, a number of these attributes should characterize the relationships in that community. People need to see that communication is open and inclusive, that all people are invited to share their views, and that no voice or class of people is marginalized. People come to recognize that when problems or matters of importance arise, everyone affected will be notified about the issue; similarly, all will be invited to share in the decision to be made. The confidence in this community would not rest on the absence of problems but rather on the firm knowledge that people in this community are able to work through problems together.

GENE: This seems to me to be the idea of sharing power in decision making. So sharing power seems to be one of your big ideas.

BILL: In most organizations, including schools, power is a function of control over other people. When we take control over people, we are in fact limiting their potential for growth and limiting our organization's effectiveness. With control, voices are muted, people tend to shelter themselves, and they are hesitant to disclose their ideas because they feel they are at personal risk. One way schools can promote democracy, both internally and in the larger community, is to create conditions in which people feel safe to speak freely and share in the decision making. The leader needs to model the value of open dialogue and the importance of hearing all voices and to instill in the district and the larger community the belief that wisdom for knowing the right thing to do can be found in diverse viewpoints. These experiences not only highlight the importance of aligning practice with belief but also come to underscore the need to be clear and articulate about our deepest values.

BARBARA: Jim spoke about the necessity of developing those conditions in Natrona County, Wyoming. What are some beliefs and values you think are critical?

BILL: When people feel that they have been left out or that a decision has been prearranged, they are not only noticing an inconsistency in practice but, more important, drawing conclusions from feeling manipulated and marginalized in what was originally purported to be an open and inclusive undertaking. The conclusions they are drawing have to do with how power and control are being exercised by the leaders of the district. In these situations people are aware that the leaders are exercising control over people to achieve the outcomes they desire.

When people feel controlled or manipulated, they become more distrustful, withdraw, or are less authentic in their interactions and relationships, which eventually can result in adversarial behavior. The structural dynamic in operation here is that people are making judgments about the fundamental values underlying the leader's and organization's intentions. When they experience the lack of genuine openness and inclusiveness and feel manipulated, they question the authenticity of the leader's espoused values and conclude that the leadership is other than well intentioned.

GENE: What, from your view and experiences, can a school district or a superintendent do to change this?

BILL: How a district exercises control and power can become very instructive for the members of the community and for those working within the organization. When people have a sense that things are fair, they are informally making a judgment about how power and control are playing out in relationships in the group to which they belong. When districts work to control for results and refrain from controlling people, it is easier to reach the conclusion that things are fair. When a diversity of viewpoints is honored and ground rules for decision making are arrived at mutually and in advance, when opportunity for input is provided to everyone and genuine consideration is given to people's thoughts and feelings, then people generally conclude that their thoughts mattered and made a difference. A greater sense of efficacy can be arrived at on everyone's part.

BARBARA: So you believe in controlling for outcomes but not controlling people. How does this work, and what does it look like in your way of doing business?

BILL: It may be important to make a clarification here about decision making. I am specifically not equating the procedure of voting with democratic practice. From this framework the focus is more on a deliberative process in which people become more open and listen more to one another. In fact, making decisions by voting (particularly by secret ballot) can over the long term cause groups to become less cohesive and less functional. Engaging people publicly in a deliberative process requires that the leaders or facilitators create conditions within the group that make it safe for people to be open with their thoughts. It requires that people are confident that each viewpoint will be respected and valued. Further, conditions need to become safe enough that people can risk trying out ideas and experimenting with possibilities. Over time, people become connected in their minds and hearts. Common views of a preferred future emerge. Thinking through things together allows people to open up one another's thinking and to arrive at richer and more effective solutions.

BARBARA: It appears that you and Jim have similar beliefs, but I need an example or two to understand them better.

BILL: When it is made clear that leaders are assuming the good intentions of everyone present and are explicit in that they value diverse viewpoints, then individuals within those groups become more trusting of one another and become more open to the legitimacy of differing viewpoints within the group. They not only are more able to find their common ground but, because of their openness to one another, can more readily discern the common good and the preferred futures that unfold in their discussion.

When leaders create the appropriate conditions, members of the community find that they can come together in an effective manner to work through current problems, make a shared decision to take collective actions, and evaluate their effectiveness. Through the opportunities that the district provides, people can experience and use more democratic practices. Schools, by the way in which they engage or convene the community, provide substantial opportunity to enhance the community's capacity to live a democratic way of life.

GENE: This seems to me to be a little too perfect. Aren't there hard political realities that make this difficult? If there were not, what you and Jim describe would be much more common than it is.

BILL: I don't mean to ignore or set aside the practical and political implications of this approach. When a large and diverse group of citizens come together and have genuine and authentic power to craft solutions for housing and school construction and when they engage the larger public in these deliberations, those very same people will be inclined to take their story to the entire community for a bond election. When large groups of a school community have been regularly involved in the policy and funding matters of a district, they will readily be available and inclined to become politically active with both their neighbors and the legislature in advocating legislative improvements. But there is a broader benefit to emerge over time within a community. Communities that have had the opportunity for open discourse and collective decision making on school matters will also use these newly developed skills in other community and neighborhood endeavors. I have seen these practices evolve to include the joint efforts of a school district and a city, the way in which a fire department works with its community, and the way in which service clubs join with the schools for community improvement. The result is that schools can be not only conveners of the community around school matters but also catalysts and conveners for public forums and decision making around matters of importance to the general community and issues extending well beyond the local community.

BARBARA: So what are some core ideas here? I get overwhelmed by the complications of implementation.

BILL: The core to this work is listening, to be fully present, to see and reflect for others the gifts and talents they have (the potential they have), and to have a profound respect for the dignity and worth of all people. Very frequently in conversations, while one person is talking, the other person is already formulating his or her response. Being fully present means working on getting rid of chatter in our head, suspending our judgments, attending fully and openly, and working to understand the legitimacy of what the other person is saying. We need to work on suspending judgment and become fully open to the legitimacy of others' ideas, even if they are different from our own ideas.

GENE: This sounds like something David Bohm would say.

BILL: Yes. These ideas come specifically from Bohm's book *On Dialogue*.[10] People who are affected by decisions have a right to have a say in making the decisions. The larger community should come to expect that they will have opportunities to participate in and discuss matters of importance concerning the schools and that they will have the opportunity to influence these decisions. Listening helps people heal and become whole. If a people feel they have been fully understood by someone fully listening, they know that what they are saying makes sense, and it makes them feel more whole.

BARBARA: Bill, please describe the Snohomish School District for us.

BILL: The Snohomish School District has nine thousand students in a semirural area of Washington State that is rapidly becoming suburban. When the district hired me in 2001, it had gone through four superintendents in five years, had experienced a serious financial crisis, and was facing its first teacher strike in over twenty years.

The school board had identified three top priorities: teaching and learning improvement, work on the maintenance of facilities, and the need for new schools to help with growing enrollment. The previous superintendent had recommended that a strategic plan be developed and had tentatively engaged a consultant to begin to develop one for that year.

BARBARA: Now for the story that connects your core ideas and ongoing policies and practices.

BILL: Rather than hire a consultant to develop a strategic plan, I moved to more of an interpersonal and community-based plan. This plan consisted of a series of meetings (which came to be called "coffees") with the members of the community. Each school principal was asked to look for diverse viewpoints reflective of the community as a whole and to find five volunteers who would invite their neighbors (not just parents, but any neighbors) to a coffee in their homes. This was an opportunity for the community to meet with the superintendent and other school representatives. Thus, microcosms of the larger community were created.

A board member, a teacher's union member, a principal, a classified union member, and I attended each coffee. The coffee started with introductions, and then it was explained that the school people were there to listen to members of the community and be a part of the conversation. I came to the meetings strictly to listen to community members. If people had particular problems with a specific school, they were instructed to take them to the school principals, as the coffees did not have the purpose of resolving local complaints. Everyone in the room was asked to take turns telling the story of how they became connected to Snohomish and the Snohomish School District.

GENE: How did you come up with the idea of storytelling as an opening?

BILL: For the first two or three coffees, the starting prompt was, "Tell us what you think about the Snohomish schools." However, this changed after a meeting with a group of Mexican-American families. This was an unusual situation in that the parents did not want to meet in a home; they wanted to meet as a group at the school. Their children also joined in the group. At other coffees, which were held in homes, children tended not to be included. The original prompt was not working with this group; no one was talking, so I told my story of why I came to Snohomish and then asked if they would tell their stories. This opened up the conversation, and a similar prompt was used in all future coffees.

GENE: A nice example of reflection in action.[11] You saw a problem and made a change that proved to be a good change for future meetings. How effective were these coffees?

BILL: They created a real connection among those in the room. Often these people had known each other for more than ten years, and the coffees provided them with the first opportunity to talk about their hopes and dreams for their community. These stories allowed people to share their values with one another. The way in which stories shape and give sense to people's journeys allows them to reflect on what they value in life. Values are boundaries and core organizers in terms of how people see and make sense of their lives and connect with others and their values.

BARBARA: What did you do after the stories?

BILL: After sharing stories, people were asked to talk about what it was that they liked or found as strengths in the school district. Last, they were asked to talk about the ways in which the district could get better and what were the priorities. Minutes were taken and sent back to each person who had attended, asking if the minutes reflected the meeting in which they had participated.

GENE: So what is the difference between asking people to share stories while being open to listening with the intent to hear, understand, and include and using this technique to manipulate others to get them to do what you want?

BILL: Is my purpose here to persuade you or inform you? Manipulation and hidden persuasion are forms of control. If this is a coffee or a meeting and I am expecting everyone to come to my way of thinking, it will only work for a while unless the audience wants to be led. Are you truly open, or are you there to control? There is a space that is frequently created in a conversation when an issue is not resolved; often leaders jump in and fill this space with a solution. A better method is for the leader to be quiet, allowing the space to be unfilled until other voices fill it with their ideas.

GENE: Why did you choose the coffee method?

BILL: As a city, Snohomish fashions itself to be a small town and not on the cutting edge of growth. The culture is very personal and inter-personal. The important thing about the coffees was that people were sharing their stories, sharing their values. We could have developed and published a large strategic model. Instead, we continued the coffees because they created conversation in the community. Everyone liked that people talked to one another about education, about things that mattered. Collectively, it became clear that the vision needed to reflect everyone's ideas. The strongest theme that came out of the coffees was that Snohomish is a small community: people know each other, want to help one another, pitch in to support, meet friends in the grocery store, and know their neighbors. They want their schools to be that way, too. This, in essence, was a good description of the culture of Snohomish.

If a leader comes in and intends to influence a culture, it cannot be done successfully through a power and control standpoint. Culture is fundamentally a moral construct, and one cannot coerce fundamental values. Within any organization, there are at least three layers of influence. The visible work is the easiest to describe and is also the easiest to change (the curriculum in a school, academic assessments, discipline procedures). The second layer is policy (procedures and process) and the underlying rules by which an organization functions. The third and deepest layer is the culture—the sets of values, the nature and quality of thinking, the relationships that guide things (how the organization develops efforts to solve problems and resolve issues), which are all geared to improving the conditions of life.

BARBARA: Can you give us an example of how the information you gained from the coffees led to some wider community action?

BILL: One of the major themes that came out of the coffees was the need for a new high school and a building bond. Following the idea of to-tal community involvement, we organized a citizen's committee on facilities that represented the diversity in the community. On the committee a division arose between long-term citizens and newer citizens. The problems with the former were a lack of trust from the financial meltdown of the district and the construction of the perceived "fancy" district office building. The newer community members, largely those using Snohomish as a bedroom community for Seattle, viewed the old-timers as antieducation.

A request to join the committee was put out to the entire community, and over seventy individuals responded. The board invited forty people to join the facilities committee, and I facilitated the committee's work, while the board retained authority for issuing the building bond. The facilities committee became a microcosm of the whole district, with all geographic and ideological sides represented.

The committee divided into small groups of three or four, and I asked them to tell each other why they chose to come and some of their history with the district. The process guidelines included the following: talk about what you heard, cherish varied views, and agree that everyone there has good intentions. No one was there to destroy the district; however, there would be some profound differences of opinion. The committee was informed that they, not school staff members, would be making the decisions about what recommendations were made to the board. The punch line here is that not only did the committee do outstanding work, but we passed the capital bond—the largest capital bond ever approved by Snohomish voters.

BARBARA: Can you sum up by reflecting on what you think are the two or three "big ideas" from your story?

BILL: I think school districts can influence the democratic practices of their community by modeling democratic behaviors. If districts model openness and inclusion, the community comes to see the district as fair, just, and willing to share decision making. This also strengthens the internal workings of the district because school staff members come to view the district in a similar fashion. They are willing to speak up because they are confident that they will be heard and their ideas will be valued. Thus, when a decision is made, even if the decision is not what some individuals thought should happen, they are more likely to support it because they believe that their ideas were considered. They will be more likely to speak up in the future and be an active part in decision making.

So I believe the real mission of schools, more than raising test scores, is the development of democratic character in the community at large, certainly including our students and staff, but also citizens in their everyday lives. Our practices have, I believe, been successful in this regard. I think that through these practices community members have come to know each other better, to come to like each other, and to have confidence in the deliberative process. I know people who met at the coffees and continued to meet in informal groups. I have had representatives from the fire department, a local men's club, and several churches approach me about how we got such effective community input on school issues. In several cases people have told me things such as, "You remember how we worked on the facilities committee? Well I took some of the things I learned from that experience, and we are using them in the arts commission." That type of comment warms my heart. We can see evidence of democratic ideals growing from our practices.

Reflections

Bill's and Jim's stories reflect only partially what happened in these two school districts. Many other things were happening concurrently. We acknowledge that these stories were told from the perspective of the superintendents. Others who were participants in these stories would have different versions of what happened and why. But from what these two superintendents reported, at least four big ideas seem to emerge.

First is the idea that school districts can reach out to the broader community in ways that promote democratic citizenship. Districts can, through modeling and shared leadership, develop community support for the schools and play a significant role in developing democratic character. This is not a small idea.

The second big idea is that deep listening is important. Listening when you are seriously curious is a powerful skill that can be taught, and, in fact, when given space and a reason to listen, most people develop deep listening skills. Listening allows others to be included in the group and helps the listener to better understand the other. Listening leads to developing a common bond and forming relationships that often extend beyond the immediate task.

The third big idea is the power of stories. As psychologist Robert Coles noted, everyone has a story and enjoys telling it to others who will truly listen. [12] Stories and storytelling build trust and develop humane connections. Stories allow both the teller and the listener to feel heard and connected to one another. Stories are powerful, and we each have our own story to tell. Providing space and time to share stories is well worth the cost in time.

The fourth idea is that shared leadership, which involves authentic decision making with an emphasis on serious listening and the sharing of stories, can establish a trusting community that allows schools and the general public to work at renewal collaboratively and with mutual satisfaction.

These stories are fine examples of community development. When people come together with some common purpose and, through democratic practices, help resolve a problem, they become bonded to one another. Thomas Bender defines community as "a network of social relations marked by mutuality and emotional bonds."[13] We like to think that the stories told here created deep and long-lasting bonds of affection. Perhaps, in the long run, the most productive thing about any work is the possibility of establishing lifelong friends—communities of friends who sustain and renew democracy.

Notes

1. William E. Hudson, *American Democracy in Peril: Eight Challenges to America's Future,* 5th ed. (Washington, D.C.: CQ, 2006).

2. Roger Soder, *The Language of Leadership* (San Francisco: Jossey-Bass, 2001).

3. Roger Fisher and William Ury, *Getting to Yes: Negotiating Agreement without Giving In* (Boston: Houghton Mifflin, 1981).

4. http://wordnet.princeton.edu/perl/webwn?s=democracy.

5. Roger Soder, "Education for Democracy: The Foundations for Democratic Character," in Roger Soder, John I. Goodlad, and Timothy J. McMannon, eds., *Developing Democratic Character in the Young* (San Francisco: Jossey-Bass, 2001), 185.

6. President Ronald Reagan, "Farewell Address to the Nation," January 11, 1989, Oval Office, http://www.reaganfoundation.org/reagan/speeches/farewell. asp.

7. Natrona County School District, Wyoming, Compact of Trust, December 2001, 2.

8. Soder, "Education for Democracy," 196.

9. Compact of Trust, 2.

10. David Bohm, *On Dialogue,* Lee Nichol, ed. (New York: Routledge, 1996).

11. Donald A. Schön, *The Reflective Practitioner: How Professionals Think in Action* (New York: Basic Books, 1983).

12. Robert Coles, *The Call of Stories: Teaching and the Moral Imagination* (Boston: Houghton Mifflin, 1989).

13. Thomas Bender, *Community and Social Change in America* (New Brunswick, N.J.: Rutgers University Press, 1978), 7.

Chapter 9

School Boards and the Power of the Public

Michael A. Resnick and Anne L. Bryant

We Americans have an abiding belief in and commitment to the principles of democracy. Those principles are exhibited in our relationship with government and in our daily interactions with one another. The shared knowledge of those democratic principles is necessary for our society to function, and so is their practice. Simply put, the active engagement of the citizenry gives life and meaning to civil society and to our democracy.

Remarkably, the three hundred million people in our vast nation share many common values that define the complex rights and responsibilities of contemporary civic life. Yet the ability to successfully negotiate the complexities of civic life is not innate. It must be taught and experienced. Where do we learn these principles? Where do we practice them and experience their application? And how do we learn to value the necessary investment of time it takes to become engaged citizens?

For many young people, school is the most significant public institution in their lives, simply because they spend so much of their time there. The public schools are therefore well situated to give students a deliberate and organized foundation of core civic principles. The schools shape students' sense of civic identity through the lessons of history, student government, team activities, and students' daily interactions with each other. They are taught that the principles of democracy apply equally to everyone, regardless of race, religion, or economic status.

The schools' role in teaching the principles of American democracy and the value of civic engagement is especially vital because of the significant number of students whose families come to the United States from countries where the premises and practices of civic life may vary from our own. It is also important because, although other community organizations can provide some motivated young people with opportunities for civic engagement, the schools can reach all children with programs and activities that engage students in community service and impart an awareness of citizen responsibility and a sense of the public interest.

The schools frequently provide adults with their first major opportunity to be involved with public institutions. In their roles as parents, taxpayers, and businesspeople, adults can get involved in decisions about what values to teach, what courses to offer, where to locate a new school, or whether to close an existing one. They may also get involved in broader decisions about the role of the schools in community life, economic development, and even issues ranging from traffic to health services and safety.

Citizen involvement in the local schools can serve both community life and participatory democracy. Vibrant civic engagement is also vital to the success of public education—and to the public's ongoing support of it. The advice and volunteerism of parents, business leaders, and other citizens can enrich the academic quality of our public schools and strengthen the schools' ability to prepare students to participate in American society. And through their involvement citizens can gain a better understanding of public education and its unique role in a free society.

Local school boards are a key mechanism in the mutually dependent relationship between education and democracy, a relationship that is played out through civic engagement. That is, beyond representing the community as elected officials, members of local school boards, as we shall see, can actually increase democratic participation by inviting citizens from the community to become more involved in the schools and empowering citizens to participate in the decision-making process. Through that engagement citizens' support for education can be strengthened. At the same time, they get a close-to-home opportunity to learn and practice democracy. Such experiences can lead to participation in other venues—and provide a powerful model for the next generation, as children watch and learn from their parents' civic involvement. For these reasons, *what* the schools do to include citizens and *how* they do it will shape public education's contribution to advancing democracy and community life.

Why Community Engagement Matters to Schools

An engaged public is important to the success of our schools for several reasons. It enables teachers and school officials to understand what parents believe is really important when it comes to what children need to know and how it should be taught. It goes without saying that academic learning is the school's primary mission, but a school is also a social environment in which most children spend six hours a day, 180 days a year. How happy their children are in school, the values they learn there, and the services they have access to are also important to parents and will strongly influence their support for the schools.

By engaging the broader public, school leaders can determine how the schools are perceived by those who, whether they are parents or not, have an interest in the schools as taxpayers, homeowners, and businesspeople. In most communities today, as many as 75 percent of households do not have school-age children. Their day-to-day interest in the local schools is not as direct or as personal as that of parents, but their perspectives are important. Not only will they vote on school budgets and other issues, but they will also interact with public school graduates as their neighbors, colleagues, and employers.

According to polling data from Phi Delta Kappa and the National School Boards Association (NSBA), the public wants schools that can provide well-rounded students who are prepared for college and the workplace.[1] But responding to national polling data is only a starting point for school systems wanting to connect with the public. Local school systems can go further to give their own communities the schools they want to match the life they envision for their children and for the broader society. Across the country a growing number of school systems are bringing the public into organized dialogues to create a vision for the local schools by addressing the big questions: What do we mean by an "educated student" in our school system? What do we want our students to know and be able to do? What values and attributes of character do we want them to possess? What do we want daily life in our schools to be?

Community engagement around such questions provides the schools with a sense of direction from their primary constituency. Without public input, these questions are often answered in terms of how policy specialists, interest groups, and others define the purposes and priorities of public education. Often these experts are primarily concerned with how they can hold the schools accountable for meeting specific goals, which usually means emphasizing areas of student learning that can be easily and uniformly measured.

That focus may narrow the schools' mission to performance on specific tests, which in turn may narrow the curriculum. Less time may be spent on developing the skills of civic engagement and democracy, on music and art, and on areas of character development that cannot be measured in ways assessment specialists and policy analysts accept as valid. But is that how community members want their children to be prepared for successful careers, family life, and citizenship? If schools do not engage the public, the mission of the schools—what they do, what they hold themselves accountable for—may become disconnected from the very constituency they are intended to serve.

In addition to helping set a vision for the local schools, the community can help ensure that expectations are met and the vision becomes reality. For example, in a Maryland program called What Counts? local school boards, working with their state association, hold kitchen table conversations to ask citizens what they value most about public education. Members of the public then explore the indicators *they* believe should be used to measure success; these may include everything from graduation and college placement rates to parent involvement to even the percentage of students enrolled in Advanced Placement courses.

In discussion groups like these, members of the public can also review the measures of success established by the state or other external agencies. Likewise, they can be involved in answering such questions as: Where do we go from here? How do we improve? Addressing these questions will lead to others: What resources do we need? What can parents do to support these improvement efforts? By engaging the community in this way, the schools are more likely not only to serve their constituents' desires successfully but also to build people's understanding of and support for the job the schools are doing. Acting on this scale requires citizen engagement far beyond a vote on taxes or a bond issue. It means recognizing and operating public education as a democratic institution.

The NSBA's publication *The Key Work of School Boards Guidebook* shows how school boards, as the elected governing authority for the local schools, can involve the community every step of the way to establish a vision for the schools, adopt standards that define the level of performance expected, hold the school system accountable for achieving those standards, and ensure continuous improvement to meet the district's vision and goals.[2] Engaged citizens bring much more to the school system than simply letting school leaders know what is important to the community. Members of the public can contribute ideas for improving the quality of education and then volunteer their time and expertise to support the education program and the activities in their schools. Although parents and others may be well versed on specific issues—especially those that involve their own children—they may not understand the big picture or the context in which a specific issue operates. Convening the community around school issues in a town meeting or a focus group gives people an opportunity to develop a broader view.

Through such activities community members can become more interested in—and gain a better understanding of—the higher mission of the schools, the challenges they face, and the successes they achieve. People who have taken part in such forums are also more likely to understand others' needs and points of view and to support decisions that can accommodate multiple concerns and the broader public interest. An engaged community, in short, is more likely to develop a deeper understanding of public education and its role in a diverse society.

In addition to helping determine how best to educate students, the community can provide insight into how the schools can best serve children and adults in other ways—for example, by becoming the neighborhood center for after-school care, adult education programs, or social services for children and families. Not only does this form of community engagement bring citizens, local government agencies, and civic service organizations together to improve the quality of life for everyone, it also defines the school as the seat—if not the heart—of neighborhood activity.

Why Engagement in the Schools Matters to Communities

Communities have a significant interest in their public schools because of the central role they play in determining their children's future. The schools also play an important part in determining the community's overall economic vibrancy and quality of life, since the caliber and range of services offered by schools will influence housing values, property taxes, and which businesses and workers choose to locate in or leave the community.

The public schools play an important though less obvious role in creating a sense of community. We live today in a 24/7 world of work, with many other priorities competing with an active civic life for our shrinking spare time. In recent decades, meanwhile, our values have shifted to place greater emphasis on individualism over the collective good. In many localities the amount of active engagement in the community at large—especially in local government activities and the political process—is diminishing. As the climate for citizen involvement is weakened, so too is our commitment to public institutions, including the public schools. And as people become separated from the decisions made by their public officials, they can become alienated from or indifferent to their government, thereby weakening the democratic process itself.

The public schools are attractive vehicles for keeping the public engaged in government and focused on the public interest. The reason is simple: the schools involve people's children. They also are more likely than most other government institutions to involve discussions and activities in which people can have a real impact, either as ordinary citizens or in their own more specialized capacities.

The schools have an advantage over most other government agencies by being close to home—it is a good deal easier to attend a meeting at your neighborhood school than at city hall, and state and federal governments are even farther away. In addition, people are likely to be familiar with the schools from their own or their children's experiences. When it comes to offering their views, many people believe they know more about education than they do about most other government functions.

Because schools are important to so many parents, taxpayers, and businesspeople, then, and because they have the capacity to convene the public, schools can play a major role in bringing individuals and community groups together to address crucial educational issues. In doing so, schools can bring citizens together to work for the common good, breathing new life into the processes of civic engagement that are essential to a participatory democracy.

A Community of Communities

When school boards convene the community around school issues, the individuals involved frequently have their own particular areas of interest and expertise. Indeed, some engagement activities may involve certain people precisely because of their specific interests. They may be leaders of civic organizations that provide community services, such as the Kiwanis; they may represent specific groups, such as homeowner associations; or they may lead student activities outside school, such as boys' and girls' clubs or scouts. They may be business leaders who have an economic interest in the schools or specialists who can provide professional advice or assistance—architects or psychologists, for example.

Communities are filled with people whose knowledge and talents can offer much to make the schools both more efficient to operate and more rewarding for students. Retirees and members of civic groups can serve as mentors for youngsters in at-risk situations, for example. The local parks and recreation department can provide facilities and resources for after-school programming. Other public or private institutions—such as church groups, libraries, museums, local universities, community colleges, and city or county service agencies—can also contribute to the educational program, the well-being of students, and the overall effectiveness of the schools.

Every community also has certain individuals who can be brought into the engagement process because of their unique capacity to build broad public support or to pull the community's social levers to make specific plans a reality. These "rainmakers" include such people as the mayor, the local newspaper publisher, or a local philanthropist. Engaging local civic and business leaders is especially important because they can use their networks to reach individuals the school system is unlikely to be able to reach directly. A school initiative aimed at improving the reading skills of low-achieving students, for example, can benefit from the involvement of business, civic, and church leaders who, in turn, can encourage their own employees or members to read to their children or to serve as volunteer tutors.

Increasingly, school districts are encouraging the creation of local foundations to help support individual students with college scholarships and to provide funding for school-based programs or program enhancements (such as career education) that might not be otherwise available. In addition to raising money, the boards of these foundations can be a rich resource for generating ideas to improve the schools, contributing to the curriculum, and developing broader public understanding of and support for the school system.

Deciding whether to convene local people in their capacity as ordinary citizens or because of their special knowledge or position is a strategic consideration. So is deciding how to bring them together. In the 2000 publication *Communities Count: A School Board Guide to Public Engagement,* the NSBA showed school leaders how to match community engagement activities with their specific needs, how to build a strategic engagement plan, and how to implement specific engagement activities, such as study circles.[3]

School leaders can also promote citizen involvement by supporting other local organizations and working with them to improve the overall quality of life in the community. By forging partnerships with local museums, theaters, and historical societies, for example, school leaders can open learning opportunities for their students and bring these institutions to the attention of students and adults alike, thereby increasing attendance and participation. Similarly, school leaders can offer vital perspectives on such issues as economic development and housing and can increase citizen participation in discussions about them.

How School Boards Engage the Public

A closer look at the concept of elected school boards and their governance function will show what they bring to the engagement process. One reason we have elected school boards is so that decisions affecting children and the school environment are shaped and approved by people who represent the community. In addition to being the school system's policymakers and governing authority, school boards hold superintendents accountable for managing the schools. School board members, in turn, are themselves accountable to the public. In effect, elected school boards are the way by which the public schools belong to the public.

When the school board becomes involved in community engagement, people know that the effort is being directed by their elected leaders. They also know that their elected leaders have access to the system and will, with the recommendations of the superintendent, make policy decisions based on the public discourse that takes place. In other words, when school boards engage the community, people know that their involvement counts and that decisions will be based on a wide range of views.

A school board's capacity to engage the community extends beyond the formal actions the board may take. Indeed, local school board members engage the community as individuals every day in their personal lives, serving as a unique set of eyes and ears attuned to the schools and the public alike. They talk with parents about their children, meet with reporters, address local clubs, and bring together citizen groups on a wide range of issues concerning the schools and their impact on the community. In effect, school board members connect what the school system is doing with what the community expects for young people in general and for individual children in particular. This is constituency representation at a personal level, a level that truly counts for individuals.

How well a school system engages the public and how the public believes its involvement will be received depend on the school board's policies and the priority it places on community engagement. It also depends on the overall climate of welcome and accessibility that the school board establishes and on its day-to-day engagement with constituents.

In addition to informal engagement, a school board conducts formal and highly focused activities that take citizen involvement to a higher level. Through these structured activities the community can help to shape the basic mission of the schools by asking crucial questions: What do community members want their children to know and be prepared to do when they graduate from school? What services do they want their school to provide? What kinds of curriculum and extracurricular offerings should be available beyond the required subjects? What size should classes be? What special qualifications should be expected of teachers? What values, character traits, and twenty-first-century skills should their students possess? And what do the schools need to look like and do on a daily basis to fulfill their mission?

The public can be formally engaged to help identify and solve—and ultimately to assume ownership of—a wide range of issues, from raising graduation rates to school construction, from the academic program to drug abuse, teen pregnancy, and sex education. The list goes on. There is no one best way to engage the public, but a number of proven practices merit discussion for what they contribute to the school system and, ultimately, to the democratic process.

Study Circles. Study circles bring together small groups of people to meet with a facilitator and members of the school staff on multiple occasions to address a complex issue, such as narrowing the achievement gap between different groups of students. These are substantive, structured meetings that involve studying documents, discussing points of view, and working as a group to develop recommendations. One Arkansas school board, for example, working with its state association, organized study circles on student achievement and family involvement. The groups' recommendations led to initiatives such as workshops designed to help parents assist their children in managing their homework assignments.

Focus Groups. A focus group meets once to consider and react to a specific issue. Unlike a study circle, the focus group is designed not to develop well-reasoned solutions but to take the temperature of the community on proposals or practices. Unlike polling, which is individualistic and private, focus groups involve a facilitated discussion that can change opinions. Through the discussion, members of the focus group can come to understand other points of view and consider the question at hand in greater depth. Focus groups can provide the school district with important feedback on school programs, advice on communicating with the public, and help in designing more broadly based engagement activities such as town meetings and polling.

Similarly, some school systems use focus groups alongside other strategies to involve the public. That was the case a number of years ago in Fairfax County, Virginia, when school leaders conducted surveys, voice polls, and focus groups to gauge community opinions on budget issues. Results of the process included a review of teacher compensation, a renewed focus on school-business partnerships, and increased staff development on technology.

Town Meetings. Town meetings offer school boards an opportunity to hear from a broad sample of the public and to engage in dialogue with participants. Because these are much larger gatherings, they are not facilitated like focus groups, nor are they structured to evoke layers of thinking or, necessarily, to identify group consensus. Nonetheless, town meetings provide an opportunity to hear varying points of view from individuals and representative groups, such as parent and civic organizations.

In addition, town meetings often draw media coverage that reaches an even wider public. The resulting community input can build support for future planning, as it did in Woodstock, Illinois. Faced with rapidly growing enrollment, this suburban district held a series of town meetings that attracted some 2,400 people. Called SchoolTalk200, the initiative led to a major facilities plan that voters approved by a wide margin.

Polling. Polling can also be used to obtain a sense of the community, although it is not deliberative and is therefore less likely than face-to-face gatherings to evoke thoughtful feedback on issues the respondents have not previously considered. Polling has several benefits, however. It provides a more statistically representative set of data than a town meeting, which may represent only the views of those folks who are sufficiently energized about the agenda issue to show up. What's more, simply posing questions to people who may otherwise not be involved at all is an opportunity to stimulate their thinking and sends the message that the school system values their opinion enough to ask. Posing the right questions can also help the school system identify issues that resonate with the community. In one New Jersey school district, for example, a poll about school facilities gave voters a forum for expressing their concern about the effect of air quality on students' health.

Virtual Dialogues. School board members can also engage the public through radio call-in programs that invite individuals to bring their thoughts and questions to public attention. Although for listeners this is a one-way channel of communication, it nevertheless identifies problems and concerns in a way that is more unfiltered, challenging, and personal than simply reading a school newsletter or the local newspaper.

Increasingly school leaders are using other avenues of public dialogue as well: audio conferences, e-mail chats, and blogs, such as the one formerly maintained by the president of the school board in Buffalo, New York. As a result of the growing number of communication vehicles, more people are being brought into the civic dialogue. When they can air their own concerns and make their own interests and ideas heard, they may be inspired to take the next steps in active public engagement.

But in order for civic engagement to be successful—especially when people are being brought together in one physical location—the process must be accessible. Location counts, and so does meeting at convenient times. Creating an atmosphere that is welcoming, conducting discussions that are positive in tone, and using language that is clear and easily understood are all equally important. People are more likely to be constructively engaged when they know their views are being listened to and when the responses are not defensive or obfuscated by professional jargon.

Successful engagement with the schools can be accomplished, but whether the activity is a one-on-one conference or a town hall meeting, it will require a deliberate effort to ensure that the public believes that the school system is accessible and interested. When the engagement is not viewed as genuine, participants who came to a meeting with neutral feelings toward the schools may leave with more negative attitudes—and no desire to engage the school system again. When community engagement activities are designed to address citizens' concerns in ways that make them feel comfortable, as well as to achieve the school system's purpose, the level of understanding and buy-in will be substantial. And when that happens, the school board is governing on a public scale.

A Living Democracy

Governance through the electoral process is the very foundation of American democracy. With 96 percent of the nation's ninety-five thousand local school board members chosen at the polls, citizens have no greater opportunity to be candidates for public office than running for a position on the school board. Moreover, because school districts generally represent a smaller population base than do other local governments, individual citizens have greater access to their elected school board members—and greater confidence that action will be taken as a result of communicating with them.

Some will claim that the relatively light voter turnout for school board elections—especially those held separately from general elections—indicates that elected school boards are not essential to advancing democracy. To that argument we say a better approach is to focus on voter turnout, not only in these elections but in American elections generally. Why not work to increase voter turnout overall to strengthen our democracy rather than use low turnout to argue that elected representation is not a necessary cornerstone of democracy?

But this discussion is about more than voter turnout at elections. Election Day is the culmination of a process that extends over months in which candidates talk to potential voters, debate one another, appear in various public forums, and have their views aired in the media. School board elections provide an opportunity for individuals, groups, and whole communities to focus on their schools and to select the candidate they wish to empower to represent them. Even the 4 percent of school board members who are appointed may go through a public vetting process in which candidates lay out their goals before parent groups and civic organizations. These bodies then convey their recommended choice to the locally elected officials who make the appointment.

As an institution, the school board also plays several other important roles to advance citizen self-government. Because a school board member generally represents a smaller number of voters than do other local and state officeholders, the cost, campaign organization, and political experience needed to run for public office are far less formidable. As a result, far more citizens can participate in the democratic process of running for public office. The overwhelming majority will return to private life after serving on the board, bringing their experience as policymakers and government leaders to other facets of civic life in which they may become engaged. For the relatively few who go on to seek another office, their school board experience provides a constituency base and public record on which to run for an office they might not otherwise consider attainable.

School boards also advance civic engagement and democracy through the way they govern. Typically school boards have seven members, although many larger systems have nine or eleven. As a result, board decisions are based on a majority vote following public deliberation rather than on the executive fiat of one person sitting alone in an office. The deliberative, public, and majority-driven nature of school board decision making helps to ensure that proposals will be well thought out, that varying points of view will be considered, and that compromises and accommodations will be made.

School board deliberation is not based solely on an exchange of views among members, especially when it comes to decisions on major educational priorities or policies affecting students' daily lives. Such decisions often follow individual conversations with constituents, public hearings, or town hall meetings conducted or attended by the entire school board, individual board members, or the administrative staff on their behalf.

When a major decision must be made—on reading strategies or dropout prevention, for example—school boards are most effective if they engage the community to understand its needs and values, take advantage of its knowledge, and gain its support for implementing the decision. Simply stated, effective school boards govern on a public scale, serving the larger public interest while sustaining the individual's commitment to participation in civic activities. The result is a living democracy.

Further, as the governing authority of local school systems, school boards can determine how democracy and community involvement are taught in their schools. Working with the superintendent, the board can evaluate current programs and decide on the appropriate emphasis and allocation of resources. Because teaching in this area can involve personal values, local culture, and activities outside the classroom, many school boards invite parents, civic organizations, and others to provide recommendations and serve as volunteers to help implement programs. Many school districts, for example, are working with local organizations to provide community service programs for high school students. Involving the public in such endeavors improves the quality of the school program and strengthens public support for it, and such involvement gives people an opportunity to renew their own interest in community engagement.

Teaching Students about Democracy

In recent years, the federal No Child Left Behind Act and state accountability systems have sharpened the focus on closing the achievement gap in essential skills like reading and math. More attention is also being paid to providing higher levels of math and science instruction to better prepare students for twenty-first-century technology, global competition, and multiple careers. As important as these efforts are, it is also essential that all students be prepared to live in a civil society in which people know how to get along with each other, value and balance the greater public interest with their own, and participate in the well-being of their community. Only in this way can we ensure that self-governance is a reality, not simply a myth to hide governance by an elite few.

Teaching living democracy reaches beyond having students memorize democratic principles and learn about important historical events that exemplify or model those principles. It involves classroom activities that teach students the values, behaviors, and expectations of life in their community—including their own responsibilities as citizens. Teacher-guided experiences in resolving conflict, student government, group projects, extracurricular activities, and class discussions can all be ways to enable students to understand and practice the elements of life in a democracy.

The importance of schools' serving this purpose was underscored by Peter Levine in "Learning and Democracy: Civic Education," an essay in the fall 2006 issue of the *Kettering Review*.[4] Adults are more likely to live democracy, Levine noted, if they experience its attributes as children—regardless of their exposure as adults. At the same time, seeing their parents and other adults engaged in the schools reinforces children's sense of community, their desire to become engaged citizens, and their sense of self-worth—including their sense of the importance of their education.

The public schools are the ideal vehicle for teaching about democracy. For one thing, their commitment to fair play, justice, equality, civic engagement, and the public good is not tempered by any specific religious, social, or economic mission. Further, because they admit all students, the public schools can offer students an opportunity to experience democracy as an interaction with a diverse, inclusive student body—not just students of one particular group or socioeconomic class.

When the public schools cease to play a leading role in preparing students to live in civil society—or when the public ceases to see the schools performing that function—the role of public education itself is diminished. At the present time some politicians and citizen groups are promoting other means of education, such as private school vouchers and cyberschools. These efforts may serve some individuals, but they are not designed to serve all students—nor, necessarily, to foster democratic principles, provide accountability to the broader community, or serve the larger public interest. It has never been more important for citizens to get involved in the public schools and to demand that civic participation become a meaningful component of their children's education.

A Case in Point

We claim that community engagement can strengthen public education and invigorate our democracy. It would be fair to ask, "What might success look like in practice?" To answer that question, we turn to the imaginary

Springvale school district, which enrolls 7,500 students in a community of 30,000 people. In 2002 the school board saw some trends emerging that were causing tensions across the school system.

On the east side of town, more students were moving in from lower-income backgrounds—including children from Central America with limited English speaking and academic proficiency. Many of their parents were concerned that their children were not learning the basics and ultimately were at risk of dropping out. Despite those concerns, some parents felt uncomfortable even coming to school to meet with teachers to discuss the education program or their own child's progress.

On the wealthier west side of town, parents were concerned that their children were not being offered adequate honors and Advanced Placement (AP) courses. Further, at the three schools enrolling students from both sides of town, there was growing concern from west-side parents that the overall climate of their school was becoming less focused on academic achievement because of increasing enrollments from the east side. Some parents were talking about redrawing attendance lines or sending their children to private school.

Meanwhile, business leaders were concerned that a school board study calling for additional programming to be phased in over several years would result in property tax increases that could limit local consumer spending. They began running an ad campaign, with a special appeal to the 75 percent of households with no children in school, criticizing the schools and the increased taxes. The school and tax issues spilled over into debates before the zoning board and town council over where to locate low-income housing and whether to offer tax reductions to attract businesses requiring higher-skilled and higher-income workers.

In viewing the situation, the school board saw a school community and town becoming more divided about their goals and less willing to address common interests. If the school board quietly voted on a staff proposal to phase in funding to meet the need for additional programming, not only would the disaffection among parents and taxpayers be likely to grow, but the energy needed to make things happen simply would not materialize.

The school board determined that it needed a plan to go to the public—not to sell a specific solution but to involve constituents in setting a vision for the school system and to participate in a process to identify needs and provide input into program proposals and measures of progress. The school board would also involve constituents in a process of reflecting on their own role in supporting the education vision they helped to create.

The process started with a series of town meetings in which individuals presented their aspirations and concerns for their children's future, including their beliefs about what the schools should do to prepare their children, their appraisal of the current instructional program, and their concerns over the climate in the schools. Based on what was said, several focus groups involving parents and the general public were convened to gain a deeper understanding of the community's education goals, its perceptions of the needs, and what citizens would be willing to do to work with their children or the schools in general.

With this public input, a broadly based advisory group of concerned citizens and civic leaders was established to work with school officials to develop their vision and expectations for the school system. They also examined the challenges they faced and reflected on their own role in achieving success. This effort included several representatives from a group of business leaders—including the publisher of the local paper and the owner of the local radio station—who, at the school board's request, met monthly to identify their goals for the school system in relation to the economic growth that they envisioned for the community at large. The school board then conducted a series of workshops to discuss the community's goals and expectations and developed a plan of action that the school system, including the board itself, would be accountable for achieving each year through a community review process.

The plan of action called for educating the "whole child" by providing all students with a wide range of courses, including music and art, as well as character development and values. Some of the measures of success were tied to the reading levels among lower-achieving students, two- and four-year college acceptance rates, AP course taking, reduction in student fighting, and enrollments in science and foreign languages.

To achieve these goals, additional programming, including summer school, would be made available for lower-achieving students and English language learners. At the same time, science offerings and Advanced Placement courses would be expanded. With these new programs and adequate parent and community participation, citizens hoped that some of the long-standing divisions would be mended and the antipathy toward the schools—including those schools serving a diverse enrollment—would be replaced by widespread enthusiasm and support.

Indeed, civic, religious, and business leaders increasingly came to value the goals developed for the schools and take ownership of them. They developed a public campaign encouraging parents who worked for them (or belonged to their organization) to support their children's studies. They also helped sponsor mentoring programs for volunteers to tutor students whose parents could not offer them the support they needed. Several employers provided flexibility to enable their employees to attend teacher conferences during work hours.

The local media covered the process. For example, the radio station ran public service announcements to promote the town meetings and re-inforce parent participation. It also conducted a series of call-in programs with representatives of the school system and the participating groups to discuss the challenges and goals of the school system. Business leaders formed a foundation to strengthen the system's career awareness program and to help parents with limited education to become better teachers of their children.

Leaders from the school board, the business community, and several civic organizations met with the town council to explain their action plan and to show widespread community support for it. As a result, the council amended the town's economic development plan to promote the community's com-mitment to the schools as a means of attracting business.

For each of the next four years, the school board and community worked together to evaluate the goals, the progress made, and satisfaction with their participation. During the intervening school board election, an informed community voted for candidates on the basis of how they would address the larger issues involving the direction of the schools. But Springvale's success with community engagement in local government was to face a new challenge from the federal and state levels.

Specifically, in 2002, the No Child Left Behind Act (NCLB) estab-lished a federal framework to hold schools accountable for students' scoring "proficient" on their state's reading and math tests. Accountability would extend to include the performance of specific groups of students, such as those living in poverty or those who were limited in their English speak-ing ability.

Although parents and school officials were satisfied with the progress being made by immigrant students at Springvale's two middle schools, not enough of those students were able to meet NCLB's proficiency requirement—es-pecially given the influx of new students over the previous three years. As a result, there was concern that the state might eventually take over these schools or require that they be totally restaffed—despite the public's support for the principals and their confidence in the teachers. For the 2006–2007 school year, school officials proposed to double the amount of class time that lower-achieving students would spend on reading and preparation for state tests—while reducing their instructional time for social studies and canceling their participation in music and art. To pay for after-school tutoring, plans to expand the honors and AP program would be canceled at all schools.

Initially, the community asked: Were the schools failing? Was the curriculum being narrowed? Was the district abandoning its mission of educating the whole child? The media picked up on these issues, and the school board began to see a renewal of the old tensions. Consequently, the school board decided to hold a series of forums to discuss these developments.

Because the community was so involved in the schools, it quickly became clear that the federal and state levels had a different set of goals than the ones they had developed and to which they were committed. They felt that NCLB was constructively challenging them to rethink the expectations they held for their children's education by requiring them to consider the issues in a context beyond their local area. However, they also felt that the federal and state officials who were implementing the federal law—and who never set foot in Springvale—were forcing their school system to move in the wrong direction. Moreover, they claimed, the federal officials did not create this program with the real-world facts of the Springvale school system in mind.

Recognizing that their state and federal lawmakers had only one vote, Springvale's community and school leaders nevertheless invited them to a town meeting to show how NCLB was failing to serve their community. As a result of that meeting, the lawmakers in attendance recommended to the congressional education committees then in the process of reauthorizing the law, that Springvale's plan be accommodated.

While not all communities were as broadly engaged in their schools as Springvale, many did become more involved when the federal program identified their schools as falling short. They too determined how best to make the educational improvements they felt were needed and to challenge their state and federal lawmakers when they felt the program was not representing their goals or reflecting the judgment of their schools' leaders.

Across the country, members of Congress were hearing from a broad range of local constituents about the same concerns that the citizens of Springvale expressed. Through these locally based conversations they recognized that, in passing the law, they had become disconnected from their constituents in establishing this national education program. In reauthorizing NCLB, Congress would address the local concerns raised with the law.

In this scenario we saw how citizens and local groups came together to advance the common good. By being active participants—rather than spectators—in democracy, Springvale's citizens were able to play a role in shaping their community and the decision making of their local government. They heard from individuals with different goals and priorities for their children. They saw the importance of achieving accommodation and consensus in building support for the action needed to advance their own interest and that of the larger community. Springvale's citizens were better informed on the issues when they went to vote for the school board candidates to lead their school system. They also were able to bring their elected officials from all three levels of government in sync with their concerns, priorities, and solutions and achieve a representative voice in policy decisions.

The Power of the Public

Public education and democracy are linchpins of our free society. How well they thrive and support each other depends largely on the civic intelligence of community members and their involvement in civic life—including their involvement in the local schools. Clearly, the public schools have a vital role to play in society. That role is enhanced when members of the community see the contribution that education makes to furthering democracy through the lens of their own firsthand experience of engagement.

The schools' role in cultivating civic intelligence is enhanced when they consciously teach the lessons of democracy and expect students to engage in its practice. Community service, for example, can teach students to value the larger public interest. By preparing students for lifelong success, the public schools hold the future in trust. To fulfill that trust, they must pass on to the next generation the values of a free, egalitarian society.

Only by inviting the community to help answer the big questions about what counts can the public schools give their constituents the kind of education they want for their children. When school boards and other school leaders engage the power of the public, the schools and the schoolchildren are enriched by the community's knowledge, resources, and energy. When they engage their community, the institutions of both public education and representative democracy are strengthened. At that point, school leaders are truly governing on a public scale, and the schools are truly the public's schools.

Notes

1. National School Boards Association/Zogby International Poll, April 2003. See also Lowell C. Rose and Alec M. Gallup, "The 38th Annual Phi Delta Kappa/Gallup Poll of the Public's Attitudes toward the Public Schools," *Phi Delta Kappan* 88, no. 1 (September 2006): 41–56.

2. Katheryn W. Gemberling, Carl W. Smith, and Joseph S. Villani, *The Key Work of School Boards Guidebook* (Alexandria, Va.: National School Boards Association, 2000).

3. Michael A. Resnick, *Communities Count: A School Board Guide to Public Engagement* (Alexandria, Va.: National School Boards Association, 2000).

4. Peter Levine, "Learning and Democracy: Civic Education," *Kettering Review* 24, no. 3 (Fall 2006): 32–42.

Chapter 10

Journalism, Schooling, and the Public Good

Richard W. Clark and Clifford G. Rowe

The fundamentals of democracy that serve as a base for this country's governance and social order have not changed for more than two hundred years. Central among these is the premise that democracy requires the enlightened participation of its citizens. While the basic principles for our system of government remain constant, changes in the world have profoundly affected the ability of citizens to participate in an enlightened fashion—to acquire sound information about the most pressing issues of the day and to take intelligent, concerted action to solve the problems of our public life.

Our world presents us with grave challenges. Globally, there are ongoing political and economic realignments, environmental threats, religious disputes, and armed conflicts. In this country, the gap between the rich and the poor is growing. We are becoming increasingly diverse, and individuals and groups seem increasingly polarized about religious, political, and social issues. Shouting at one another seems to be obscuring other forms of interaction. At the same time there are new and highly complex technologies available for communicating. There is truly an explosion of available sources of information about all these changes and challenges facing society.

In these times citizens of a democracy require an ever-expanding knowledge base, and they need to be able to make up-to-date observations of the world around them. As important as their initial education is, they cannot expect to go to school as children, learn the "correct answers," and then function for the remainder of their lives with a static information base. Furthermore, they need more than an abundance of information. They need to be able to analyze the information coming their way, to sort useless and/or dangerous information from that which is potentially constructive. They also need to learn to engage in conversations that lead to agreement regarding how to act on the multitude of issues facing the nation in such a way that the common good is served.

Journalism Today and in the Future

Because citizens rely on the media for much of the information they use in making decisions in a democratic society, it is important to understand the present state of journalism. The nation's news media are in flux, to phrase it as neutrally as possible. There is speculation over the fate of "traditional" or "mainstream" media, as they are routinely labeled. We can look at these as the remnants of our parents' media—newspapers, magazines, radio, and network television, predominantly. Their demise has been documented and denied, both their deaths and their longevity foreseen, and their diminished or expanded roles in self-governance anticipated accordingly.

This situation is not entirely new. One of this chapter's authors remembers hearing a teacher who was coordinating a remedial writing workshop tell the assembled junior college applicants who had been denied admission to the school that it was unfortunate that they had been born when they were. They were the last generation of young people who would have to learn to write, she said; textual communication was on its way out. This was in the mid-1960s, when television was emerging as the exciting new kid on the media block. Her prediction was based on a logical interpretation of what was happening, at least to some degree. Hand-in-hand came the even bolder pronouncement that the print media were a disappearing breed.

Forty years later, the demand for skilled readers and writers prevails, and print media, while working with new formats and delivery systems, continue to claim influence and revenue that, depending on the day and the analyst, put them in the front ranks of societal importance—or somewhere not too far behind.

Whatever forms journalism takes in the future, its educative function in a democratic society remains constant. Our democracy provides schools to help educate the young, but schools are not the only source of education for the young and certainly not the only source for the continuing enlightenment of the people. The health of our democracy depends on the ability of all of our educative social institutions to perform the job of enlightening citizens. In chapter 2 of this book, Alan Wood makes these points clear with the following comment (see p. 43):

> For human society to succeed, it first needs to be open to whatever information is relevant to its health and survival. Second, that information has to be accurate. Third, it must be communicated without interference. Fourth, it has to be understood. Fifth, it needs to be acted upon effectively, that is, by educated and responsible citizens and by wise leaders. Without freedom of speech, the various parts of society cannot respond to challenges effectively because they have been denied the knowledge and information they need to function. Without education, the information cannot be fully understood. Without democracy, a society lacks the freedom to act in its own best interests. Without a willingness to accept moral responsibility by an educated citizenry, a society cannot achieve synergy among the parts.

We believe strongly that for all five of the needs that Wood mentions to be satisfied the various forms of mass media must join with the schools as continually renewing vehicles of learning. We believe that, just as it is important to understand the problems of schools and to address how renewal should be occurring in them, it is important to understand the problems facing the media as they seek to fulfill their educative role, and to consider the actions journalists must take to renew their practice. Moreover, we will attempt to demonstrate that, in spite of the many challenges facing today's media, the roots of promising renewal are present in certain journalistic practices and, if nourished, these practices can play a big role in securing a healthy future for our democracy.

In order to describe the educative role of the media more completely, we turn next to consideration of each of the five requirements that Wood identified for a democratic society to succeed.

Ample Information

Bill Kovach, former editor and current chair of the Committee of Concerned Journalists, and Tom Rosenstiel, director of the Project for Excellence in Journalism, identify journalists' responsibility for disseminating information in their book, *The Elements of Journalism: What Newspeople Should Know and the Public Should Expect.* They assert that "the primary purpose of journalism is to provide citizens with the information they need to be free and self-governing."[1]

The overwhelming majority of contemporary journalists who contribute to the nation's news media would likely agree with that statement of purpose. Journalists often speak in those terms, for example, as they gather at conventions of their colleagues, as they speak to their readers, viewers, and listeners in editorials and broadcast commentary, and as they lobby for legislative and judicial endorsement. In spite of the idealism represented by this point of view, many who are responsible for mainstream publications and broadcasts demonstrate by their actions that they see the main purpose of journalism to be making money for those who own the media.

While there is general acceptance of Kovach and Rosenstiel's purpose statement, an increasing number of journalists question whether the purpose of producing informed citizens is being fulfilled and whether there might not be better ways of doing it than present media practices. Discussions of these better ways tend to focus on the interaction—or lack thereof—between citizens and the media and between the media and other institutions, such as government, business, and schools.

Those who see serious flaws in the way media meet their obligations to give the public all the information it needs put the blame on a range of causes, from a need to redefine news as necessarily involving an emphasis on conflict to a need by media producers to put corporate profitability ahead of journalistic quality.

Accurate Information

To realize the vision of a better-informed democratic society, journalism worthy of its mandate in such a society also must adhere to principles of accuracy and fairness. This is an instance in which the role of the schools and the role of journalists become joined. Responsible educators model such principles in their own communication, teach future citizens the rewards and challenges of accurate communications, and teach all students to be discriminating readers, viewers, and listeners.

Election campaigns, rife with claims and counterclaims, are newsworthy events in a democracy. They are also too often characterized by inaccurate reporting. In the rush to cover events, journalists sometimes make mistakes. During the 2000 presidential campaign, students at Concord High School in New Hampshire demonstrated the potential power of good instruction in media literacy. After Vice President Al Gore addressed their school, the students in Joanne McGlynn's English class were dismayed to see the inaccuracies in reports published about Gore's remarks. When major newspapers such as the *New York Times* and the *Washington Post* and network television shows reported that Gore had given a speech at their high school taking credit for having discovered the Love Canal, the New Hampshire students demanded and obtained retractions. Their further study of the journalists' tendency to report hearing what they expected to hear has been the subject of continuing discussion in such publications as *Brill's Content* and on WBEZ Chicago's *This American Life*.[2] There need to be more exemplary instances such as this one.

Teachers should be developing in students an expectation that they will find in print and broadcast journalism adherence to basic principles such as truth (accuracy), humaneness, justice (fairness), stewardship, and freedom. These are not theoretical flimflam, but practical concerns for how journalists should collectively and individually do their jobs. They are standards of professional performance for journalists that all citizens should learn to apply.

Universities, which are often engaged in debates regarding the nature of the general education experience for all students, also need to consider the importance of developing a critical approach to the media. If critical analysis is applied only to historical passages or allowed only for faculty, there is little reason to believe that college graduates will be much more able consumers of the news media than their peers who are not college educated.

Meanwhile, accuracy and fairness continue to be essential standards for journalists. Numerous polls have demonstrated that the public doubts the accuracy of media reports.[3] Round-the-clock coverage of news on cable channels and twenty-four-hour-a-day posting of news on Web sites by newspaper and broadcast stations seem to be leading to even more problems of accuracy, as media outlets compete to see who can break the news first. (This is true even if what passes as news is no more significant than the latest gossip about the death of a *Playboy* playmate of the year or "breaking news" regarding the schooling of a potential presidential candidate discovered and reported two years prior to the election.) Candidates are declared winners in elections, and then more complete information indicates they are not. Death tolls are exaggerated or downplayed based on erroneous early information about disasters. Few who watched, riveted, to the unfolding scene at the 2006 Sago mine disaster in West Virginia will forget the look of absolute horror on the television reporter's face when he learned that his reports that a number of the miners had been found alive were wrong and that rather than numerous survivors in relatively good condition, there was only one, and he was in critical condition.

Freely Expressed Information

Accuracy in reporting information is not enough. Journalists must be free to report all the news and to offer opinions regarding the issues of the day. Shortly after the destruction of the World Trade Center on 9/11, the publisher of the *Sacramento Bee* was invited to give a graduation speech at a local university. When she suggested that we need to be concerned about protecting freedoms such as those guaranteed under the First Amendment to the Constitution, some students and adults in the audience made so much noise in opposition that she was unable to complete her remarks.[4] Reports in the campus press and city newspaper of the ensuing dialogue revealed that many believed that the students and adults who disrupted the speech were in the right and the publisher was wrong.

In voicing this viewpoint, these Californians seemed to share the opinion of many, if not the majority, of their contemporaries throughout the nation. In a 1999 survey "53 percent of Americans said they believed the press has too much freedom."[5] More recently, the *Chicago Tribune* reported results of a national poll that "found that five or six of every 10 Americans 'would embrace government controls of some kind on free speech, especially if it is found unpatriotic.'"[6]

Such views are inconsistent with conditions necessary to a healthy democratic society. While Americans may know that the First Amendment to the United States Constitution guarantees freedom of the press, they may not be aware that this freedom is also one of the fundamental rights agreed on by the founders of the United Nations in 1948: "Everyone has the right to freedom of opinion and expression; this right includes freedom to hold opinions without interference and to seek, receive and impart information and ideas through any media and regardless of frontiers."[7] Statements such as this one reflect widespread recognition that the freedom we want and need for individuals and for effective democratic governance depends on broad protection of freedom of expression.

As Bill Moyers has written, "I am reminded of the answer the veteran journalist Richard Reeves gave when asked by a college student to define 'real news.' 'Real news,' said Richard Reeves, 'is the news you and I need to keep our freedoms.' I am reminded of the line from the news photographer in Tom Stoppard's play *Night and Day*: 'People do terrible things to each other, but it's worse in places where everybody is kept in the dark.'"[8]

Information providers are currently pursuing two contradictory courses. On the one hand thousands of individual bloggers and special-interest advocates provide more independent voices. Unfortunately, at the same time, traditional media are being wrapped into mergers that leave large corporations in control of more and more media content. The consequent increase in reporting that is beholden to corporate interests threatens the independence of inquiry essential for a free press to meet its responsibilities to society. Continuation of this trend poses a threat to the nation of a loss of authoritative, professional, and ethical journalistic practices.

University of Washington president Mark Emmert spoke to the connection between a free press and the maintenance of an enlightened, well-educated citizenry:

> Think about young people coming to a university. Young people who have seen only single points of view in the media, who have been fed only cultural perspectives that are about as rich as fast food—if they have never heard a free and open debate of ideas—what kind of students are they going to be? What is the probability that they are going to challenge views and opinions in the classroom? What is the probability that they are going to be open to the diverse opinions that they are going to hear in the university? What's the probability that they, themselves, are going to be creative and invent new ideas going forward?
>
> I have had the opportunity to go to universities in nations where homogenized opinions are, in fact, the only opinions that go forward. You can find students there who are very good at math. You can find students who are very good at reciting the scientific facts of the day. But you will not find students who are creative. You will not find students who are pushing forward new scientific borders. You will not find students who want to debate issues with their classmates, let alone with their faculty. In short, you will not find the makings of democracy in those places.
>
> The free flow of ideas, the diversity of opinions, the capacity to hear ideas locally and nationally, are absolutely critical to the educational enterprise.[9]

Understood Information

Ample, accurate, freely expressed information and opinion are of little value unless the audience understands them. Two things are necessary for this understanding to occur:

1. The journalist needs to be knowledgeable and to possess the skill of translating his or her knowledge into language that is understandable to the audience.
2. The audience member needs to be broadly educated and have the capacity to engage in critical thought concerning the material.

Knowledgeable Journalists. A knowledgeable journalist must be well educated. Not surprisingly, there are debates about whether people preparing to be journalists should focus on professional studies emphasizing technique and process or on academic studies. As is the case with teacher preparation (the other profession that has a responsibility to communicate the content of the disciplines, not just develop a theoretical or procedural appreciation of them), there are those who argue that journalism schools' emphasis on process and theory are misplaced. Jonathan Last, writing in the *Wall Street Journal,* claims that "instead of educating future journalists on the nuts and bolts of journalism—because let's be honest, it isn't rocket science or even carpentry—it would make more sense simply to teach them things. Facts, it turns out, are useful."[10]

Many of those who have been the subject of an ill-informed reporter's story—whether about education, politics, economics, or some other important field—would probably agree with Last's argument. But others would point out that it is unlikely that any journalist can be so well educated that he or she is fully informed about all topics that are apt to be assigned. What can be hoped for, and is not always the case, is that the reporter on a particular beat will be at least knowledgeable enough to know whom to talk with and how to sort sense from nonsense concerning the topic. The broadcast industry has been particularly delinquent in ensuring that its reporters are adequately informed on the subjects about which they are asked to report, and budget limitations at print media outlets have left newsrooms without enough knowledgeable reporters.

Knowledgeable Audience Members. Unfortunately, even if a print or broadcast journalist provides a well-written and knowledgeable story, there is still no guarantee that it will be understood by even the majority of the audience. Some of this can be traced directly to failures within the educational system.

If, for example, students do not learn basic scientific concepts, have no understanding of probability theory, or are unable to apply fundamental principles of logic to their analysis of information, it will be difficult if not impossible for a journalist to write a story about global warming that is well understood by the audience. Some problems of understanding can also be traced to the powerful influence of cultural beliefs that shape audience members' interpretation of a story. For example, those whose value systems cause them to distrust science also find it difficult to understand accurately written stories on global warming.

Action Growing Out of Information

An abundance of accurate information freely disseminated and fully comprehended is of little importance unless enlightened actions follow from it. Journalists and educators face a common question in this regard: To what extent is action the journalist's or educator's responsibility rather than the student's or media consumer's? If students score poorly on a test, was it the teacher's fault? If voters cast their ballots for a candidate who is a convicted felon (or, as has been the case more than once, a dead person), is it the fault of the voters or of the media for having failed to communicate effectively?

A teacher might purport to teach about how the federal government is supposed to function but disavow responsibility for students who fail to engage in the political process. This is an example of teachers who say that it is their responsibility to present the information and the students' responsibility to learn it. Similarly a journalist might report critics' complaints about mismanagement in a school district and deny responsibility for efforts in the community to "throw the rascals out" by claiming that he or she was simply reporting what others were saying. This serves as an example of journalists who claim that their responsibility is to report the news, but what is done as a result is up to the reader, viewer, or listener. In such instances, professionals who refuse to accept a significant responsibility for the actions that stem from their work fail to serve the interests of a democratic society. Those who are sources of our information need to model responsibility for the consequences of the understandings they generate if we are to expect responsible behavior from the citizenry at large.

These then are the challenges facing journalism as an ally of schools in ensuring the presence of an enlightened citizenry. We turn next to an examination of some trends in the field that we believe offer hope for the future.

Hope for the Future Found in the Practices of Today

For eight years the Institute for Educational Inquiry in Seattle engaged in dialogue with educators and journalists about the state of journalism and its role as a contributor to a well-educated citizenry, because education and journalism seem to offer the best hope of jump-starting our sputtering democracy. One of the most rewarding results of this effort was the discovery of how many talented, ambitious, motivated professionals there are in both camps, eager for the opportunity to enlist in this campaign. From our interactions with them, we have learned about the state of journalism today and found in their enthusiasm and commitment hope for the future.

Public Journalism

During recent years journalists and others have been actively engaged in discussing how to strengthen the contributions of journalism to an enlightened citizenry. Out of these discussions have come experiments with "public" or "civic" journalism and most recently "citizen journalism." These forms, in one way or another, emphasize closer involvement with the public in all stages of producing news. They encourage more context for news stories rather than presenting them as isolated incidents. And they often take the lead in exploring how to combine newspapers, Internet news sources, and television and radio broadcasts as a means of telling the entire story to a broad audience.

This approach openly calls for the news media to emphasize journalism that not only will help citizens become more informed and active in community decision making but will encourage them to pursue such a role. It invites readers, viewers, and listeners not only to pay attention to current issues but to help define those issues and their outcomes.

An example of such an undertaking is A Starting Point, a project introduced on June 4, 2006, by the *News Tribune* in Tacoma, Washington.[11] The newspaper had invited nine leaders from Tacoma's East Side, "an area coping with poverty, scarce jobs, language barriers and gang violence," to meet and discuss what could be done to restore the neighborhood. Included among the leaders were a high school principal and a teacher. The resulting report started on the front page and continued on two pages inside with excerpts of what the participants had said. The newspaper also put on its Web site a video and full transcript of the discussion and invited—and received—responses from readers. Prominently displayed in the newspaper package was a summary of "what can be done," where participants suggested actions "whose results could be measured." They called for involvement from the community, the city, businesses, schools, police, and families.

That is public journalism. Its proponents believe that such journalism results in news that more closely reflects the needs and desires of citizens. In the process, it is seen as reconnecting citizens, media, and society's processes of governance.

Jay Rosen, a prominent educator and advocate for public journalism, offers a simple formula for this kind of journalism: "Try to get people engaged, then step back when they do. Start where citizens start, but don't end where citizens end."[12] Critics of public journalism, on the other hand, see it as journalists' stepping outside the bounds of objectivity, of "making news" rather than reporting it. They have viewed it as ivory-tower idealism at best and an erosion of First Amendment freedoms at worst, since it invites "outsiders" into the news-making process.

But more media are experimenting with it, spurred in part by evidence of declining audiences for the so-called traditional or mainstream media and in part by the availability of new technology that enables them to present a more expansive and interactive news package.

A key point here is that the advent of public journalism provides an opportunity for those who see shortcomings in how our democratic institutions communicate (with each other and with citizens) to explore new ways of serving the public interest.

Peace Journalism

A lesser-known approach to contributing to the enlightenment of a society flies under the banner of peace journalism. British journalists Jake Lynch and Annabel McGoldrick credit professor Johan Galtung with providing the original peace journalism model. Lynch and McGoldrick offer the following definition: "Peace journalism is when editors and reporters make choices—of what stories to report and about how to report them—that create opportunities for society at large to consider and value non-violent responses to conflict."[13]

They explain that peace journalism involves insights from conflict analysis, suggests new considerations regarding the connections between journalists and their sources (connections that are much like those of participant observers in social science research), and builds on awareness of nonviolent alternatives to resolving conflicts. Speaking directly to the issue of ensuring that the audience understands journalists' work, Lynch and McGoldrick ask,

How does journalism shape the lives of people and nations? What are journalists responsible for? Is the meaning of a news story generated chiefly at the moment of production, or the moment of reception? Does the reporter load, as it were, a hypodermic syringe which is then injected into the consciousness of anyone reading, watching or listening? Or do the messages communicated by newspapers and programming depend on broader cultural conditioning, and its influence on the way they are interpreted? ...

[This book, *Peace Journalism,*] is unavoidably based on the proposition that public understanding of key issues depends, at least to some extent, on how they are reported.[14]

Peace journalism, like any sophisticated effort to understand and explain conflict, emphasizes context and considers multiple perspectives on issues (avoiding framing a conflict as "good guys" versus "bad guys"). In order to be accurate and useful, peace journalists are encouraged to "develop a critical self-awareness."[15]

Peace journalism is offered as an alternative to common approaches to reporting on wars. Understanding of conditions surrounding potentially or actually violent conflicts is important for the citizenry. Being able to report with an understanding of conflict analysis, providing the audience with context for stories, and accepting responsibility for the consequences of the story told are qualities desirable in all journalists. The notion of the journalist being critically self-aware is very similar to the expectation expressed throughout this book that educators be engaged in renewal processes.

Whether emergent theories of peace journalism will influence mainstream reporting on a broad range of important issues remains to be seen, but it offers hope for greater contributions to an enlightened citizenry than can be found in much of contemporary media.

Equity and Access

In 2005 the Institute for Educational Inquiry and the First Amendment Center cosponsored a roundtable in Washington, D.C., at which journalists and educators discussed what they had learned in eight years of talking and working together for the public good. In one of these sessions they talked about problems of access to classrooms by journalists and to newsrooms by educators. One administrator said she had solved the problem of access to her schools by television journalists: she refused to allow their presence. A television journalist responded that her station was receiving an increasing number of photos out of classrooms submitted by students using their cell phone cameras. While neither approach was likely to produce greater insight into the community's classrooms, the exchange did point out a computer-driven system for alerting those living in the region of Mount Rainier of volcanic action and potential mudflows. As a result of the malfunction, the system broadcasted an erroneous warning of volcanic activity on a low-power radio station. A woman, hearing the warning at home, used her cell phone to call a relative at work. Word of the pending "disaster" spread through the workplace and shortly into the general public, mostly through cell phone conversations and well ahead of the "regular" media.

School officials have experienced similar consequences from the presence of new technologies. Many reported having first learned of potential problems in their schools not through phone calls from angry parents, but through calls from news organizations that had received the information from angry parents or even from cell phone communications from students at the sites of the problems. To paraphrase an old song, communication channels are a-changin'.

Again, what is viewed by some as a frustration can also be seen as an opportunity. Do you have information you want to get out to the public? Report it, either through existing media or by creating your own media. A school district superintendent at the 2005 Washington, D.C., roundtable reported that his schools were producing and distributing their own television reports on two of their own channels. Also, school district Web sites are expanding their array of online messages far beyond the listing of bus schedules and school lunches to include their reports on school events and issues. As long as the source of such communication is transparent (unlike efforts by some governmental agencies to produce propaganda that masquerades as independent, objective reports), these messages can play an important role in educating the public.

Intriguing possibilities exist for traditional sources of information (such as schools) and traditional producers of news (such as newspapers and broadcast facilities) to collaborate in producing the best possible information product, whether as conventional journalism or something else. The technology exists to do this, but the ways in which to bring it to bear in an organized, accessible, and—yes—marketable product are still being tested. It is time for imaginative, bold ideas to emerge from journalists committed to the renewal of their profession.

Balance

The changes under way that are redefining news provide opportunities for new voices to be recognized and projected into the public arena. At its most optimistic, this could be viewed as a rebirth of the free-speech

significant fact about the flow of information in modern society: it
become more difficult for persons in positions of power to control ac
to information.

The ubiquitous computer is an obvious focal point in assessing the
pact of changes in this flow, but one can no longer stop there, as news
other information is transmitted and arrives on a rapidly expanding a
of electronic devices, none of which leave ink on your hands. Howe
they do put in the hands of citizens greater control of the informatic
their disposal, including what is commonly referred to as "news."

News no longer arrives just with the morning or evening paper, or
the five A.M., five P.M., or eleven P.M. news. It is more likely that it is g
to be there all the time and in the format in which people want it a
given moment.

This is why news organizations, whether print, broadcast, or electroni
gearing up for 24/7 operation, if they are not already there. While this n
that deadlines for reporting, packaging, and distributing the news are con
it also means that there can be greater flexibility in the way news is proces:
is not necessary to have all of the information right now. Journalists can p
some now and present more of it later, when they are able to find the cc
for a better, more complete story. In winter 2007 the *Washington Post*
a story about deteriorating conditions at Walter Reed Hospital.[16] Follc
reporting by media throughout the country revealed that the problems
much more widespread than the first report implied. Not only were wo
victims from Iraq and Afghanistan being treated in rundown facilitie
there were problems at military hospitals throughout the country, and ve
of past wars were complaining about the treatment they were receiving a
While the first story did not provide the entire picture, it opened up a
inquiry that was vitally important for the nation to pursue.

New technology allows this kind of in-depth coverage—it almo
mands it. What results from it will be determined, as always, by those
it. Will it be used to reveal flaws in the action of government offic
to obsess on strange behavior by celebrities? Will it be used to provi
kind of context that peace journalists advocate or to share shrill pa
rant? Will the technologies be joined in the best of public journali:
will the entertainment potential of "reality" television usurp more and
of broadcast time? How such questions are answered will go a long v
determining the extent to which we have a truly enlightened citize

As indicated earlier, those using new technologies need not be em
at news organizations. The means for getting information into the
arena is at the fingertips of all who have the electronic tools. Co
what happened early in spring 2006, when there was a malfunctic

metaphor (originally attributed to Oliver Wendell Holmes)—the "market-place of ideas." What some envision here is a greatly expanded arena for the exchange of information and ideas, an arena whose capacity is limited by neither publication space nor available air time. Theoretically, it is an unlimited space that could guarantee access for every point of view. For example, no school would be dependent on the approval of an editor or news director for access to the local newspaper or television station. Community members with hot issues would not have their contributions screened. The traditional role of the newsroom as the gatekeeper of information would be diminished, if not eliminated.

Should such a transformation take place? Some would argue that, with the sheer volume of information already being created and published on the Internet, there is a great and growing need for systems to organize material and guide consumers to and through it. Existing media are in a position to serve that function as they develop their own Web sites and invite the public to plug into them and interact with them. For one thing, these media are known by name and inherently bring a certain amount of credibility to the exchange.

One can foresee both positive and problematic consequences if the newsroom's role as gatekeeper were diminished or eliminated. Deborah Howell, ombudsperson for the *Washington Post* newspaper, touched on a possible positive benefit in her May 21, 2006, column, "Have You E-Mailed the *Post* Lately?" In it she points out that "reporters today get more daily feedback from readers than any journalists in history."[17] That feedback not only results in readers' having the opportunity to agree or disagree with journalists but also, as Howell reports, provides those journalists with story tips and may lead them to sources that they otherwise would not have uncovered.

Another possible result of reducing the mediating presence of editors and newsrooms is seen in the blogging phenomenon in which "plain folks" post whatever is on their minds. Some of it is magnificent; some of it is mundane. While those with more to say and more ability to say it may continue to have greater access to the hearts and minds of all of us, it seems obvious that more voices will be heard and become part of the democratic conversation. Will that ensure greater balance in the range of ideas and opinions? Not necessarily, but it should provide more opportunity for those who feel their side of the discussion is being ignored to at least make that point.

So while conventional forms of media serve as recognized sources of up-to-date information and opinion, and thus are natural collecting points for public discourse, under the new scheme of mass communication they should not be considered the only ones. Other collecting points—particularly in topic areas of vital importance to a democratic society such as education, the environment, or health care—could serve the same function. For instance, parents who are seeking a wide range of information on a topic such as charter schools, academic testing, or the education of teachers should be able to go to a school district Web site for links to far-ranging expertise as well as suggestions on how to work for improvement in their own schools.

Reminding ourselves once again of the fundamental need for citizen awareness and knowledge in a self-governing society, we can applaud the diverse world of information coming to life through the Internet. It opens up possibilities of an entirely new way of thinking about how the public is enlightened. But we also have to recognize the shortcomings and frustrations that come with the free-for-all of unorganized dialogue. Many individuals in the news media recognize the difficulty of bringing accepted standards and principles of responsible journalism into this new marketplace. But there are also many outside the media with the same standards and principles; the solution, once more, may lie in the willingness of institutions, public and private, to join forces for the greater benefit of the public.[18]

Control and Accountability

All citizens have a stake in the conduct of their news media, and they are ultimately responsible for ensuring media accountability. That is a big responsibility, and there is evidence that many Americans are losing interest in taking on that burden, which is, in the final analysis, the burden of citizenship. As noted previously, both educators and journalists can help increase civic understanding through expanded and vigorous efforts at media literacy. The media also need to be more transparent in their work—they must let the public look in on the practices of journalism and the obligations that go along with it. Fortunately, there is evidence that more news organizations are experimenting with ways of doing that. Those on the outside who benefit from that transparency can make its presence even more likely by taking advantage of it. For example, one long-standing principle of responsible journalism has been that of correcting errors and accepting criticism and complaints from the public. That will be more likely to happen if those in the public, including institutions such as schools, insist on such openness. At the same time, students, the next wave of citizens, should be learning in advance how to use and to challenge the media.

One way that lesson is learned and advanced is through vigorous, well-coached student media (for example, newspapers and webcasts). These venues permit students to learn responsibility to their respective communities and experience at the same time the processes of accountability. Exemplary schools recognize that providing such experiences for students enables them to fulfill their obligation to fortify our democracy. Responsible professional news media are eager to assist the schools in maintaining an environment for such student endeavors.

Finally, many media show a willingness to be more responsive to public requests for accountability, whether through management and staff efforts to provide access to newsrooms or through external mechanisms, such as news councils, citizen advisory bodies, or media critics. Journalists should take the lead in putting such systems in place, and educators should be among those eager to employ them and to educate others in their use.

Money and Resources

In spite of promising trends, obtaining the necessary resources is a primary concern of those attempting to meet their obligations as a free press in a complex, multifaceted society. It is a concern not only for the journalists functioning at the "street level" but also for many editors, publishers, and other media owners at the top. As noted above, while journalism in the United States is a vital player in the democratic process, it is also a business. While many in the media and their observers do not see the two functions as being in opposition, in recent years there has been increased criticism of the trimming of budgets and resources in newsrooms in the name of greater profitability in the corporate offices.

This trend should worry us. The media are supposed to be serving us as we attempt to govern ourselves. Citizens, including educators, should insist on no less than quality journalism in their dealings with the media. They also should realize that good journalism results in part from opportunities to obtain accurate, complete information from reliable sources—and often under tight time constraints. Efforts should be made by those on both sides of the citizen/media equation to provide and maintain reliable and effective channels for the exchange of such information.

The reporter is one of the keys to ensuring effective communication channels. For example, not only should those covering schools be skilled reporters and writers (as should any journalist), but they should also be knowledgeable about the history of schooling and its role in U.S. society. Ideally they should be aware of the differences between education and schooling and comprehend that they share with people who work in schools a responsibility to educate. They should keep up not only with trends in school management, particularly finance, but also with trends in teaching and with the latest developments in relation to underlying questions of equity, governance, and purpose for our educational systems.

Obviously, a newsroom that does not have a reporter assigned on a regular basis to the education beat is unlikely to meet that criterion. Yet even though frequent surveys show that news on education is at the top of the list of topics of interest to the public, there is no guarantee that any given news organization will have such a reporter on staff on a regular basis, particularly in the case of broadcast newsrooms. In our experience, we have found that even those who have a full-time education writer often are reluctant to provide the time and other resources necessary for that reporter to keep current on major educational issues. Nevertheless, educators can help keep channels for the reporting of education effective by routinely making available the human sources and relevant information that reporters need in order to explain clearly and in a timely fashion what is going on in the schools.

When the needs of a democratic society are taken into account, politics and national security—at least the conflicts associated with political ballots and ongoing warfare—rightly receive much attention from the media. But similar concerns to those mentioned regarding education can be raised for other vital areas—such as religion, environment, science, transportation, economic conditions, and health. Coverage on these topics is often spotty, too often in the hands of poorly informed reporters, and limited to sensational or conflict-laden stories.

Media independence is vital to a free press. This independence requires that journalists never be beholden to any party other than the public interest. But that does not mean reporters should fail to explore ways to work closely with people who have specialized knowledge or special commitments if doing so is of benefit to the public good. Fortunately, our experience with journalist fellows from around the country has convinced us that there are many excellent reporters who, with the right support, can be well-informed contributors to the continuing renewal of our media.

Media as Educational Forces in Society

As we seek to describe what needs to be done to approach the challenges of creating and maintaining an enlightened society, much of the inspiration for this quest comes from the writing of those seeking renewal in education as well as those who are advocating changes in journalism. An obvious example would be that of John Goodlad, who more than twenty years ago in his book *A Place Called School* outlined goals for schools in developing citizen participation. Schools, he said, should aid students to:

- Develop historical perspective.
- Develop knowledge of the basic workings of the government.
- Develop a willingness to participate in the political life of the nation and the community.
- Develop a commitment to the values of liberty, government by consent of the governed, representational government, and one's responsibility for the welfare of all.
- Develop an understanding of the interrelationships among complex organizations and agencies in a modern society, and learn to act in accordance with it.
- Exercise the democratic right to dissent in accordance with personal conscience.
- Develop economic and consumer skills necessary for making informed choices that enhance one's quality of life.
- Develop an understanding of the basic interdependence of the biological and physical resources of the environment.
- Develop the ability to act in light of this understanding of interdependence.[19]

Goodlad might just as well have been outlining educational objectives for the media in a free society. As we said at the outset, and as many have argued in this book, schools play an important role in providing the initial education of the young, but education for a democratic society does not end with schooling. Citizens must continue to learn. Of the various educational forces in a democracy, none is more powerful than the mass media. Inevitably they will shape the views that are held by the people with regard to their government and the critical issues of the day. Senator Barack Obama made this clear in his *New York Times* best seller, *The Audacity of Hope*:

> Simple math tells the tale. In the thirty-nine town hall meetings I held during my first year in office, turnout at each meeting averaged four to five hundred people, which means that I was able to meet with maybe fifteen to twenty thousand people. Should I sustain this pace for the remainder of my term, I will have had direct, personal contact with maybe ninety-five

to one hundred thousand of my constituents by the time Election Day rolls around.

In contrast, a three-minute story on the lowest-rated local news broadcast in the Chicago media market may reach two hundred thousand people. In other words, I—like every politician at the federal level—am almost entirely dependent on the media to reach my constituents. It is the filter through which my votes are interpreted, my statements analyzed, my beliefs examined. For the broad public at least, I am who the media says I am. I say what they say I say. I become who they say I've become.[20]

Journalists can and should contribute to the accomplishment of educational goals such as those Goodlad described above. If they actively pursue that goal, then, as the world continues to change, they will contribute to an enlightened society. Journalists will have such an impact to the extent that they attend to the renewal of their profession. As we learn more about public journalism, see new developments such as peace journalism, observe the potential of new technologies for increasing equity and access to information, and recognize efforts to achieve balance in reporting, we are optimistic about the promise of journalism as a renewing enterprise that will continue to contribute to the enlightenment of participants in a democratic society. We hope that threats of monopolistic practices, misplaced financial greed by ownership, or failures by the schools to produce a critically literate public do not derail these positive trends. The political, scientific, philosophical, and ideological issues facing our democracy and the world are so important and complex that only an initially well-schooled citizenry continually enlightened by the best of journalistic practices can hope to deal with them.

Notes

1. Bill Kovach and Tom Rosenstiel, *The Elements of Journalism: What Newspeople Should Know and the Public Should Expect* (New York: Crown, 2001), 17.

2. Joanne McGlynn provided the authors and a group of Journalist Fellows from the Institute for Educational Inquiry with a firsthand account of her students' experiences in March 2000. Mike Pride, "Just One Word," *Brill's Content* (March 2000): 48–49; *This American Life* (WBEZ Chicago) provided additional commentary on the incident on January 28, 2000 (episode 151).

3. Robert J. Haiman, *Best Practices for Newspaper Journalists* (Arlington, Va.: Freedom Forum, n.d.), 9.

4. "President Comments on Commencement Ceremonies," December 17, 2001, http://www.csus.edu/news/121701commencements.htm.

5. Kenneth A. Paulson, "Fairness and the First Amendment," in Robert J. Haiman, *Best Practices for Newspaper Journalists* (Arlington, Va.: Freedom Forum, n.d.), 72.

6. Cited in Bill Moyers, "Media that Set Us Free," *YES! A Journal of Positive Futures* (Spring 2005): 5.

7. General Assembly of the United Nations, *Article 19, Universal Declaration of Human Rights,* adopted and proclaimed by the resolution 217 A (III) of December 10, 1948.

8. Moyers, "Media that Set Us Free," 16.

9. Mark Emmert, "Consolidation of Media Is Unhealthy for Education," *Seattle Times,* December 22, 2006. This op-ed by President Emmert appeared on the editorial pages of the *Times* after he offered a similar statement to a federal hearing regarding monopolistic practices in the media. He also later shared the statement electronically with the University of Washington community.

10. Jonathan V. Last, "Schools for Scribblers: Newspapers Dwindle, But Journalism Graduates Keep Coming," *Wall Street Journal,* May 19, 2006.

11. Sean Robinson, "A Starting Point," [Tacoma, Wash.] *News Tribune,* June 4, 2006, 1.

12. Jay Rosen, *What Are Journalists For?* (New Haven, Conn.: Yale University Press, 1999), 8.

13. Jake Lynch and Annabel McGoldrick, *Peace Journalism* (Stroud, U.K.: Hawthorn, 2005), 5.

14. Ibid., xix.

15. Ibid., xvi.

16. Dana Priest and Anne Hull, "Soldiers Face Neglect, Frustration at Army's Top Medical Facility," *Washington Post,* February 18, 2007, A1. This initial article identified online links and references to video. It was followed by numerous articles and editorials in the *Post* as well as follow-up reports by many other media outlets.

17. Deborah Howell, "Have You E-Mailed the *Post* Lately?" *Washington Post,* May 21, 2006, B6.

18. For more information about the blogging phenomenon, see Amanda Lenhart and Susanna Fox, *Bloggers: A Portrait of the Internet's New Storytellers,* Pew Internet & American Life Project, July 19, 2006.

19. John I. Goodlad, *A Place Called School* (1984; repr., New York: McGraw-Hill, 2004), 53.

20. Barack Obama, *The Audacity of Hope: Thoughts on Reclaiming the American Dream* (New York: Crown, 2006), 121.

Chapter 11

From Here to There:
What Really Matters

Roger Soder and John I. Goodlad

Part One by Roger Soder

This chapter begins with a memorandum from me to the head of a fictitious political consulting firm requesting a critique of the preceding ten chapters of this volume. The response from the head of the consulting firm analyzes the formulation of problems, solutions, and strategies and also comments on the rhetoric of the authors' presentations.

Much of what follows may be seen as critical and thus unsupportive of the basic objectives shared by my fellow chapter authors. But criticism can be seen as supportive. In the "Notice" to the second volume of *Democracy in America,* Alexis de Tocqueville warns that readers might be astonished that he addresses "severe words" to the societies that the democratic revolution has created. But, he says, "I shall respond simply that it is because

I was not an adversary of democracy that I wanted to be sincere with it. Men do not receive the truth from their enemies."[1] Or, following the old adage, friends don't flatter. And thus the critique offered here.

Memorandum

To: Creative Advertising and Political Consultants
         (Seattle and Florence)
From: Roger Soder

During our recent telephone conversation I indicated to you that I am representing authors of chapters in a forthcoming volume on renewing America, its democracy, and its schools. The authors, desirous of seeing their views of the world and their recommendations for action made real, have asked me to send you an advance copy of the manuscript, which is enclosed. I have highlighted portions of their analyses of problems and their approaches to solutions.

We seek your professional opinion here because we know that what we might take to be self-evident is not necessarily self-evident to others. We know that although the publication of the volume is a necessary first step toward renewing America, it surely is not a sufficient step. Much will have to be done to help persuade others that what is self-evident to us should be self-evident to them. Hardly an easy task, getting people's attention to begin with, and then getting them to see that what we have in mind is important not only to us but even more so to them. We know this, but we need insights into how we might transform that knowledge into a deeper understanding of just what is going to have to be done to get from here to there. Thus, what we need from you and your colleagues is an analysis of what the next steps might be, what it might take to achieve what is outlined in the chapters. We await with interest your analysis.

Memorandum

To: Roger Soder
From: R. Paulo, Head, Creative Advertising and Political Consultants
         (Seattle and Florence)
Re: Response to request for analysis

Thank you for the opportunity to comment on the problem statements and approaches to solutions in your forthcoming volume on renewing education and democracy in America. What you have here is interesting and challenging, to be sure, ranging from the macro and the global to the micro and the very immediate local. We have reviewed the volume with care, and I am pleased to share with you and your colleagues the results of our review.

I begin with the analysis of specific problem statements and approaches to solutions. It should be noted that we did not analyze all of the dozens of problems and solutions brought to the fore in the volume. We decided to deal with selected claims, ones that highlight the opportunities and challenges. Should you find our work satisfactory and wish to continue, we would of course deal with the whole. Following the analysis, I present some general comments.

Analysis of Selected Problem Statements and Approaches to Solutions

In providing this analysis, let me note that I am not denying the potential good aspects of what is being advocated in these chapters. The analysis of difficulties is provided to give us a prudent assessment and understanding of what will most likely have to be done in order to realize those good aspects. Let us turn, then, to the analysis. I begin with a discussion of four large-scale issues identified by chapter authors that bear on the basic character of the American people and its institutions.

The first problem we will deal with centers on perceptions that the American people are limited in their ability to engage in thoughtful democratic discourse and action. Goodlad (chapter 1, pp. 19–20) provides a summary of these perceptions:

> Nonetheless, even most of those who graduate from secondary schools are still early and limited in their apprenticeship into the social and political democracy of which they are a part. And there is little on the road of life lying ahead to ensure that the passage of time will move them beyond this apprenticeship. In general, the populace is, at best, well informed about a quite narrow range of the social, political, and economic issues with which the nation must continuously grapple. Most of us, in addressing the domains of human discourse and endeavor, are informed by the friends and colleagues with whom we associate daily, among whom none may be well informed in the rubrics of the ongoing conversation.
>
> In other words, we are much guided in what we store in our mental ecosystems by conventional wisdom, not the books and papers that arise out of serious inquiry into our habitat and behavior. A disturbingly high percentage of voters are so unclear about their own beliefs that on Election Day they are unable to sort out candidates on the ballot who appear to align with them from those who do not. The most cleverly scripted and presented television message wins the day.

The difficulties here are legion. If the great hordes of people actually are as limited and uninformed as opined here, there is little hope. If the people are so limited, so gullible, then how can they be smart enough to know how limited they are and how much they need in order to do what is wanted of them (that is, go to town hall meetings, read serious books, and take part in discussions in cafés)? On the other hand, if they are not that limited and gullible after all, then perhaps something can be done. But great care must be taken here. I know of no advertising campaign, no matter how well funded, that ever succeeded by implying that people were limited and suckers for the best television pitch put before the barely comprehending masses. If there is a way out of this difficulty, it probably lies somewhere with the strategy outlined by Alexander Pope:

> 'Tis not enough your Counsel still be true,
> Blunt truths more Mischief than nice Falsehoods do;
> Men must be taught as if you taught them not;
> And Things unknown propos'd as Things forgot.[2]

The second problem we will deal with relates to the one immediately above. It deals with the many agents actively seeking enculturation antithetical to democracy and is found in chapter 3 by Martin: "It would require volumes to document all the sources and the full content of the political education and miseducation occurring in the United States today. For now, it suffices to note that with young children being exposed to political miseducation at home and in the community and with mature men and women developing traits at work that run counter to democracy, education for democratic citizenship is best thought of as a lifelong process" (p. 54). Martin goes on to claim that miseducation and opposition to democracy begin at home and are reinforced by the "hidden curricula" of "government, religious institutions, corporations, the military, the Boy Scouts, and neighborhood gangs," all of which "inculcate belief in the sanctity of hierarchical structures and unquestioning obedience to authority" (p. 53).

The difficulty here is that we hardly know where to begin. There is hardly a societal institution, according to the assertion here, that is not on the wrong side of democracy and is in fact consciously aware that it is on the wrong side and proud to be so. If the assertion has any basis, then we might be better off fading into the shadows. Martin proposes an approach to a solution here: "We need to persuade the wide range of educational agents ... other than school, to acknowledge their status as educators and to agree that, like school, they therefore have an obligation to contribute to the making and maintaining of a democratic citizenry" (p. 60). But my colleagues and I fail to understand how these "educational agents" can begin to stand up against the formidable array of opponents posited here. To take on all of these institutions will require work on an impossibly large scale. As part of the advertising/political strategy, I suppose we could consider remolding some of these institutions, perhaps starting with the Boy Scouts. It will be much more difficult to remold the military (after all, even the volunteer colonial militias fighting the British had hierarchical structures) and religious institutions.

The third problem, related to the first two, deals with control over communication, as opined by Theobald (chapter 4, p. 67): "The vast majority of Americans are simply unaware of how precarious our circumstances have become. Once again, leaders of democracies, no less than kings and dictators, crave the control of information. Because of the corporate-controlled development of mass media, today's democratic leaders can exercise a degree of control nearly as complete as that of kings during the feudal era." Again, more difficulties: if the mass media are not to be controlled by corporations, then they are to be either not controlled at all or controlled by the state, I presume. Mass media left to their own devices will be bought and sold, of course, and will be back in the hands of conglomerates within days, assuming that we somehow wrested media out of their hands to begin with. But if the mass media are controlled by the state, then we are right back to square one, for what is the difference between control by a king or dictator and control by a state?

Theobald would have us circumvent this problem by apparently modest actions. "Create study groups composed of teachers, community members, administrators, and school board members. Read a book.... Make a bold step.... Declare independence from educational policy ill-suited for local circumstances.... We need schools that specifically target new ends for education. Create those schools, and economic and political reform will unfold in their wake" (p. 81). But it is difficult for my colleagues to see how these actions, however laudatory, will help deal with the problem he identifies.

The fourth problem is that we in America (and the world) are burdened with a serious anachronism and serious defects in how we think about the world, as illustrated by Wood (chapter 2, pp. 30–31): "The central ideology of our time—nationalism—and the central institution of our time—the nation-state—are inadequate to the task at hand. Both grew out of a highly competitive, bloody stage in European history that is long since past. We face the twenty-first century, in effect, with eighteenth-century tools." Wood goes on to claim that we must discover "the centrality of education not only to our national welfare but also, and far more profoundly, to our very humanity. To do that will require more than just a minor recalibration of our national priorities. It will require, to some degree, a fundamental rethinking of the intellectual assumptions of the modern world" (p. 31). Related here is the claim made by Theobald that "the great error of would-be political and economic reformers of the past century is that they made their attempts without recognizing the degree to which their chances of success hinged on educational effort" (p. 65).

The difficulties here are again legion. It is no small task to fundamentally rethink assumptions of transportation planning for a Seattle suburb, let alone the intellectual assumptions of the modern world. Wood may indeed be correct in his analysis. And his novel solution is of interest: "What we need now is a new statement of principle—a kind of Declaration of *Inter-dependence*—that realigns our national and global priorities to respond to our present array of challenges. We need nothing less than a new constitutional convention that would bring together representatives of all the chief institutions in American life to rededicate the nation to the renewal of the human potential through education" (p. 32). But my colleagues and I are less sanguine than Wood is as to what needs to be done here. The international political structure, however out of date, seems to be quite resilient. So, too, our intellectual assumptions. As for the "chief institutions" being rededicated, we must juxtapose Wood's institutions to the broad array of Martin's institutions poised with their hidden and perhaps not-so-hidden attempts to secure uncomprehending and unquestioning obedience.

Thus far, we have considered claims dealing with the larger society and the world. The next part of our analysis will focus on three claims dealing more particularly with education and America's schools.

The first claim deals with lack of common democratic purpose, as suggested by Goodlad: "What the disconnected array of individual schools scattered like seeds across the landscape most need to serve the people and this nation well would be what our so-called system of schooling lacks: a common public democratic purpose. What we would then expect of our schools is common commitment to this purpose and creative attention to the personal, social, vocational, and academic development of the young" (p. 19). The "lack of purpose" theme is echoed by Theobald: "It is past time to put an end to our century-long amnesia related to what schools are for" (p. 80). Whether the problem is seen as lack of purpose or, as Theobald suggests, the need to recover something we once had, there are difficulties. Goodlad talks here of what we should expect of schools, but again the challenge is surely daunting, for although people might say they want a democratic purpose, their limited views of the world are going to get in the way of achieving that purpose.

Theobald claims to be optimistic about recovering purpose: "Though the current policy context yields little reason to be optimistic that this [ending our long-term amnesia regarding schooling's purpose] might happen, the larger scholarly trends under way all point to a renewed interest in the role played by community in what it means to be human, a development that suggests that the insertion of community in public school curriculum may not be as far off as one might think" (p. 80). Here we have several difficulties to deal with. First, with Theobald, the mass media are under the control of either the conglomerates or the kings. Second, with Martin, most of our society's institutions are intentionally antidemocratic. Third, scholarly interest is hardly a warrant for policy change; if it were, we would be just as likely to base decisions on postmodern, poststructuralist deconstructionism. Given these views, it is difficult for my colleagues and me to hold out much hope for those contributing to "larger scholarly trends."

There is yet another difficulty. If purpose as existed in the old days is lacking, there is still the suggestion that schools currently have a purpose—economic utility. Theobald suggests that we need to move "the educational narrative in this country away from what the late Neil Postman called the 'god of economic utility'" (p. 80). Moreover, Theobald argues that we need to "educate citizens rather than self-interest pursuers" and "students so educated will be far more likely to shoulder the burden of democracy and to interrogate sham public relations campaigns sponsored by corporate media" (p. 80). So not only have we amnesia and need to recover what was once the purpose of schools, we also need to counter what is claimed to be the current central purpose of schools since the early part of the twentieth century.

The second claim centers on the failures of American schooling. Mc-Daniel (chapter 5) asks, "Why is it [democracy, teaching students how to handle conflicts, how we resolve conflicts, how we have our voices heard] not more common?" (p. 93). She concludes that "one reason is that deeply entrenched structures of schooling that took shape over one hundred years ago militate against it," leaving us with a schooling system that "values compliance more than critical thinking and responsible action" (pp. 93, 94). And although "reformers throughout the twentieth century tried to change the system to make it more capable of providing an authentic education fit for a free people, . . . the system has proved to be remarkably difficult to change" (p. 94). And "even when educators manage to embrace a new vision for their schools, the powerful pull of community expectations can undermine their efforts" (p. 94). This claim is reiterated in somewhat different form by Clark and Rowe (chapter 10, p. 200) with their notion of "failures by the schools to produce a critically literate public," failures that might well be expected of a system that values compliance more than critical thinking.

One can feel overwhelmed by the difficulties that emerge from a consideration of these claims. Perhaps what McDaniel suggests as modest strategies will ultimately have some impact: "The first step is to start talking. . . . Invite your local school principal or school board member to join the conversation. Talk about the issues that matter most to you. Decide together what can be done to improve your local school, and then do it. Form an online community with other active civic groups working to improve education. Share stories, suggestions, and resources" (p. 97). We can hardly gainsay these suggestions. But we would suggest in turn that it will take a lot to remove or radically change these deeply entrenched structures of schooling. And, too, the expectations put forth by Clark and Rowe—for example, "teachers should be developing in students an expectation that they will find in print and broadcast journalism adherence to basic principles such as truth (accuracy), humaneness, justice (fairness), stewardship, and freedom" (p. 185)—are reasonable, but a sober analysis must juxtapose these expectations to the claims of school failure to produce a critically literate public. As part of that sober analysis, one must ask what it would take to shift schooling so radically from failure to success in creating, with Clark and Rowe, "knowledgeable audience members."

A third claim about American schooling centers on the difficulties of doing anything about it. Goodlad suggests that "simply returning schooling to where we thought it was at the beginning of this century is unacceptable. It needs comprehensive overhaul: mission, educational conditions, structures and systemics, and, above all else, the development of a renewing mode throughout" (p. 22). Further, Goodlad claims, "the story of seeking to break new ground in schooling has been an exceedingly disappointing one, overshadowed as it has been by reform eras addicted to an ill-guiding linear model of change. There has been reluctance on the part of reform leaders to challenge the long-standing symbols, structure, and systemics of our system of public schooling" (p. 25).

More difficulties emerge. McDaniel would like us to think of educators as trying, over the last one hundred years, to provide an authentic education for a free people, but even when these educators, armed with a new vision, try to reform, they are beaten back by an undermining community. Goodlad appears to have less faith in educational reformers, let alone the community. It would appear, though, that even if we can sort out what educational reformers have or have not done for whatever reason, we must consider the political and practical implications of what Goodlad is claiming here. If leaders are to challenge the long-standing symbols, structure, and systemics but have been reluctant to do so, either we will have to have new leaders, or the old leaders will have to be comprehensively overhauled.

Five Key Issues

Following is an analysis of five key issues related to language and the process of political change as raised by the other contributions to the volume.

1. Abstract Language and the Need to Define Terms

Many of the problem/solution statements are couched in language so general or abstract as to make the meaning difficult to discern, or to allow all sorts of meanings to be read into the statements by all sorts of folks to serve their own ends. Here we are faced with a difficulty addressed by Seymour Sarason in his *Revisiting "The Culture of the School and the Problem of Change."* Sarason notes the difference between "analyzable and unanalyzable abstractions," suggesting that the former is a sentence or proposition that "enables us by the use of certain rules or inference to derive other statements that direct us to do certain things and to make

certain observations."[3] He cites as an example of the latter a recommen-
dation from James B. Conant's *The Education of American Teachers*: "If
the institution is involved in educating teachers, the lay board of trustees
should ask the faculty or faculties whether in fact there is a continuing and
effective all-university (or interdepartmental) approach to the education of
teachers; and if not, why not?" Sarason asks what Conant might believe
are the "defining characteristics of an 'effective' approach, so that one can
decide whether or not one agrees with the characteristics so that, *regardless
of agreement,* one knows how to test for the presence or absence of these
characteristics." Sarason goes on to note that "it is the case with many of
Conant's recommendations that he is most clear about unimportant matters
and most vague about the important ones."[4]

I share Sarason's concerns. I recognize that often one must begin with
generalities and broad propositions. If every book stating problems and
advocating changes were to incorporate every necessary version of analyzable propositions, every book would be far too long and far too unreadable.
What I am suggesting, however, is that in the business of problem analysis
and political change we must always have first the necessary follow-up, the
careful dissection of propositions. Sooner, rather than later, every proposition must be dissected. If we want to say "effective approach," then we are
duty bound to define what "effective" means. If we do not take the trouble
to define, other people will have difficulty following our reasoning, and the
only ones we will persuade (superficially) are those who are content with
vagueness.

2. Alignment of Problem Statements and Derived Approaches to Solutions

There needs to be close attention to the relationship between a given
problem statement and what appear to be the consequent approaches to
solutions. If we say in a report that "the problem is that the principal is not
allowing effective teaching of reading in the school," then the approaches to
solutions must surely bear somehow on the principal's alleged behavior. If
the approaches to solutions appear to veer off in other directions, with our
report talking about the need to teach math, the reader will quite reasonably wonder what happened to the problem, regardless of what he or she
might think of math teaching.

Let me note two particularly telling examples of lack of problem/solution
alignment. As discussed above, Martin puts on the table the claim that
"the government, religious institutions, corporations, the military, the Boy
Scouts, and neighborhood gangs all have hidden curricula that inculcate
belief in the sanctity of hierarchical structures and unquestioning obedience
to authority." Whether that claim has any basis in fact is a matter I will not
address here. Martin's approaches to solutions, as noted in the analysis
above, bear on the matter of schools needing to "take multiple educational

agency into account in decisions about the education of school children" and needing "to persuade the wide range of educational agents other than school to acknowledge their status as educators."

Perhaps more useful ways for us to consider the problem/solution alignment can be found in the notions outlined in other chapters of the volume. Daynes (chapter 6) describes the origins of four different education models, concluding that they advanced approaches to civically engaged education worthy of consideration and possible emulation, without necessarily linking these approaches to large-scale statements of problems. In chapter 7 Strickland and Suiter present localized strategies at the classroom level for getting students engaged in thinking. What those strategies will lead to remains open and the results uncertain, but what is central here is that the authors, in carrying out those strategies, make but modest claims as to the results and do not link the strategies to global statements of global problems. Likewise, Lowham and Mester, in conversation with Lippke and Edgar (chapter 8), describe how they found ways to get conversations going in their respective communities; the work suggests that "serious listening and the sharing of stories, can establish a trusting community" (pp. 159–160). That is to say, there is at least the potential that something good might come of the work, but the claims are modest, not reaching too far beyond the grasp.

The suggestion here, then, is that one approach to the problem/solution alignment is to make sure that if we make explicit problem statements, then we had best recognize that the audience is going to expect solution statements directly bearing on those problem statements, and we had best meet audience expectations if we want to be persuasive. Another strategy is to be far more muted in stating problems and let discussions of approaches to solutions focus on the good of the approaches on a small-scale rather than large-scale basis. By this strategy the audience can consider in depth the "goods" in and of themselves without pressing immediately to align those "goods" with gross and global problem statements and without wondering why the approaches do or do not meet expectations created by those kinds of problem statements.

3. The Need for Persuasion and the Recognition of Competition

I can agree with the sentiment attributed to Margaret Mead, "Never doubt that a small group of thoughtful, committed people can change the world. Indeed, it is the only thing that ever has." But in considering problem statements and approaches to solutions, we need to remember that all of this involves a political process, and political processes one way or another involve persuasion. (Even war, a variation of a political process, involves the art of persuasion. Recently the Pentagon commissioned a report from the RAND Corporation entitled, "Enlisting Madison Avenue: The Marketing Approach to Earning Popular Support in Theaters of Operation."[5]) Your small group of determined activists can do what they will. But if you want to move even a smidge beyond the immediate, you will have to figure out how to get your points across to become known *and listened to.*

Consider the competition for time and space and attention. Consider all the blogs out there. Making yourself heard is not an easy task. (Simply look at the number of blogs and other kinds of attention-getting strategies that can be found in just two or three newspapers or magazines, say, the *New York Times,* the *Washington Post,* and the *Economist.*)

Moreover, there will always be considerable competition with other political groups, each having what might be seen as a legitimate agenda.[6] You and your colleagues might not see competition among environmental issues and health issues and income distribution issues and foreign policy issues and education/schooling issues. Are they not all related? Are we not all trying to achieve a better world? Well, yes and yes. But from the perspective of the audience member, the television viewer, the mail receiver, there is the very real possibility of overload, what with all the din. Overload can lead to audience fatigue—fatigue that if sustained will result in little attention being paid to any of the pleas, no matter how worthy.

4. The Need for Reasonable Possibility

Whatever collections of problems and approaches to solutions, they must be seen by the audience as being within the range of real world possibility. Problems that are seen as impossible to solve will not long engage the audience. Why waste the time? Solutions that appear to involve magic or the tooth fairy rather than reality will be dismissed out of hand.

Perhaps it might seem better to not know the level of difficulty. For example, Lewis and Clark and Jefferson all thought that the Rockies would be like the Alleghenies—rolling hills, walk up one side, amble gently down the other side, all the way from Montana to the Pacific Ocean. Had they known (and had a conservative and parsimonious Congress known) that the Rockies were, well, the Rockies, they might not have wanted to support the planned expedition.

Selling the possibilities sometimes leads to going past reality in order to make the sale. Here we might consider the admonitory example of how Lyndon Johnson and his staff attempted to sell the War on Poverty. They were faced with a dilemma, one they never transcended. Try to sell the War on Poverty on the basis of reality and they would most likely fail: why, Congress would ask, should we allocate all that money for such a small return? But try to sell by making grandiose claims (which is the strategy they ultimately used) of solving all sorts of complex societal problems, and you lose in the long run, with support dwindling because those complex problems were not solved.[7]

The need here, then, is for us to balance reasonable possibility and real-ity. It will be a challenging but necessary task to determine how to couch the many problem statements and approaches to solutions in the volume in ways that achieve this balance.

5. Conceptions of Time

Many of the problems and the solutions put forth by the authors invoke or imply large-scale action taking place over a long period of time. A "funda-mental rethinking of the intellectual assumptions of the modern world" (as with Wood, p. 31) is not to be accomplished in a week or two. Goodlad (p. 11) would have the masses "become good listeners, learners, crap-detectors, and decision makers," but that task extends over a good many years, es-pecially when the people are apparently so limited and gullible.

In gauging strategies and their probabilities for success, we need to have some sense of the general conception of time in America. In *The Clock of the Long Now,* Stewart Brand argues that Americans have a foreshortened sense of time.[8] Americans tend to think of a "long time from now" in terms of months, maybe a year or two. Americans lack the kind of foresight, say, that led the British navy in the 1400s to plant oak trees that would not be ready for harvesting (and then turning into sturdy ship timbers) for hundreds of years.

The rhetorical and political (and ethical) issues here are those discussed by Gregory Bateson in considering how to maintain original insights in long-range plans. Should a later group of planners understand the original insights? Or should "the original planners put into the very fabric of their plan collateral incentives which will seduce those who come later into car-rying out the plan for reasons quite different from those which inspired the plan?" Bateson concludes that "it will not pay in the long run to 'sell' the plans by superficial *ad hominem* arguments which will conceal or contradict the deeper insight."[9] But the challenge is immense. It is going to be very difficult but very necessary to ask people to support and see through to completion a long-term program for radical social, political, and educational change with payoffs so far off in the distance that we (or anybody else) cannot even imagine what lies over the horizon.

We will be pleased to work with you and your colleagues should you wish to retain us. I will work up a task analysis along with a budget and get back to you. To achieve what this book's authors wish to do, renew education and democracy in America, will not be cheap: you do indeed get what you pay for. And what you are going to pay for is a struggle. The struggle may be rewarding, but it will be a struggle all the same.

Let me note in closing that we are not speaking for or against any of the problem statements or the approaches to solutions. We are, of course, in accord with your desire for a healthy and free society. And surely we are strongly in accord with your views of education as an end in itself and as a means leading to the greater likelihood of creating and sustaining that healthy and free society.

Part Two by John I. Goodlad

The authors of the preceding chapters are engaged in activities from which they expect themselves as well as others to learn. Their writing here is directed to a moral good: the care and renewal of the American democracy. They view this work-in-progress as not fulfilling its promises, of falling short in implementing moral concepts and principles articulated in its founding.

They share belief in and hope for the power of education (for young and old) to shape a political and social democracy that is truly of, by, and for the people. Further, they view this shaping as a nonnegotiable agenda for the understanding and participation of everyone, not just the policymakers presently in power. All of these authors are educators, whether or not they are professionally engaged in teaching in schools or colleges. For educators not to have hope for the success of what they envision is an oxymoron.

Like most people, these colleagues and I view education to be a good thing. We know that education can be a bad thing, but we usually employ another word in discussing it—miseducation. Actually, the word "education" is a neutral term. Philosophers such as John Dewey, Alfred North Whitehead, and R. S. Peters, whose writing has been influential over recent decades, define education as a process of becoming—of continuously developing as a person—that has no end other than itself. This becoming can be laced with good and bad learnings. The culture in which this shaping of human belief and action takes place defines which is which. The good and the bad reside in the context of one's life: thievery, compassion, deceit, caring, envy, thoughtfulness, or whatever. Learning encompasses one or the other or both. The hope of those who wrote this book is, of course, for the good to prevail over the bad, the moral over the immoral.

Before writing this section, I decided to check, without conducting a national poll, on whether the duality of meaning embedded in the word "education" has or has not survived the passage of time. I turned to encyclopedias because of their role in identifying the conventional wisdom regarding such matters. Whether defined and discussed on the web or between the covers of a text, there appeared no *direct* reference to education being inclusive of both the good and the bad. However, moral duality can be inferred in citations such as "*Education,* the process by which people's abilities and talents are developed. *Education is about everything that is learned in a lifetime* [italics mine]: habits, knowledge, skills, interests, attitudes, and personality."

We tend not to think negatively about such words as "people's abilities and talents." They set a tone here of education's being a good thing. Similarly, much of what I read conveyed a positive tone about schooling—elementary, secondary, and tertiary—which commonly becomes a major part of articles under the heading of education. Schools conduct bad as well as good education. To be much schooled is not necessarily to be well educated. For schools to serve the democratic public purpose thought necessary by the authors of this book, they must be highly selective in what and how they teach, especially since they are not the major agencies in the intentional and, especially, nonintentional education of the populace.

I was pleased to encounter in my reading various versions of the following: "People become educated not merely in attending schools but by the total experience of life. They learn through direct experience, imitation, and self-teaching. They learn from parents and friends, from such institutions as churches and libraries, from recreational and social agencies such as clubs, and from the press, motion pictures, radio, television, and the like."

In chapter 3 Jane Roland Martin makes clear that variables beyond schools are the major educators in one's life. To ignore this fact is folly. Asking schools to do what they cannot do well or at all, what other agencies and enterprises could do much better, has contributed to both a loss of public confidence in schooling and inattention to its potential for sustaining and renewing our democracy.

I think three things in particular motivated Roger Soder to write as he did in the first part of this chapter: the centrality of hope in preceding chapters, the educative orientation of the authors, and the fear that the combination of these two would lead readers to believe that the many positive activities reported in some chapters indicate that significant renewal of our schools and perhaps even our democracy is well under way. By introducing the voice of an outside critic, he was able to sound an even stronger warning than he might otherwise have presented.

I think Roger and I would agree that there is currently in this nation a great deal of discontent and even fear. The blessings of this land are such that threats to our well-being are often met with a shrug and the expectation that "these things too shall pass." But waiting too long to act or not acting at all can be costly. The time has come for a great awakening; the calls are many and varied. We should be grateful to Roger Soder for warning us that implementation of the call in chapters 1 through 10 of this book must not be lost to underestimating the challenges we would face.

I already have addressed what I think many readers would agree are correct assumptions about Roger Soder's presentation of a rather harsh critique of our manuscript: the centrality of hope for a great turning in the present culture of our democracy and the high expectations for a strategy of changes heavily dependent on the education of children, youths, and adults. There is, I think, some subtle evidence of other reasons for Roger to write the fictitious critique as he did. To these I now turn.

★ ★ ★

Roger knows about the nation's general failure over a long period of time to effect so-called reform, let alone renewal, in schooling. I write "the nation's failure" because blaming public schooling and especially teacher education programs for their failure to implement the ill-guided and underfunded recommendations of national commissions, governors' summits, and the like has been so often in fashion. I will not take educators off the hook for their shortcomings, but it is necessary to remind readers that little in the systemics and regularities in which they work is of their doing.

Soder is also well aware of findings from research that discourage one from being sanguine about the ability of schooling, let alone the American democracy, to renew itself. He, the late Kenneth Sirotnik, and I studied in depth and breadth a purposefully representative sample of teacher education programs in the United States. Our major findings have since been supported by other studies. He is also versed in the findings of two equally comprehensive studies of elementary and secondary schools and of educational change that Sirotnik, other colleagues, and I conducted earlier. Three findings in particular probably influenced his reactions to the first ten chapters of this book.

The first is that we found little to encourage us to believe that, over time, the schools and university-based teacher education programs in our sample would evolve into mission-driven renewing entities, open and responsive to the inquiry-based educational ideas that were then extant. These findings were readily accessible in books, professional journals, and the agendas of district, state, and national conferences. What the educators we studied heard and read, apparently, was theater to be variously experienced, but not potential reality to replace present structures and practices.

The second disturbing finding, a close kin and probable cause of the first, is the lack of cohesion among the component parts of the schooling enterprise, including the top tier of colleges and universities. Colleges of education and departments of the arts and sciences in universities, as well as elementary and secondary schools where student teachers gain teaching

experience, make contributions to the conduct of teacher preparation but
rarely join together in setting common goals and designing curricula.
Until they do—and at least awareness of this need is growing—a considerable chunk of what the preceding authors envision for the renewal of the
American democracy will continue to be regarded as theater to be enjoyed,
perhaps, but ignored in practice.

The third major finding from the three comprehensive studies with
which Roger is more than a little familiar pertains to the very core of the
ten preceding chapters: the goal of educating a democratic public is almost
entirely absent from the recommendations that have emerged over the past
half century from highly touted, nationally commissioned school reform
reports and those emanating from state governors' "education summits."
And that nonnegotiable agenda introduced in the introduction and chapter
1 certainly is not presently guiding schools and teacher education in our
country.

Given this awareness (and much more of similar ilk) in Roger Soder's
mind, are his trepidations and cautions well taken? Ought they not be
widely heeded as we steadfastly move forward with an agenda of developing
a democratic public—an agenda of clear mission, the conditions necessary
to the advancement of this agenda, and strategies for its implementation?

How Do We Clarify Our Educational Agenda?

Here is where the writing of a book such as this one on educating a democratic people arouses frustration. As I mentioned, reference to "education"
conjures up in the minds of many people "schooling," and schooling, in
turn, conjures up good thoughts that often border on the virtuous. More
schooling becomes a good thing. Over the past couple of decades, conventional wisdom tells us that the goal of our elementary and secondary
schools is to prepare everyone for college. Then, higher education, in turn,
will prepare everyone for a good job and ensure for the nation a highly
competitive role in the global economy. Embedded here is a powerful
implicit contract with the young: succeed in this journey, and doors to the
benefits of our democracy will open before you.[10]

Is this the mission we should want for our schools? I think not. Is this
the message we want stewards of our schools and teacher educators to
internalize? No. And is this not a message of cruelty for all those young
people whose circumstances give them and their parents little hope? Yes.

Finally, is it an honest message? It might be well intentioned, but even
if I should yield to this possibility (which I am not now prepared to do), I

must challenge its validity. The academic learning that goes on in schools correlates poorly with the learning one needs to make the most of oneself in life and be a responsible, participating citizen in a democratic society. Further, the present extreme narrowing of the school curriculum and the accompanying criterion of test scores as the measure of school quality (might one say "virtue"?) give us little hope that much schooling will ensure a well-educated public.

It should come as no surprise that Roger Soder, well informed and active as an educator and an involved citizen, would worry about the possibility of readers' taking seriously the agenda presented in earlier chapters, being impressed with the success stories presented, and getting caught up in the tone of hope, but not being adequately aware of the magnitude of significantly changing the mission and conduct of our schools and democracy. Or, worse, they might conclude that the work to be done is for others, especially our elected representatives in local, state, and federal offices. Then, of course, there is the worry about stirring folks to involve that old chestnut: blame. Taking all of this into consideration, how is it still possible for education to make a truly democratic people?

As I wrote in chapter 1, David C. Korten's book *The Great Turning* provided me with a sweeping view of five thousand years of moving from what he calls "Empire to Earth Community" and grassroots strategies for continuing the work-in-progress we call democracy.[11] My sense of hope for a present turning was heightened by the bold critique of Harvard University in *Excellence without a Soul* by Harry R. Lewis, a former dean of Harvard College.[12] He sees his own and other prestigious universities steadily losing their sense of educational purpose (more or less as I defined it earlier) to customer satisfaction—to economic utility. I always take hope from keen analyses of what is healthy and what is decaying in our culture. They are essential to the well-being of democracy.

For cultural renewal to occur, more and more people must become aware that others in the groups with which they are associated have similar concerns. There is in this realization a sense of belonging, of being human. Then, when this awareness matures to include the realization that some of the undesirable things of yesterday and today are being replaced with things more desirable, there sometimes comes a kind of epiphany of desiring both to share and to help. In regard to being educated into democracy, Alan Wood, author of chapter 2, wrote in 2001, "To be fully human means to accept limitations on one's negative freedoms in order to realize more fully one's positive freedoms."[13] Positive stirrings in the context of one's life attract positive stirrings nearby and frequently elsewhere. The process begins with conversation.

Beyond the fact that I am an educator, what stirs my expectations for a great turning in the mission of our schools, a great turning that will bring with it a great turning in the care and renewal of the American democracy? First, because the widespread, palpable discontent across this land is now accompanied by the increasing awareness of our considerable educational and, indeed, general cultural shortcomings. Second, because of the nature of the fingerposts that not only point to these shortcomings but also to paths for dealing constructively with them. Third, because of the kind and amount of inquiry engaged in by the creative cultural analysts who study them. Fourth, because of the apparent lack of some monster plan or planning of a plan to fix whatever it is that our political and corporate leaders think needs fixing. Fifth, because of the multitude of thoughtful people in relatively small groups and settings who are restlessly awaiting the tipping point that will bring them into the work that increasingly is calling out for attention. Sixth, because of the growing willingness of young and old to take personal risks if this work appears to be sufficiently worthy. Seventh, because of the stirrings in other countries of people who are increasingly challenging the gross inequities and injustices of their cultures. And eighth, because so many people now accept the old adage: we have met the enemy, and he is us.

In chapter 1 I referred to the great turning taking place over fifty centuries described by David Korten, with democracy now the core of unfinished business. His is the long view in which lifetimes of sixty to a hundred years are the short terms on which each little turn depends. Each is only a brief moment in time, but Korten views the present era as a historic opportunity to advance a society based on democratic principles. But what will trigger the actions that will convert these principles into the behavioral virtues of a democratic public?

In *The Tipping Point* Malcolm Gladwell describes and analyzes activities and fashions that unpredictably take off from modest beginnings to become what he aptly calls epidemics: the unexpected resurgence of sales in the mid-1990s of the brushed-suede shoes named Hush Puppies, the sudden drop-off in crime over about the same period of time in New York City, the extraordinary success of televised early childhood programs such as *Sesame Street,* and more. He addresses the power in marketing of whatever is seen by adolescents as "cool." In an afterword he writes about challenges that would be impossible to overcome by one person alone that suddenly become surmountable when tackled in close-knit groups.

What especially caught my attention in Gladwell's afterword had to do with the immunity people develop to such communication technologies as the telephone, the fax, and now e-mail that were initially useful and became overwhelming: "They turn instead for advice and information to the people in their lives whom they respect, admire, and trust." Gladwell explains that "the fact that anyone can e-mail for free, if they [*sic*] have our address, means that people frequently and persistently e-mail us. But that quickly creates immunity, and simply makes us value face-to-face communications—and the communications of those we already know and trust—all the more." In regard to the quality of group decisions, they are best made when communication is face-to-face. "The fact that expressing a dissenting view in person is much harder socially ... gives that opinion much more credence in the group's deliberations."[14]

One of the overarching conclusions regarding the change process that I take from Gladwell (who draws from a variety of sources) is that many small groups are more effective than a large one involving the same number of people. This aligns, I think, with my conclusion, after years of inquiry, that the renewal of schooling best proceeds school by school. Along with other of Gladwell's conclusions, it strengthens the community-by-community, face-to-face dialogue, decision making, and action described and recommended in several chapters of this book.

What will trigger the tipping point when millions of people realize that caring for our democracy is a nonnegotiable agenda for all of us and rise to the challenge of being caregivers? Will it be fifty-five human connectors (Gladwell's term) picking up from Bill Moyers's charge (see chapter 1) and calling out from wherever they are and whenever they can, "The promise of America leaves no one out"? Might it be thousands of schoolteachers convening with parents and others in their communities over the public democratic purpose of schooling? Or might it be adolescents nationwide deciding that joining in a nonnegotiable agenda for the common good is cool?

Notes

1. Alexis de Tocqueville, "Notice," in *Democracy in America,* vol. 2, trans. Harvey C. Mansfield and Delba Winthrop (Chicago: University of Chicago Press, 2000), 400.

2. Alexander Pope, "Essay on Criticism," in E. Audra and Aubrey Williams, eds., *Alexander Pope: Pastoral Poetry and an Essay on Criticism* (London: Methuen, 1961), 395–96.

3. Seymour B. Sarason, *Revisiting "The Culture of the School and the Problem of Change"* (New York: Teachers College Press, 1996), 38. Another useful approach to ways of understanding change is found in Paul Watzlawick, John Weakland, and Richard Fisch, *Change: Principles of Problem Formation and Problem Resolution* (New York: Norton, 1974).

4. Sarason, *Revisiting,* 40.

5. See Karen DeYoung, "The Pentagon Gets a Lesson From Madison Avenue," *Washington Post,* July 21, 2007, A1.

6. For a useful discussion of agendas and how they are established and compete, see John W. Kingdon, *Agendas, Alternatives, and Public Policies,* 2nd ed. (New York: Longman, 1995).

7. The dilemma of how to sell the War on Poverty is discussed in depth by David Zarefsky, *President Johnson's War on Poverty: Rhetoric and History* (Tuscaloosa: University of Alabama Press, 1986). See also James L. Sundquist, ed., *On Fighting Poverty: Perspectives from Experience* (New York: Basic Books, 1969).

8. Stewart Brand, *The Clock of the Long Now: Time and Responsibility* (New York: Basic Books, 1999).

9. Gregory Bateson, *Steps to an Ecology of Mind* (1972; repr., Chicago: University of Chicago Press, 2000), 512–13.

10. For more on this contract, see Neil Postman, *The End of Education: Redefining the Value of School* (New York: Knopf, 1995).

11. David C. Korten, *The Great Turning: From Empire to Earth Community* (San Francisco: Berrett-Koehler, 2006).

12. Harry R. Lewis, *Excellence without a Soul: How a Great University Forgot Education* (New York: PublicAffairs, 2006).

13. Alan T. Wood, *What Does It Mean to Be Human?: A New Interpretation of Freedom in World History* (New York: Peter Lang, 2001), 3.

14. Malcolm Gladwell, *The Tipping Point: How Little Things Can Make a Big Difference* (Boston: Little, Brown, 2002), 274–75.

About the Editors
and Contributors

Kenneth Alhadeff is chair of Elttaes Enterprises, chair of the Kenneth and Marleen Alhadeff Charitable Foundation, and owner of the Majestic Bay Theatres. Additionally, he serves as a member of the board of regents for Washington State University, as board president of the Northwest School for Hearing-Impaired Children, as a trustee of Key Bank National Association, and as a board member of the 5th Avenue Theatre Association. He was also cochair of Governor Booth Gardner's Commission for Dr. Martin Luther King Jr. Holiday events. He has a strong passion for the arts, the value of teachers, the importance of philanthropy, and the promotion of social justice.

Anne L. Bryant is executive director of the National School Boards Association (NSBA). She served on the Simmons College Board of Trustees (1972–2007) and was the chair of the board (2001–2004). She is vice chair of the Schools and Libraries Committee of Universal Service Administrative Company. Prior to joining NSBA in July 1996, she was executive director of the American Association of University Women. Bryant's awards and honors include honorary doctorates from the University of New England and Middlebury College and the Chancellor's Medal from the University of Massachusetts.

Richard W. Clark is a senior associate of the Institute for Educational Inquiry and an auxiliary faculty member at the University of Washington Bothell. He served as the executive director of the National Network for Educational Renewal from 2000 to 2003. Clark was deputy superintendent of Bellevue Public Schools in Bellevue, Washington, from July 1980 to July 1991. He is the author of various books, articles, chapters, and papers on professional development schools, school–university partnerships, curriculum, collective bargaining, school-centered decision making, and administrative preparation programs. Recent publications include *Kids and School Reform* with Patricia Wasley and Robert Hampel, *Effective Professional Development Schools,* a chapter in *Teacher Education for Democracy and Social Justice,* and, with Ann Foster and Corinne Mantle-Bromley, a chapter in *Boundary Spanners.*

Gary Daynes is an associate professor of history and director of the Center for Civic Engagement at Westminster College in Salt Lake City, Utah. Prior to joining Westminster in 2006, he was a faculty member and administrator at Brigham Young University. His research and writing focus on the intersection of history, education, and community life. He was a producer of the documentary *The Best Crop* on the history and culture of orchard communities. Daynes is the author of *Making Villains, Making Heroes: Joseph McCarthy, Martin Luther King, Jr., and the Politics of American Memory* and the editor of *Fulfilling the Founding: A Reader in American Heritage.*

Eugene B. Edgar is a professor of education at the University of Washington with a specialization in special education. He teaches courses on exceptional children and families. His research interests have included early childhood education, secondary programs for youths with disabilities, and post-school follow-along studies of youths with disabilities. His current interest is in how best to ensure that public schools are for all children and how citizenship education can become a more integral part of public schools.

John I. Goodlad is president of the Institute for Educational Inquiry and a cofounder of the Center for Educational Renewal at the University of Washington. He held professorships at Agnes Scott College and Emory University in Georgia, the University of Chicago, and UCLA (where he was dean of the Graduate School of Education from 1967 to 1983) before coming to the University of Washington in 1984. He is the author, coauthor, or editor of approximately forty books on education; has received numerous national awards in recognition of his work; and holds honorary doctorates from twenty colleges and universities in the United States and Canada.

Barbara A. Lippke is senior project manager consultant for Seattle Public Schools in the department of technology services. Prior to taking this position, she held several positions with the Seattle Public Schools: principal at View Ridge Elementary School, regional coordinator for

Seattle Public Schools, and special education elementary coordinator for sixty-eight Seattle elementary schools.

James R. Lowham is the superintendent of schools for the 11,600-student Natrona County School District in Casper, Wyoming. He assumed that role in July 2002 after serving as associate superintendent (2001–2002) and executive director (1997–2001) of Curriculum and Instructional Services. Over the past thirty years he has worked as a teacher and school administrator and had a career as a commissioned officer in the U.S. Army and the Wyoming Army National Guard.

Jane Roland Martin is professor emerita in the Philosophy Department of the University of Massachusetts, Boston. She is a past president of the Philosophy of Education Society; a recipient of fellowships from the John Simon Guggenheim Foundation, the National Science Foundation, and the Bunting Institute of Radcliffe College; and the holder of honorary degrees from Salem State College and the University of Umeå in Sweden. Her books include *Reclaiming a Conversation: The Ideal of the Educated Woman, The Schoolhome: Rethinking Schools for Changing Families, Cultural Miseducation: In Search of a Democratic Solution,* and most recently, *Educational Metamorphoses: Philosophical Reflections on Identity and Culture.*

Bonnie McDaniel is a research associate with the Institute for Educational Inquiry. Her research interests are in the philosophy of education, democratic theory, and most recently in the history of American education. She has taught foundations of education courses at the University of Washington and Western Washington University. She was the recipient of the 2004 Gordon C. Lee Dissertation Award from the College of Education at the University of Washington in Seattle.

William Mester is superintendent of the Snohomish School District in Snohomish, Washington. Prior to taking this position in 2002, he was superintendent of the Mead School District near Spokane, Washington, for thirteen years and before that served as a principal, teacher, and school psychologist.

Michael A. Resnick is associate executive director of the National School Boards Association (NSBA), where he oversees the organization's advocacy program and Center for Public Education. He has written extensively about policy issues in education, including *Communities Count: A School Board Guide to Public Engagement* and *The Educated Student: Defining and Advancing Student Achievement.* Prior to joining NSBA in 1969, he was an attorney in the Office of General Counsel at the U.S. Treasury with responsibilities in the area of international trade.

Clifford G. Rowe is a professor in the Department of Communication and Theater at Pacific Lutheran University in Tacoma, Washington. He held various positions with the *Seattle Times* between 1969 and 1980. He began his career as a reporter with the *Oregon Journal* and then worked for the *Chicago Sun-Times* and *Paddock Publications* (Arlington Heights, Illinois). As a member of the Society of Professional Journalists, he helped draft the society's first major revision of its code of ethics. He has judged regional journalist competitions, including those for educational reporting.

Roger Soder is a research professor of education in the College of Education at the University of Washington. His undergraduate, graduate, and teacher education courses focus on education, schooling, democracy, and leadership, as well as the ethics and politics of rhetoric. Soder's current research and writing interests center on these topics, specifically the role of the university in a free society, the culture of leadership succession, and the rhetoric of teacher education. His most recent book is *The Language of Leadership.*

Jim Strickland is a community-based educator at Totem Middle School (formerly Marysville Junior High School) in Marysville, Washington. He has been teaching students with disabilities for the past seventeen years. He assists other educators in exploring the implications of democratic values for curriculum, school organization, and professional practice. Strickland's current work is driven by the commitment to create schools that are functionally integrated with their surrounding communities and that enable all children to experience, understand, and actively engage in the democratic way of life.

Dianne Suiter is principal of Central Academy Nongraded School in Middletown, Ohio. She has studied and worked with public and private progressive schools in many states for more than thirty-four years. She has taught and supervised high school special education classes, designed and directed a democratized K–12 gifted education model, directed and helped found a progressive religious elementary school, and supervised K–12 curriculum and instruction in several districts. She has also taught at the McGregor School of Antioch University, Antioch University, and Miami University of Ohio. Her research has focused on women in leadership and school reform.

Paul G. Theobald is a senior fellow of the Institute for Educational Inquiry. He currently holds the Woods-Beals Endowed Chair in Urban and Rural Education at Buffalo State College. He is an educational historian whose work frequently crosses disciplinary boundaries and has appeared in distinguished research journals. His first book, *Call School: Rural Education in the Midwest to 1918,* has remained the definitive study of the history of rural education in this country. His second book, *Teaching the Commons: Place,*

Pride, and the Renewal of Community, is an intellectual history that weaves in philosophical themes to build a new vision for educational ends.

Alan T. Wood is a history professor at the University of Washington Bothell. He was associate dean for academic affairs there from 1995 to 1999 and also served as interim vice chancellor for academic affairs at the University of Washington Tacoma from 2006 to 2007. His academic field is Chinese history, and for the last ten years he has taught and published in the area of world history. He is working on a global history for a general audience, tentatively entitled *One World: A Biography of Humankind.* His other books include *Limits to Autocracy: From Sung Neo-Confucianism to a Doctrine of Political Rights, What Does It Mean to Be Human?: A New Interpretation of Freedom in World History,* and *Asian Democracy in World History.*

Index

academic development, 14, 19, 22, 77, 163, 175, 219

access, 192–194, 200

accountability, 41, 78, 79, 131, 135, 164, 165, 168; media, 196–197; NCLB and, 173, 177; test scores and, 15

accuracy, 67, 184–185, 185–186, 188, 189

achievement, 135, 169, 175

achievement gap, closing, 12, 128, 169, 173

Addams, Jane, 108, 110, 112

Addams, John Huy, 108

Advance Placement (AP) programs, 164, 175, 176, 177

Agenda for Education in a Democracy (AED), 21, 23, 25, 139

Aristotle, 35, 89

atomistic model, 33, 35

at-risk youth, 119, 121, 127, 167

Bailyn, Bernard, 48

balance, 194–195, 200

Barber, Benjamin: on education for democracy, 55

Barnard, Henry, 80

Bateson, Gregory, 214

Beecher, Catharine, 107

Beecher, Henry Ward, 107

Beecher, Lyman, 107

Bender, Thomas: on community, 160

Berman, Morris: political/economic theory and, 81n1

Berry, Wendell, 3, 10, 73, 81

Bohm, David, 155

Bongart, Sergei, 13

Boyer, Ernest: on adult expectations/ schools, 21

Brand, Stewart, 214

Bryant, Anne, 6

Bush, George W.: NCLB and, 15

Central Academy, 118, 126–136

change, 16, 28n31, 93–98, 194, 221; leadership and, 18; linear models of, 18, 25; political, 210

character education, 161, 176

charter schools, 105, 196

Child Rights Information Network, 52

Churchill, Winston, 144

citizens, democracy and, 84, 85, 89, 166, 169

citizenship, 31, 108, 164; corporate, 79; education, 57, 58–59, 89–90, 103; global, 42; nurturing, 140; responsibilities of, 117; testing and, 96. *See also* democratic citizenship

civic acts, 104, 106, 111, 112

civic engagement, 80, 104, 111, 112–113;